D0386427

Anaxandra (*fl. c.* 2nd century BC)

An Hachette UK Company
www.hachette.co.uk

First published in Great Britain in 2018 by Cassell Illustrated, an imprint of
Octopus Publishing Group Ltd
Carmelite House
50 Victoria Embankment
London EC4Y 0DZ
www.octopusbooks.co.uk

Distributed in the US by Hachette Book Group
1290 Avenue of the Americas
4th and 5th Floors, New York, NY 10104

Distributed in Canada by Canadian Manda Group
664 Annette St, Toronto,
Ontario, Canada M6S 2C8

ISBN 978 1 78840 063 3

A CIP catalogue record for this book is available from the British Library.

Printed and bound in China
10 9 8 7 6 5 4 3 2 1

Commissioning Editor Romilly Morgan
Senior Editor Pauline Bache
Copy Editor Alison Wormleighton
Assistant Editor Ellie Corbett
Research Assistants Jane Birch and Samantha Cracknell
Art Director and Designer Yasia Williams-Leedham
Illustrators Hélène Baum, Lauren Simkin Berke, Miriam Castillo, Winnie T Frick, Tanya Heidrich, Grace Helmer, María Hergueta, Shreyas R Krishnan, Allegra Lockstadt, Sara Netherway, Marcela Quiroz
Senior Production Manager Peter Hunt
Production Controller Katie Jarvis

Forgotten Women

The Artists

Contents

n the opening scene of the documentary *!Women Art Revolution (!W.A.R.)*, the artist and filmmaker Lynn Hershman Leeson approaches people in New York and San Francisco and challenges them to an unusual task: to name three women artists.

"Frida Kahlo, that's one," a woman with a blonde ponytail says triumphantly. Then she falters: "I need two more women artists," she beseeches a passer-by. Everyone around her looks mystified.

Later in her film, Leeson says that she is on a mission to honour the lost feminist art of the 1960s and 1970s. "When artists are battling for space in the cultural memory," she says, "omission – or, even worse, eradication – becomes a kind of murder."[1]

I watched *!W.A.R.* one spring evening in 2017 at London's Barbican Cinema, when I was still in talks about writing the *Forgotten Women* series. A friend had invited me to a screening, and the film was only ten minutes in before I was convinced that, if there was ever to be a *Forgotten Women: The Artists* book, the opening sequence of Leeson's powerful and much-needed documentary had to be in the introduction. (One of the subjects of her film, the painter Sylvia Sleigh, also made it into the book.)

It wasn't because I wanted to make fun of the hapless interviewees that Leeson cornered on the street. It's because I think their struggle is actually pretty easy to relate to – and it is relevant to the whole of *Forgotten Women*. Women can be forgotten out of pure vituperative nastiness, but they can also slip out of public consciousness because they are so rarely commemorated. Nobody wants to be the person who awkwardly fails to come up with a second or third female artist, yet here we are.

It's not just people on the street who struggle to think of women in art. Omission can extend all the way into higher education. Recently, an art historian friend who lectures at a university sent this text to my group chat: "I have to teach a course called Masterpieces of Western Art next year," she said in despair, "and they've managed to devise a syllabus from Parthenon to Andy Warhol with not a single woman."

The view is equally dispiriting for those currently on the ground, working as artists. A report from the Freelands Foundation in the UK found that though women made up 62 percent of art and design graduates between 2011 and 2012, an audit of 134 commercial galleries in London a year later found that 78 percent represented more men than women. Between 2014 and 2015, only 25 percent of shows at major art institutions were by women.[2]

The situation is just as dire outside of the UK. According to the National Museum of Women in the Arts, based in Washington, DC, only 30 percent of artists represented by US commercial galleries are women – and for every dollar a male visual artist makes, a woman artist makes only 81 cents. Those in the arts professions can expect to earn almost $20,000 less than their male peers every year.[3]

None of this would come as a surprise to the activist artists known as the Guerrilla Girls, nor would it have to the late feminist art historian Linda Nochlin. Both have mounted powerful defences of the position of women in art; the

Guerrilla Girls with droll wit, activism and gorilla masks, and Nochlin with her 1971 masterpiece of criticism, the essay "Why Have There Been No Great Women Artists?"

"The fault lies not in our stars, our hormones, our menstrual cycles, or our empty internal spaces, but in our institutions and our education," Nochlin argues of women's history-of-art no-show. "The miracle is, in fact, that given the overwhelming odds against women, or blacks, that so many of both have managed to achieve so much sheer excellence, in those bailiwicks of white masculine prerogative like science, politics, or the arts."[4]

Or, as the Guerrilla Girls ask in a 1990 poster: "Q. If February is Black History Month and March is Women's History Month, what happens the rest of the year? A. Discrimination."[5]

The true history of women in art stretches back thousands of years. The Ancient Roman author Pliny the Elder tells us of a woman who, heartbroken by the departure of her lover, sketched the outline of his shadow on a wall. Thus, bas relief was created. Some believe that, even earlier, primitive cave women left behind ochre handprints on the walls of damp caves and grottos – the first traces of the artistic impulse in humanity.

Until the 19th century, however, women were barred from art schools and institutions where they might develop their artistic skills. A few, such as the 5th-century BC Ancient Greek painter Timarete and the 17th-century Italian painter Elisabetta Sirani, were lucky enough to be born into artistic families, and grew up assisting their fathers in their studios, where their talents were recognized and encouraged.

Women were doubly cursed in art; not only were most unable to seek professional training, but they were also barred from studying the nude male form, which was seen as essential to mastering the art of drawing. Instead, they leaned toward still lifes and self-portraits. Some artists developed an indefatigable tenacity and laboured in obscurity for decades before they found success. Others, like the enigmatic 20th-century photographer Vivian Maier, were self-taught talents who died without ever gaining recognition.

Choosing women for the book was not an easy task. I was assisted in this by my editors Romilly Morgan and Pauline Bache, as well as Gina Luria Walker, the founder of the New Historia initiative at the New School in New York City (*see page* 219). As with all books in the *Forgotten Women* series, we have tried to select a range of artists from around the world and across the ages. After all, one of the pitfalls of the so-called public record is how much it favours white heterosexual men from rich countries – and how little that captures the true richness and diversity of history.

If there is anything that connects the 48 women in this book, it is that they possessed the drive and self-understanding that connects all great artists. They were not motivated by the need for public adulation or money – in fact, many of them didn't make a penny from their work.

Instead, they had a certain way of seeing the world – a force of understanding that could translate light and shade into tempera paint or marble, imbuing whatever medium they chose with enormous power, emotion and depth. You can see that in the explosive colours of Corita Kent, the nun-turned-artist who saw joy everywhere in God's creation, or the deep, soulful wanderlust that infuses the *Bildungsroman* work of the German artist Charlotte Salomon.

There is tragedy in this book, too. It is in the stories of women like Jo Hopper, who gave up a promising career to assist her spouse's artistic ambitions, and painters such as Tina Blau and Marlow Moss, whose works were lost in the chaos and destruction of World War II.

There are missed opportunities by the dozen, in which interlocking forces of racism, sexism and economic circumstance have held women back from achieving their full potential as artists. Who knows what Harriet Powers, the former slave who sewed quilts of celestial perfection, would have become if she wasn't so constrained by the segregation of her time? Would drip painter Janet Sobel have become just as famous as Jackson Pollock if she hadn't had to take a job at her family business?

Happily, there is joy to be found, too – for example, in the lives of Alma Thomas, the schoolteacher-turned-artist who achieved unexpected fame in her seventies, and of Clara Tice, whose husband gave up *his* career in art to support her own. There are also stories of bravery and recklessness, sensuality and sex, scandal and mystery. Sometimes, as in the case of the occultist and painter Marjorie Cameron, a single life can combine all six.

Change is happening now, albeit with the imperceptibility of shifting tectonic plates. The director of the Tate art museums and galleries in the UK is Maria Balshaw, Lisa Phillips heads up the New Museum in Lower Manhattan and Laurence des Cars is chief of the Musée d'Orsay and Musée de l'Orangerie in Paris. But unless you have your ear pressed close to the ground, these changes might be difficult to register.

Other museums have taken drastic action to diversify their collections. At the time of publication, the Baltimore Museum of Art had just announced plans to sell seven works by white male artists, including Andy Warhol and Robert Rauschenberg, to fund a "war chest"[6] for acquiring works by women and people of colour.

"The decision to do this rests very strongly on my commitment to rewrite the postwar canon," the museum's director, Christopher Bedford, told the art market website Artnet. "To state it explicitly and act on it with discipline – there is no question that is an unusual and radical act to take."[7]

I hope that *Forgotten Women: The Artists* can form a modest part of this sea change in art; to show that, beyond the Frida Kahlos and Georgia O'Keeffes, there is an entire universe of women's art to discover, explore and remember. At the very least, it will help you to name more than three women artists.

Abstract

JANET SOBEL

When Janet Sobel (1893–1968) died at the age of 75, her obituary in the local paper listed her as the vice-president and director of Sobel Brothers, Inc., the costume jewellery business founded by her late husband, Max. But Janet hadn't just manufactured cheap trinkets for a living. When she was in her mid-forties, she taught herself art and became one of the most talked-about painters in New York. Today, this Abstract Expressionist is regarded as the mother of drip painting (the technique that made Jackson Pollock famous).

Born Jennie Olechovsky in Ekaterinoslav, Ukraine, Janet was one of the hundreds of thousands of European immigrants who had fled hardship and persecution for America's promised land. When her father was killed, possibly as a result of one of the anti-Jewish pogroms that swept Ukraine, the rest of her family promptly boarded an ocean liner for Ellis Island. On arrival, in 1908, the Olechovskys abandoned their last name and became the Wilsons. In Brooklyn, Janet married Max Sobel – also a Ukrainian Jew – and sold potato knishes on Coney Island beach to tide them over during the

Depression. When Max's jewellery business took off, the Sobels and their five children traded up to chichi Brighton Beach in Brooklyn, and Janet became a full-time homemaker.

In 1938, she began experimenting with a new hobby. One version of the story holds that she took a shine to art after she started doodling over her son Sol's drawings from art school. Another claims that when she tried to convince Sol to stick with an art scholarship, he told her: "If you're so interested in art, why don't you paint?"[1]. In any case, Janet began drawing on anything she could get her hands on, co-opting scavenged seashells, used envelopes and empty boxes in the name of art.

Sol wound up taking his mother's early attempts to his teachers at the Educational Alliance Art School in Manhattan. When he was told that Janet possessed undisputed talent, he immediately became her greatest champion. He showed his mother's work to artistic figures such as the collector Sidney Jarvis and fellow artists Marc Chagall and Max Ernst. They, in turn, introduced Janet to influential critics and gallerists like Peggy Guggenheim, who gave Janet her own solo show in 1946.

Nobody quite knew what to make of Janet. The newspapers called her a "palette packin' grandma"[2] and leaned hard on the attention-grabbing image of a Brooklyn housewife who stumbled into artistic genius. Others described her as a primitivist savant and a top-drawer American Surrealist. "Mrs Sobel's colours are unfailingly good, her imagination absolutely unrestricted, and her compositions hang together into well-knit and decorative units on the wall," wrote *New York Sun* critic Henry McBride. "Of all the so-called primitives to come to light, she is the gayest."[3]

Janet herself was far removed from the art world – she had no artistic training whatsoever and stayed that way for the rest of her life. "No, I never went to museums much," she once said. "I didn't have time and I didn't understand these things."[4] Her early work mainly consisted of folksy, figurative paintings that recalled her peasant childhood in Ukraine. Within a few years, however, the jewel-like orchards and women in patterned headscarves in her paintings began melting together into something fantastically new.

Mixing sand into paint, she began to blow and pour colour in expansive loops and curlicues, using glass pipettes to shoot the mixture across the canvas. There might be an occasional glimpse of a face or a pair of eyes through the intricate lattice of paint, but Janet had otherwise fully embraced abstraction.

This was, apparently, much to the delight of one Jackson Pollock, who began exhibiting similar "drip paintings" a couple of years later, in 1947. "Pollock (and I myself) admired these paintings rather furtively,"[5] recalled art critic Clement Greenberg of Janet's show. Greenberg later told Sol that Pollock had been impressed by his mother's work and that he thought she outclassed Mark Tobey, the man who many believed had influenced Pollock's own signature style.

However, Janet's fame was not destined to last. When the family moved to New Jersey to be closer to their jewellery factory, Janet lost touch with the art world. It didn't help that she had also developed an allergy to paint, forcing her to use crayon and pencil instead. When her husband Max died, work at the family business took over her life completely. Soon, her name became more of a whisper and then it faded out altogether – her monumental artistic contributions to Abstract Expressionism reduced to being perceived as the work of an amateur and hobbyist. When she died, the obituary summed it up plainly: "The widow of the late Max Sobel, who died in 1953, she was 75 and a self-taught artist."[6]

EMILY KAME KNGWARREYE

When Emily Kame Kngwarreye (*c.*1910–1996) came face to face with the work of American painter Sol LeWitt and other Modernists from the West, she had only one question: "Why do those fellas paint like me?"[7]

It was a good question, even though most art critics tended to ask it the other way around: how did Emily, an elderly Aboriginal woman who spent most of her life in the outback, paint like those fellas? "When you consider that she never studied art, never came into contact with the great artists of her time and did not begin painting until she was almost 80 years of age, there can only be one way to describe her," Japanese curator Akira Tatehata said when considering Emily's monumental, punchy canvases of indigenous life. "She was just a genius."[8]

Emily was born in the arid Australian desert of Alhalkere, where the nearest town, Alice Springs, was roughly 250km (150 miles) away. She was only about ten when she saw a white man for the first time, after German settlers moved to the area and renamed it Utopia. Like other Aboriginal people in the region, Emily was forced from her ancestral lands and found work on the cattle stations that dotted the sparse landscape.

In 1977, Emily was among a group of Alyawarr and Anmatyerre women who learned to make batik cloth, a traditional Javanese method of decorating fabric with hot wax. The government-sponsored programme sought to raise money to fund their legal claim to Utopia, and the resulting work was instrumental in proving the women's ownership of their land during the hearings. Thanks in part to the Utopia Women's Batik Group, the Australian government restored the land to its original owners two years later.

After a decade of producing batik, however, Emily grew tired of making the cloth. "I didn't want to continue with the hard work batik required – boiling the fabric over and over, lighting fires, and using up all the soap powder, over and over," she explained. "My eyesight deteriorated as I got older, and because of that I gave up batik on silk – it was better for me to just paint."[9]

As an Anmatyerre elder, Emily was custodian of the sacred Dreaming sites for her tribe – elders before her had passed on their knowledge of the ceremonial body markings, songs and ancestral stories. Even her pierced nose was a symbol of her ancestor rock, Alhalkere. The red-orange deserts of Utopia, with its native yam and white-trunked ghost gum trees, was the stuff of her Dreaming, and Emily painted it all. Her first canvas, *Emu Woman*, painted when she was in her late seventies, was a sensation – nobody in Australia had seen anything like it.

"*Awelye* (women's dreaming), *arlatyeye* (pencil yam), *arkerrthe* (mountain devil lizard), *ntange* (grass seed), *tingu* (dog), *ankerre* (emu), *intekwe* (emu food), *atnwerle* (green bean), and yam seed," she said when asked to explain the bold lines and fizzing colours that saw her compared to Jackson Pollock and Mark Rothko. "That's what I paint, whole lot."[10]

Emily's work arrived just in time for an explosive takeoff of interest in Aboriginal art. Hailed as "the greatest colourist in Australia's artistic history",[11] Emily was also extraordinarily productive – she made an estimated three thousand pieces of work over her brief painting career, which was just short of eight years. Her artistic routine involved spreading her canvas on the ground and sitting cross-legged, switching between her left and right hands for her signature "dump dump dot" brushstrokes. Up until her death at the age of 86, she painted at least one canvas a day.

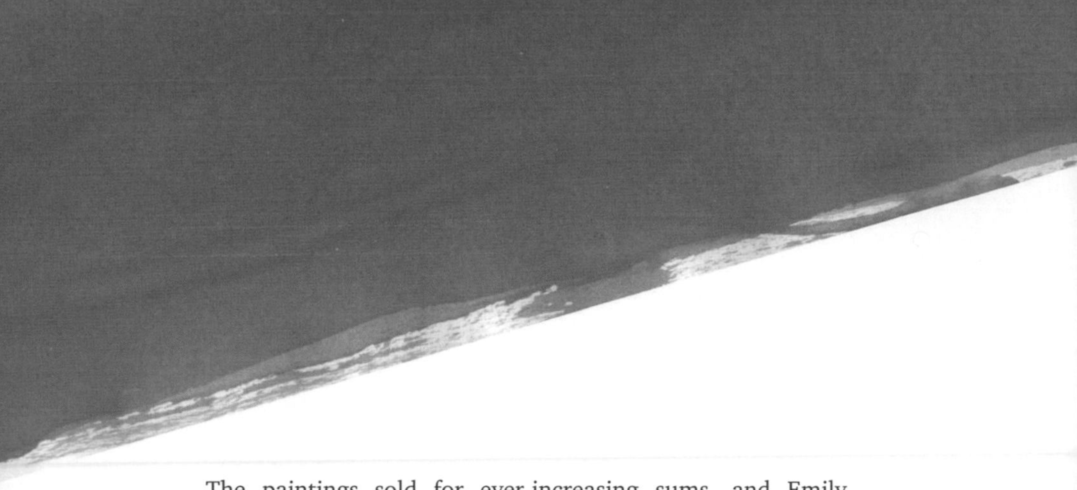

The paintings sold for ever-increasing sums, and Emily was soon earning up to A$500,000 a year. In keeping with tradition, this wealth was communally shared with her kinspeople to buy necessities like food and clothing. Then came the carpetbaggers – the wheeler-dealer agents, gallery owners and all-round hustlers who wanted to cash in on the Emily phenomenon. Even some of her own family thought she was being worked into the ground. "I don't want to end up like that old lady," the artist Kathleen Petyarre said of her aunt. "Everybody fighting over canvas all the time."[12]

The demand for her work was so high that it prompted a boom in forgeries, with one collector telling the British newspaper the *Sunday Telegraph* that he had been offered a fake for about £12,000 (roughly A$27,500 at that time). "It wasn't her style, it wasn't even her brushwork, it just wasn't subtle enough," he said. "Prices are rocketing and as soon as there's a market like this there'll always be conmen."[13] These accusations of exploitation and unscrupulousness dogged Emily even after her death, with some believing that highlighting a single Aboriginal artist to such a degree went against the collective tradition of her people.

Just over a decade after Emily's death, her monumental work *Earth's Creation* was sold for A$1,060,000 – at the time, a world record for an Aboriginal artist and the highest price ever paid for a female Australian artist. But her greatest legacy lies in those who succeeded her. Today, the artistic community of Utopia continues to thrive – and that is thanks to women like Emily, who said simply of her work: "I keep on painting the place that belongs to me."[14]

HILMA AF KLINT

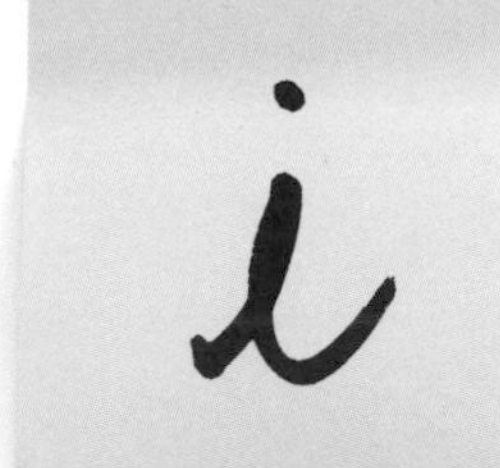

In her lifetime, Hilma af Klint (1862–1944) was known for turning out technically accomplished, if conventional, botanical illustrations and landscapes. But the Stockholm-born artist – one of the first women to be admitted to the Royal Swedish Academy of Fine Arts – had an all-consuming secret. She believed that she was communing with higher beings from a different, astral plane, and that one of them had appointed her to undertake her greatest artistic commission yet. The series known as *The Paintings for the Temple* would become her masterpiece and would prefigure abstract art pioneer Wassily Kandinsky's work by half a decade.

Like many people in the 19th and early 20th centuries, Hilma developed an interest in spiritualism. She attended seances as a teenager, and the early death of her youngest sister only served to reaffirm her devotion to Theosophy, a school of mysticism pioneered by Madame Helena Blavatsky. Among their various theories, Theosophists preached Neoplatonism – the belief that there was a more enlightened, abstract plane of existence from which all things descended – and asserted that mediums like Blavatsky could speak to the inhabitants of that plane to gain esoteric knowledge.

Blavatsky's work was enormously popular – everyone from Piet Mondrian to W B Yeats knew of her. Hilma, however, took it one step farther. At the age of 34, with four other women artists, she set up a group called The Five, which was part sisterly collective and part mystical sect. The

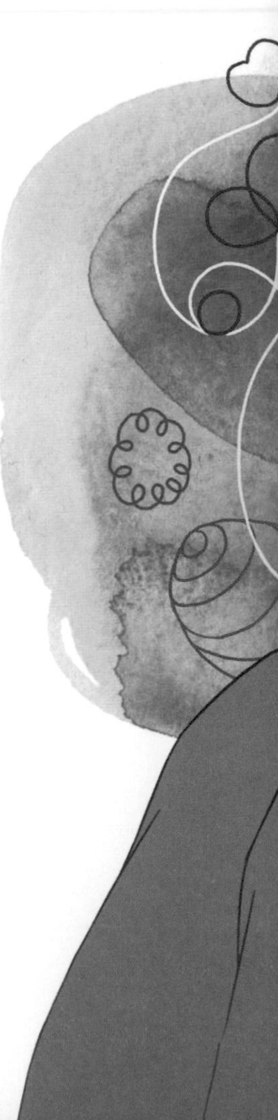

would-be cosmonauts held regular seances to explore the realms that lay beyond the senses. They believed that they were contacting spirit leaders known as the High Masters, and, much like the Surrealists three decades later, they made automatic drawings and writings in which they allowed their hands to spontaneously write and paint without conscious control.

In 1904, Hilma received a special message from a High Master she called Amaliel: she had been selected to create paintings "on the astral plane" that would represent the "immortal aspects of man".[15] This marked the beginning of *The Paintings for the Temple* – a monumental work that eventually grew to encompass 193 paintings, some more than 3m (10ft) tall. "The pictures were painted directly through me, without any preliminary drawings and with great force," she claimed. "I had no idea what the paintings were supposed to depict; nevertheless, I worked swiftly and surely, without changing a single brushstroke."[16]

The results were a world away from the illustrations she had made as a professional draughtswoman for a veterinary institute. By painting an abstract world that nonetheless communicated all the power of the physical form, Hilma found a way to translate the philosophy of Theosophy into art. Her images dance and sing with dazzling psychedelic colours and the movement of celestial spheres. She painted no less than 111 of these pieces between 1906 and 1908, imagining that they would hang in a never-to-be-constructed spiral building called The Temple.

Hilma did not exhibit the paintings during her lifetime. It is thought that social reformer and fellow esotericist Rudolf Steiner, upon visiting her studio, told her it would take the world half a century to understand the pieces. Reportedly heartbroken, Hilma decreed that she would only allow her art to be exhibited 20 years after her death. In her will, she also declared that nobody should be allowed to purchase individual paintings from *The Paintings for the Temple* and split up the series.

Recognition of this proto-Modernist would take far longer than the two decades she had envisaged. After her death at the age of 81, Hilma's work languished unloved for many years. In 1970, Sweden's Moderna Museet director Pontus Hultén even rejected a donation of the whole collection on the grounds of her association with spiritualism. (Never mind that Kandinsky was also an avid follower of Theosophy.) It was only in the 21st century that Hilma was rediscovered and hailed as a precursor to abstract art; a spiritual foremother who somehow divined the radical swerve of Modernism years before anyone else.

"You are to proclaim a new philosophy of life and you yourself are to be a part of the new kingdom. Your labours will bear fruit,"[17] Amaliel told her. More than a century later – and roughly half a century after the Moderna Museet's rejection – that is only just beginning to happen.

NASREEN MOHAMEDI

hen Nasreen Mohamedi (1937–1990) began her career in art, most of her contemporaries in India were strict adherents of realism. With only pencil and graphite as her tools, Nasreen executed a one-woman mutiny against the artistic orthodoxy of the day. With geometric, grid-like sketches that sing with luminous movement, her radical exercise in austerity eventually saw her proclaimed one of her country's most important abstract artists.

Nasreen was born in Karachi and moved to Bombay with her family four years before Partition cleaved the Indian subcontinent in two. In London, she enrolled at St Martin's School of Art and worked at a printmaking atelier in Paris. She was well travelled – there were trips to Tokyo and a stint teaching art in Bombay – but her visits to relatives in Bahrain and Kuwait were the ones that left the biggest impression on her work. Nasreen was hypnotized by these countries' traditional Islamic architecture and repeatedly photographed their deserts on stark black-and-white film.

A tiny dot, a grain of sand

A dot

All leading to the same

A whole[18]

With her poetic work reflecting on the importance of the miniscule, over time Nasreen's sparse line drawings grew smaller in size and ever more abstract. Like many of her artistic peers, she started out in watercolour and oils – but as other artists began moving on to bigger and more expansive canvases, Nasreen rebelled. "I feel the need to simplify,"[19] she wrote in her diary. She was looking to, as she put it, "break the cycle of seeing [so that] Magic and awareness arrives." Unsurprisingly, she was interested in Zen Buddhism and Sufism, recognizing in them the same search for stripped-back unity; her desire, she said, was to get "the maximum from the minimum"[20].

In 1972, Nasreen was offered a teaching job in the fine arts faculty at the Maharaja Sayajirao University of Baroda, in the seaside Indian state of Gujarat. She made an obvious impression on her students by getting them out of the studio and teaching them outdoors: "She wanted to let the students know that they should observe minute details in nature, and not simply imitate them," explained Vivan Sundaram, a painter who was taught by Nasreen. "She looked for the essence in simplicity and form and that was her main work."[21]

She would also show her work to her students on the floor of her living room in complete silence; her audience would quietly observe the art and then leave with a hug, all without uttering a single word. "Silence didn't mean lack of communication to her,"[22] remembered curator Roobina Karode, a former student turned lifelong friend.

Her studio was equally sparse, its only furnishings a low light and a simple drafting table. Sometimes she would ditch the desk altogether in favour of drawing on the floor. It was a monastic life, best summarized by Roobina: "Nasreen mopped the floor of her studio/home several times in a day. The daily rituals of cleansing before sitting down to work were as mandatory for her as rituals of ablution before the offering of prayers."[23]

When Nasreen Mohamedi passed away of Huntington's disease at the age of 53, she was at the tail end of a long battle with the illness that robbed her of motor function. "It was like mortality in cruel play to see this elegant woman in an inadvertent display of the body-soul, stubbing knocking tapping hitting lunging through space,"[24] art critic Geeta Kapur said of her friend toward the end of her life.

Nasreen had already watched the genetic disease claim the lives of two brothers and her father; she was only in her thirties when she, too, received the fatal diagnosis. Still she persevered with her art, using an architect's table and precision tools to steady her hand and control any involuntary tremors. She rarely discussed her own work or practice; her notebooks provide the only evidence of her thoughts on art. In May of 1990, having finally succumbed to her illness, she was buried by the Arabian Sea. "One day all will become functional and hence good design," Nasreen once wrote. "There will be no waste. We will then understand basics. It will take time. But then we get the opportunity for pure patience."[25]

ALMA THOMAS

ost people tend to view retirement as a chance to kick back and relax, but not Alma Thomas (1891–1978). At the age of 69, the Washington, DC, art teacher left work and began a dramatically new chapter in her life as the creator of joyously vivid abstract paintings. "Through colour," she said, "I have sought to concentrate on beauty and happiness, rather than on man's inhumanity to man."[26] The resulting work was compared to everything from Byzantine mosaics to the pointillism of Georges Seurat.[27]

Alma was born in Columbus, Georgia, at the tail end of the 19th century, or the "horse and buggy days",[28] as she put it. Her father was a churchman and her mother a seamstress, but the pair decided to uproot their family of four girls and head for Washington, DC, away from the racial segregation of the Deep South. Alma wanted to be an architect and, in 1924, became the first student to graduate from Howard University's new fine arts department. But there was little opportunity for Alma to pursue her childhood dream, even in relatively progressive DC. Instead, she entered teaching and did painting on the side.

Her early work was considered proficient enough to merit inclusion in group shows, but it failed to dazzle the art world. It was only when she abandoned still lifes and realism in her retirement – partly as a result of her creeping arthritis and failing sight – that she hit upon her own inimitable style.

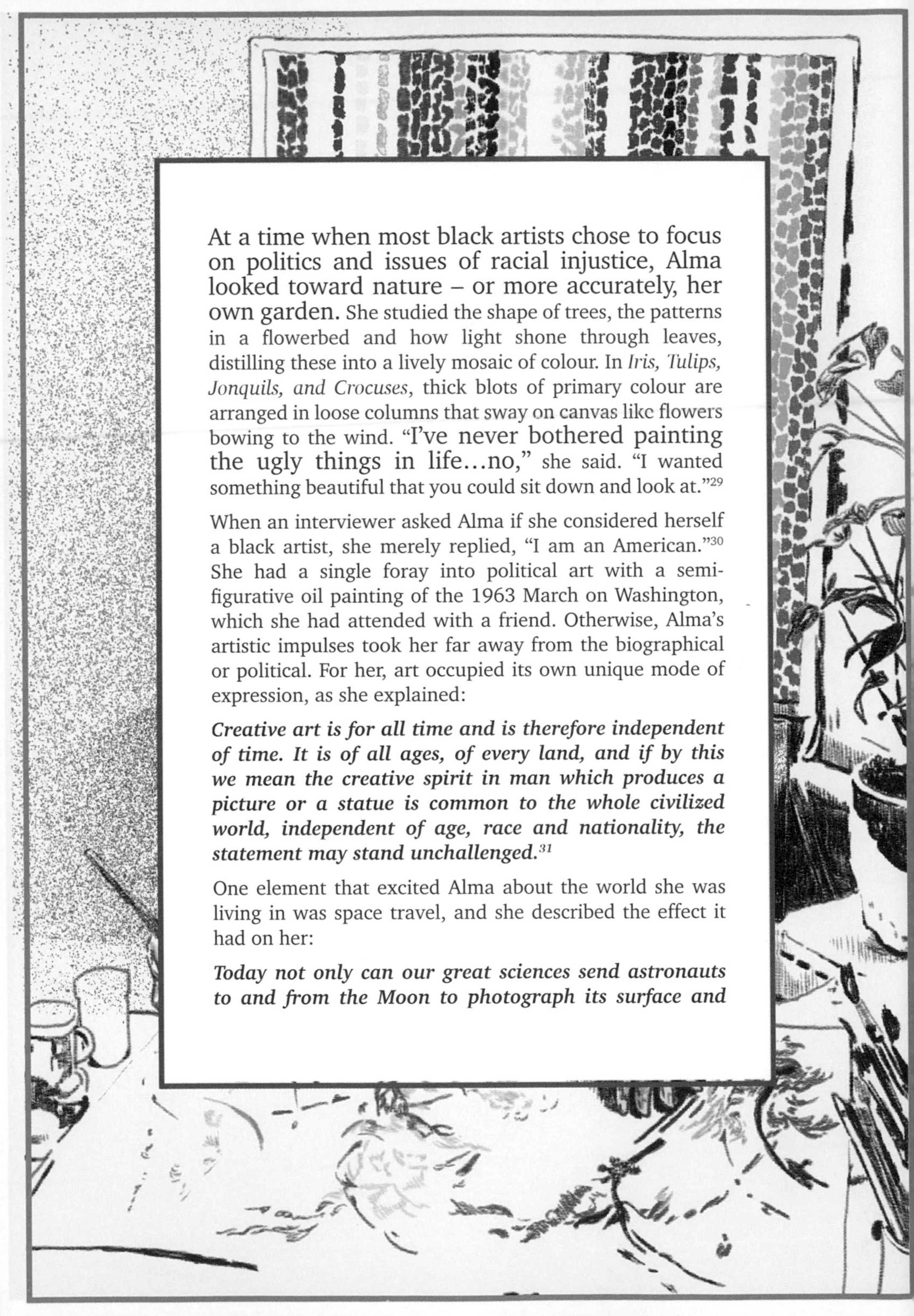

At a time when most black artists chose to focus on politics and issues of racial injustice, Alma looked toward nature – or more accurately, her own garden. She studied the shape of trees, the patterns in a flowerbed and how light shone through leaves, distilling these into a lively mosaic of colour. In *Iris, Tulips, Jonquils, and Crocuses*, thick blots of primary colour are arranged in loose columns that sway on canvas like flowers bowing to the wind. "I've never bothered painting the ugly things in life…no," she said. "I wanted something beautiful that you could sit down and look at."[29]

When an interviewer asked Alma if she considered herself a black artist, she merely replied, "I am an American."[30] She had a single foray into political art with a semi-figurative oil painting of the 1963 March on Washington, which she had attended with a friend. Otherwise, Alma's artistic impulses took her far away from the biographical or political. For her, art occupied its own unique mode of expression, as she explained:

Creative art is for all time and is therefore independent of time. It is of all ages, of every land, and if by this we mean the creative spirit in man which produces a picture or a statue is common to the whole civilized world, independent of age, race and nationality, the statement may stand unchallenged.[31]

One element that excited Alma about the world she was living in was space travel, and she described the effect it had on her:

Today not only can our great sciences send astronauts to and from the Moon to photograph its surface and

bring back samples of rocks and other materials, but through the medium of colour television all can see and experience the thrill of these adventures. These phenomena set my creativity in motion.[32]

From her house on Fifteenth Street, she imagined what it would be like to look down on Earth from the vantage point of an Apollo mission. "You look down on things," Alma surmised. "You streak through the clouds so fast you don't know whether the flower below is a violet or what. You see only streaks of color."[33]

It was perfect fodder for an abstract artist with a singular view of the world. In 1969, she began her *Snoopy* series, inspired by the cartoon nickname that NASA astronauts had given their spacecraft. In paintings like *Blast Off* and *Snoopy Sees Earth Wrapped in Sunset*, conventional space imagery – the pointed tip of a rocket, the blue-green orb of Earth – are injected with Alma's jet-fuel vision and transformed into columns of colour and shimmering balls of light.

At the age of 80, Alma was given her own retrospective at the Whitney Museum of American Art in Manhattan – the first black woman in its history to receive the honour of a solo show. She remained characteristically humble about the achievement: "One of the things we couldn't do was go into museums, let alone think of hanging our pictures there," she said on the eve of the opening. "My, times have changed. Just look at me now."[34]

CAROL RAMA

omen with beady-eyed snakes emerging from their genitalia, their oversized vulvae pulsating hot pink and red with desire; tortured patients in hospital beds and wheelchairs, squeezed into heels and tormented by men with a bushel of penises…you could never accuse Carol Rama (1918–2015) of being prudish. "I paint by instinct and I paint for passion," she once said. "And because of rage and because of violence and because of sadness. And for a certain fetishism. And for happiness and melancholy together. And especially for anger."[35]

The painter, from Turin, Italy, had plenty to be angry about. Her father's car-and-bicycle factory had failed amid the economic turmoil of the 1920s, prompting her mother's breakdown and his subsequent suicide in 1942. With the family bankrupt and her comfortable middle-class existence shattered, Carol spent her childhood visiting her mother in a psychiatric institution. Even as a girl, she felt strangely at home there – there was something liberating being among people who cared little for social convention. "It was then I began to make indecent drawings,"[36] she remembered.

Artists in Turin were mainly producing figurative art when Carol first picked up a paintbrush and began creating watercolours of nude women and men in the throes of ecstatic torment. She was entirely self-taught and, barring a dalliance with a group known as Movimento Arte Concreta, remained a fiercely solo flyer. "I discovered that painting freed me from the anxiety I felt after what happened in my family," she said. "It transformed my feelings of anxiety about everything that society classified as transgressive."[37] According to Carol, she felt safe only when standing in front of a blank canvas.

Carol's gutsy lewdness was not received well by patriarchal Italian society. In 1945, her first exhibition, at the Faber Gallery in Turin, was shut down on charges of obscenity. Carol persevered regardless, transforming her nudes into assemblages, which she made out of oozing layers of paint, teeth, strips of fur and even glass eyes from an embalmer's. Her *Mad Cow* series was inspired by a newsreel clip of the convulsions of a dying cow during an outbreak of "mad cow disease" in England, with rubber sliced into teat-like shapes and arranged on a mail sack. "The death shudder has become an echo of the orgiastic one,"[38] she told the *New York Times*.

Carol was never fully embraced by the outside world in her lifetime. The woman who called herself a "premeditated lunatic",[39] and accessorized with a necklace bearing a gold double penis pendant, spent most of her career working out of her cramped, dark top-floor apartment on Via Napione in Turin, where the walls crawled with antique knick-knacks and found objects.

She was admired by a small yet sincere group of overseas fans, including Man Ray and Andy Warhol, but was ignored by the Turin art scene. (Her commanding personality probably scared some off.) She once declared:

I could never be with normal people, was never at home with the middle classes. I am so lucky to declare this kind of madness. It means I can shift my moods. I have been tortured because I had always painted subjects or things, like naked women, or my father with shaving blades, or flower crowns, like the kind my mother used to make picking up the leaves from the garden of the psychiatric clinic. I don't come from educated painting, I come from feeling.[40]

Carol was finally recognized in 1978, when Italian critic and curator Lea Vergine encountered and fell in love with her taboo-busting work, subsequently becoming her fiercest champion. For the group show *The Other Half of the Avant-Garde: 1910–1940*, Vergine found and exhibited a dozen of Carol's banned 1945 watercolours, singlehandedly resuscitating interest in the painter's career.

"I want to shock and stir up trouble," Carol once said. "Causing outrage around myself became almost an obligation."[41] True to form, she retained her sharp tongue and dirty mind all the way into her old age. When someone asked her how five people from different nationalities would feel about her work fifty years from now, she simply replied: "I would fuck all five. Because instinct and pleasure are universal."[42] In 2003, when the rest of the world finally caught up with Carol and awarded her the Golden Lion for Lifetime Achievement at the Venice Biennale, her only question was: Why had it taken them so long?

CHARLOTTE POSENENSKE

***t**hough art's formal development has progressed at an increasing tempo, its social function has regressed.*

Art is a commodity of transient contemporary significance [...]

It is difficult for me to come to terms with the fact that art can contribute nothing to solving urgent social problems.[43]

The history of art is littered with people who gave up and threw in the towel, but less so with those who chose to leave for political reasons. Charlotte Posenenske (1930–1985) was one of them. Shortly after publishing the above words in 1968 in Swiss magazine *Art International*, the German artist ditched art and became a sociologist.

In one sense, her departure was a long time coming. That same year, she had been in Kassel, Germany, to protest against *Documenta*, the mega-contemporary art show held there every five years. Charlotte handed out flyers to the "culture vultures" in attendance, informing them that events like *Documenta* "blind us to social misery and the deplorable state of affairs in society [...yet] here you are, all gathered together to chat and lie and talk crap so as to gain the upper hand".[44]

She came of age during the Third Reich in Wiesbaden, the capital of Hesse in western Germany. Her father was a Jew who had married a Gentile woman. Preferring suicide to execution, he took his own life when Charlotte was nine years old. Charlotte herself survived only thanks to a kindly policeman who had concealed the file identifying her as half-Jewish – the Nazis called people like her *mischlinge* ("half-breeds") and conscripted them into forced labour. Charlotte grew up on the run from the Nazis, hiding in a basement laundry and on a farm.

Aged 15 when the war finally ended, she began studying art under Willi Baumeister at the Stuttgart Art Academy. Baumeister had emerged as one of Germany's most important leaders in abstract art and theory – his work had even appeared in the 1937 *Degenerate Art* exhibition, which sought to deride Modernist work, art that Hitler felt fell short of Nazi ideals.

Charlotte's early work consisted of abstract paintings in bright primary colours, but her encounter with American minimalism on her visits to New York crystallized a new approach to art for her. Ditching paint and colour, she began bending simple construction materials like sheet aluminium and corrugated cardboard into sculptures. Everything she made was produced in orderly series, from A to E, infinitely reproducible, and all the work was sold at cost.

Her best-known sculpture, *Square Tubes [Series D]*, could be described as a series of hollow galvanized steel forms that resembled ventilation pipes or ducts. Charlotte instructed viewers and exhibitors – whom she called "consumers" – to do whatever they wanted with the component pieces. In a 1967 exhibition, entitled *All This, Sweetie, Will One Day Be Yours*, Charlotte hired four men in Lufthansa overalls to transport a cardboard version into the gallery and rearrange the sculpture in response to the audience.

In Charlotte's 1968 Statement, she also wrote:

The things I make are

variable

as simple as possible

reproducible.

They are components of a space, since they are like building elements,

they can always be rearranged into new combinations or positions,

thus, they alter the space.[45]

Increasingly, however, Charlotte felt uneasy with the function of art in a politically unstable and unequal world. Within a year of her Statement, she had stopped producing any new work. By 1970, she had packed away all her unsold art and exiled it to her attic, turning down an attractive opportunity to pitch a public art project in Germany. She declared in *EgoIst*, an art magazine based in Frankfurt:

> ***Each investment exceeding the minimum satisfaction of the actual needs [of the tenants] serves only to pretend these needs are met completely. That is why 38,000 DM are to be invested [...] for a fountain or a sculpture. That which is supposedly no longer merely useful – art – gives a good return for the developer. [Art] is meant to make believe that these rabbit holes have fulfilled all needs, and that one can now afford the beautiful. Art is supposed to advertise the slums of the future [...] Art here has the function of an alibi.***[46]

Can art make a difference? By the end of a 17-year career in art, Charlotte thought not. She got a place on the graduate programme for sociology at the University of Frankfurt and spent the rest of her life researching industrial labour and acting as a union organizer. In doing so, she staged her final and most dramatic statement on art: quitting.

FAHRELNISSA ZEID

ven without her remarkable career as an abstract artist, Fahrelnissa Zeid's (1901–1991) life was already the stuff of fairy tales. Dubbed the "painter princess",[47] the Turkish artist was one of the first women to attend the Istanbul Academy of Fine Arts. She took tea with Hitler, married a Hashemite prince, fled a military coup in Iraq and threw notorious parties that were the talk of the town among London's avant-garde elite.

Fahrelnissa was born near Istanbul into a well-to-do Ottoman family. When she turned 12, their world was shattered when her elder brother shot and killed their father. Tragedy struck again when Fahrelnissa and her first husband lost their eldest child, Faruk, to scarlet fever in 1924. Despite her early heartbreak, Fahrelnissa travelled widely during her marriage, taking art classes at the Académie Ranson in Paris. Along with her education at the Istanbul Academy, this made her one of the few Turkish women at the time to have received formal training as an artist.

In 1934, Fahrelnissa divorced her husband and married Prince Zeid Al-Hussein of the Iraqi royal family. She gamely took on the duties of an ambassador's wife when he entered diplomatic service – a responsibility that included meeting Adolf Hitler when the couple lived in Berlin. (They talked painting, but history is otherwise silent on what she thought of the Führer.)

Thanks to her very first brush with air travel, Fahrelnissa had a life-altering experience en route from Berlin to her husband's next posting in Baghdad. "I did not 'intend' to become an abstract painter; I was a person working very conventionally with forms and values," she once said. "But flying by plane transformed me…The world is upside

down. A whole city could be held in your hand: the world seen from above."[48] Like Alma Thomas (*see* page 30), Fahrelnissa's earthbound vision suddenly soared into the abstract.

In Baghdad, she allied herself with an avant-garde collective known as the d Group. But it was Prince Al-Hussein's next posting, to the UK, that set her on course to becoming an artist. She turned a servant's room at the Iraqi Embassy in London into her studio, organizing lavish salons and parties with guest lists that read like a *Who's Who* of European art, including André Breton, Henry Moore and Lee Miller. "As long as I had lived and worked in Turkey, I had seemed to distrust my own artistic initiatives. I was too isolated, too unsure of myself," Fahrelnissa said. "Now I feel that I am at least understood and accepted, whether in London or in Paris, as an artist rather than as a kind of freak."[49]

She began to refine her approach to painting, too. In her 1947 work *Fight Against Abstraction*, balled fists appear to punch their way out of a tiled backdrop reminiscent of stained glass. Fahrelnissa was clearly undergoing a battle between her old figurative impulses and her instinct toward a new visual style. By 1948, she had made a breakthrough with the fittingly named *Resolved Problems*, a purely abstract canvas depicting a brilliant kaleidoscope of reds, yellows, blues and greens. "Often, I am aware of what I have painted only when the canvas is at last finished,"[50] she said. Critics praised Fahrelnissa for injecting her love of Islamic architecture and design into Western Abstract Expressionism. She exhibited in Paris, New York and London, including a solo show at London's Institute of Contemporary Arts.

The events of 1958, however, brought an end to life as she knew it. Iraq's Hashemite royal family was overthrown in a military coup; King Faisal II was machine-gunned to death and his body strung up in public. Most of Fahrelnissa's in-laws met the same fate. She and her husband were ordered to depart the embassy. Already prone to bouts of depression, Fahrelnissa was left traumatized by the sudden fall from grace. "It is as if I had suddenly become afraid of colours and of life," she said. "Instead of the brilliant kaleidoscope that once seemed to surround me, I can only perceive, all around me, a winding labyrinth of hard and heavy black lines."[51]

Fahrelnissa never returned to the giddy heights of Abstract Expressionism. Driven into exile, she returned to her less masterful, figurative work, and the woman who had once exhibited in major cities across the West now faded into obscurity. In 1975, she moved to Jordan to be closer to her son and founded a studio at home to teach young female artists. "You must forget what you know because what you know is what you have learned," she instructed her students, "but what you do not know is what you really are."[52]

When London's Tate Modern gallery mounted the first retrospective of her work in the UK in 2017, her son Ra'ad bin Zeid said he was "floating on air". "My mother worked so hard in her life and it wasn't always very easy being a woman and being the wife of a diplomat and coming from the Orient," he said. "People did not pay attention to her in the beginning. But she persisted and she kept on."[53]

MARLOW MOSS

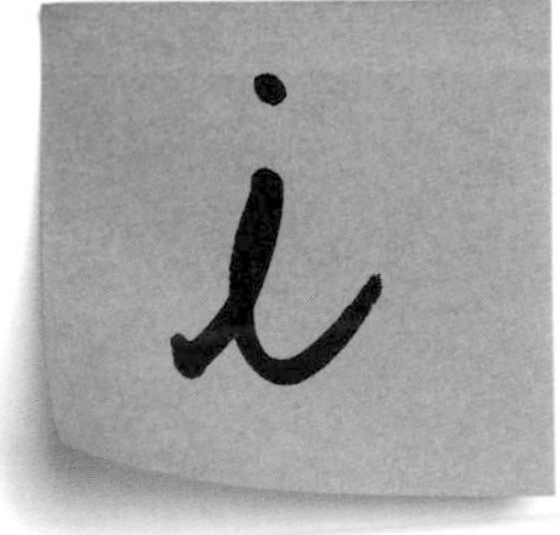

n 1919, London-born Marjorie Jewel Moss (1889–1958) was not doing great. Although she had attended the Slade School of Fine Art in London, she had suffered a nervous breakdown, abandoned her studies and retreated to Cornwall, where she had spent time convalescing as a child. At her seaside sanctuary, she made a solemn vow to herself: she would never give in to depression again. Instead, she reinvented herself – and so the middle-class daughter of a Jewish clothier and a homemaker became Marlow Moss, the cross-dressing lesbian and abstract painter whose paintings were exhibited alongside those of Piet Mondrian and Wassily Kandinsky. "I destroyed my old personality," Marlow later said, "and created a new one."[54]

On her return to London, Marlow chopped off her hair and plunged into the glitz and glamour of the Roaring Twenties. She wore suits and silk cravats, partying by night and reading philosophy by day. Her niece recalled: "My memory of seeing Marlow, then Aunt Marjorie, was a person in a tailored double-breasted suit with short hair, then called an Eton Crop. My sister and I couldn't make out if she was a man or a woman, and I don't remember if we asked anyone about this, probably not!"[55]

Marlow may have reinvented herself in London, but it was in Paris where she met the love of her life, the Dutch novelist A H "Nettie" Nijhoff, who introduced Marlow to Mondrian. The Dutch painter had coined the term Neoplasticism to express a dramatic new method of painting: one that was distilled down to, as he put it, "the straight line and the clearly defined primary colour".[56] Marlow, however, went one better by introducing parallel double lines in her work. She wanted to capture, as Nettie put it, "space, movement and light".[57] Double lines appeared in Mondrian's painting a year later, leading to an ongoing debate over whether Mondrian's apprentice influenced her tutor, or the other way around.

Marlow's vivid and coolly elegant paintings were admired regardless, and she became a founding member of the influential Paris group known as Abstraction-Création. "Her work," one friend said, "is immaculate, scrupulously honest: fractions of the Absolute which have been captured in matter."[58]

When Hitler's troops began marching across Europe, Marlow realized that Paris was no place for a half-Jewish lesbian and her Dutch lover. The couple left for Normandy and then the Netherlands, futilely hoping to outrun the Germans. When

Nettie's homeland was invaded, Marlow escaped on a fishing boat to England. The two lovers hoped their parting would only be temporary. Marlow was in her fifties when she arrived back in London, alone in a now unfamiliar city. Mondrian attempted to convince her to move to New York with him, but she departed for her old haunt in Cornwall instead. Nettie, meanwhile, went on the run and waited out the war in the south of the Netherlands.

By 1944, Marlow had found a studio near the Cornish fishing village of Lamorna and was attempting to make inroads into the British art scene. She was cruelly rebuffed. Her time in France had made her too much of an outsider to fit in with her British contemporaries; regarded as an eccentric loner, she grew increasingly isolated. "I'm convinced it's for the individual himself to create his own life despite any obstacles," she wrote to a friend back in Europe. "I am very much alone in my ideas here."[59] Most of her art had already gone up in flames – the Germans had bombed the French chateau where she had lived with Nettie and had stored her work.

The couple's reuniting in 1946 prompted Marlow's most productive decade yet. She continued painting and began to experiment with sculptures in brass and steel, making enough work to have two solo exhibitions in London. But, as in the Cornwall art scene, Marlow was too many steps ahead for her English peers. It didn't help that she was still proudly flouting the conventions of femininity – she wore cuffs and a riding jacket everywhere, accessorized with cigarettes or a riding crop. Several art critics thought she was a man; others sneered at her as a second-rate Mondrian. One review was cruel in its praise: "The sculptures are superb, objects of austere, calculated beauty. The exhibition deserted and not one work bought."[60]

Just a month after her second show, Marlow was diagnosed with stomach cancer and she died only two months after that. She remained resolutely herself even as death approached, fastening her shirt with a brooch and keeping herself groomed and her face powdered. "Leave me alone," she said shortly before she died. "I have to get accustomed to space."[61]

Figurative

PREHISTORIC CAVE PAINTERS

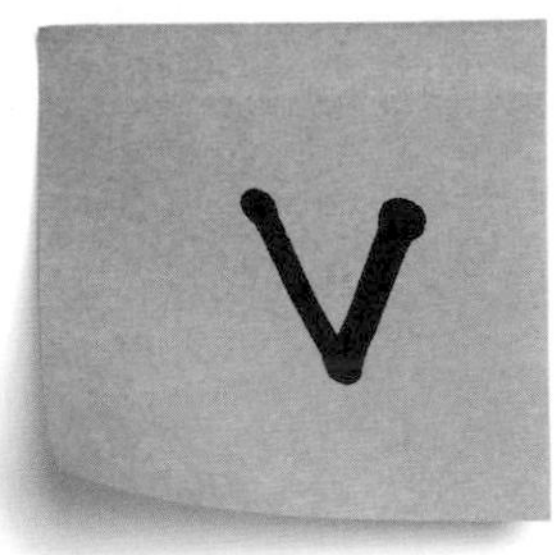

Venturing into the labyrinthine El Castillo cave in Cantabria, Spain, is like stepping back in time. When your eyes adjust to the flickering light, you'll be able to spot ancient cave paintings daubed by anonymous prehistoric artists. The millennia-old rock art traces the outlines of bison and ibex so gracefully that Pablo Picasso was moved to declare "we have learned nothing in 12,000 years"[1] when he first laid eyes on them.

The UNESCO World Heritage Site was discovered by Spanish archeologist Hermilio Alcalde del Río in 1903 and is considered one of the wonders of pre-civilization. It is also home to several handprints, thought to have been made by their ancient creators, the prehistoric cave painters (*fl.* *c.*38,00 BC), by blowing paint over hands tightly pressed to the surface of the rock – a kind of prehistoric stencil.

It is not the only cave that is home to such handprints. Ancient nooks and crannies, littered with hundreds of these markings, usually tucked next to paintings of animals, have been discovered in places ranging from Indonesia and Borneo to Argentina, and are thought to date from about 40,000 years ago. Nobody knows what they mean – scientists theorize that they could operate as some kind of artistic signature, imprinted thousands of years before the dawn of written language. For decades, however, scientists were certain of one thing: the handprints were male.

Not so fast, said Dean Snow. In 2013, the Emeritus Professor of Anthropology at Pennsylvania State University published a decade's worth of handprint analysis that showed many of these handprints to be female. Mankind's first artists, he suggested, might have been predominantly female. "There has been a male bias in the literature for a long time," Snow told *National Geographic*

magazine. "People have made a lot of unwarranted assumptions about who made these things, and why."[2]

Snow's leap into the unknown was down to a chance encounter with the work of John Manning, a British scientist who discovered that women and men tend to have differing lengths of fingers. Men's index fingers are usually longer than their ring fingers, whereas both fingers on women tend to be the same length. When Snow looked through a book on Upper Paleolithic art and spotted a handprint from the Pech Merle cave in France, he knew that Manning was onto something.

"I thought, man, if Manning knows what he's talking about, then this is almost certainly a female hand,"[3] Snow said. When a further tally of more palm-print images suggested that two-thirds were female, he added: "I thought here was a neat little one off science problem that can be solved by applications of archaeological science."[4]

Snow built an algorithm that could distinguish whether a handprint was male or female, and he crunched data from 32 of the clearest prehistoric stencils from Europe, including 16 from El Castillo. When the results came in, 75 per cent of the handprints belonged to women.

When the findings were published in the scientific journal *American Antiquity*, the news was immediately picked up by newspapers around the world. Not everyone was persuaded by the results – one scientist suggested that the smaller finger ratios could come from adolescent boys who climbed into the caves for fun. But Snow remained convinced. "Given the size of the sample used here, it will be surprising if the predominance of females does not hold up as hand stencils and handprints are examined in additional caves located in southwestern Europe,"[5] he wrote in his study. He cited a *New Yorker* cartoon from 1980 that shows a group of cavewomen huddled around a wall of prehistoric art, one of whom asks: "Does it strike anyone else as weird that none of the great painters have been men?"[6]

"The humorous irony in 1980 was, of course, based on the generally accepted view that cave artists must have been males," Snow said. "Now, more than three decades later, the cartoon still seems funny, but the focus of the irony has been shifted."[7] In other words, the historical myth of the great male artist had gone the way of the woolly mammoth.

There are, of course, still more mysteries to uncover, and more evidence is needed to back up what we now know. Were these deep, dark caves sites of religious pilgrimage for primitive mankind? Were the cave paintings of bison and other food sources a form of ritual invocation – the Paleolithic equivalent of "if you paint it, they will come"? And just how many of these prehistoric handprints belong to women?

In 2017, a European team of archeologists began building an online database of three-dimensional handprints, hoping to answer some of these questions. For the price of an admission ticket, you can even visit El Castillo yourself to take a look. Until then, however, the writing remains on the wall – we just have to learn how to read it.

CHEN SHU

ccording to her family records, Chen Shu (1660–1736) entered the world blessed by no less than the Chinese god of literature himself. Sometime before the Qing dynasty painter's birth in Jiaxing, her father had donated money to repair a temple and was said to have been rewarded with a thank-you visit from the heavenly deity in his dreams. Chen Shu herself was born on the birthday of the god of literature.

Appropriately, she grew into a book-smart and quick-witted child. When eight-year-old Chen Shu saw the boys in her family troop off to school to learn to read, write and paint – the skills they needed for their future positions as scholars and government officials – she got them to parrot their lessons back at her so that she could pick something up. By the age of ten, she was able to draw and recite from the *Book of Songs*, the revered anthology of classical Chinese poetry. Her mother banned her from further participating in such unladylike behaviour, but this failed to discourage Chen Shu, who proceeded to make a perfect copy of a painting from her father's study just to prove that she could.

After giving her daughter a good beating, Chen Shu's mother went to bed and dreamed of none other than the god of literature himself. "I have given your daughter a brush," he thundered. "Some day she will become famous. How can you forbid it?"[8] As Chen Shu's son, Qian Chenquin, says in his biography of his mother, things changed quickly after that. A teacher was hired to tutor Chen Shu in a classical education, and she was able to paint as she wished, though it didn't stop her father from making passive–aggressive comments. "It's a pity she's female," he said. "Were she male she would exalt the family name."[9]

Chen Shu's own family had no artistic connections to speak of, but that changed once she married into the Qian family in neighbouring Haiyan. Her father-in-law was a renowned calligrapher and poet, and her husband occasionally added lines of poetry to Chen Shu's paintings. The couple entertained widely and mingled with the great and good of Chinese literati, though not without significant cost – at one point, Chen Shu had to pawn some of her clothes to keep up with their lifestyle. But most of her life remained taken up by the demands of family and child-rearing – she had three sons and one daughter – and caring for her parents-in-law and her own mother.

It was only in the last three decades of her life that she was truly able to pursue painting, and all of her extant work is dated to this period. She painted everything from summertime landscapes to exquisitely detailed images of flowers and birds. In *White Cockatoo*, a melancholy pet bird is chained to a perch, with its eyes trained on an insect buzzing into view on the lower third of the scroll. At the top of the scroll is sweetly and subtly painted white blossom.

At the time, women were not allowed to make a living from their painting, but this was not for the reasons you might expect. The Qing dynasty believed that the greatest art was created only by educated amateurs who painted in the privacy of their home for leisure and enjoyment, and didn't seek to profit from it like common tradesmen. Women of a certain class and rank could be recognized as painters in their own right, though they were always expected to put their family and domestic duties first.

Thankfully, Chen Shu was repaid in kind for her devotion to her children. Her son Qian Chenquin grew up to be a high-ranking official and her greatest champion – he showed off much of her work to the Qianlong Emperor, prompting him to collect her "divine work".[10] Thanks to her son's efforts, Chen Shu is still the woman with the highest number of works in the palace collection today. Her legacy also lives on in another way: as the matriarch of her family, she trained male and female members of her direct and extended family in the art of painting. All told, no less than twenty of her descendants, including five women, became artists themselves – her influence echoing down the generations, from one master to another.

TINA BLAU

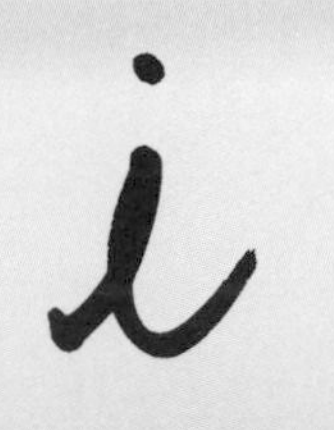

In the years after Tina Blau's (1845–1916) death, the Jewish-born painter's work hung in Austria's greatest public museums, and the Wiener Frauenakademie (Vienna Art School for Women and Girls), which she co-founded, was turning out talented artists by the bucketload. She even had an Austrian street named after her: Tina-Blau-Weg. By 1938, however, Nazi Germany had annexed Austria and ordered the systematic erasure (and attempted genocide) of its Jewish population. Tina's artworks came down from the walls, her school lost its funding and – in one final indignity – the street that had been named after her was renamed after a male artist.

The news would have broken her heart. While she was alive, Tina had triumphed in the face of overwhelming sexism to earn a living as an independent artist. She had dragged Impressionism into Austrian art, infusing the country's gloomy landscape-painting tradition with space and light. Critic A F Seligmann hailed her as a Modernist pioneer: "If a history of the development of Austrian painting, especially landscape, should be written," he said, "then Tina Blau must be named as among the first to practice Impressionism."[11]

Born in Vienna, Tina was fortunate enough to have a father who invested everything in her art. Although Simon Blau had once harboured artistic ambitions of his own, he ended up training as an army doctor. Women at the time were barred from formal training, but Simon paid for

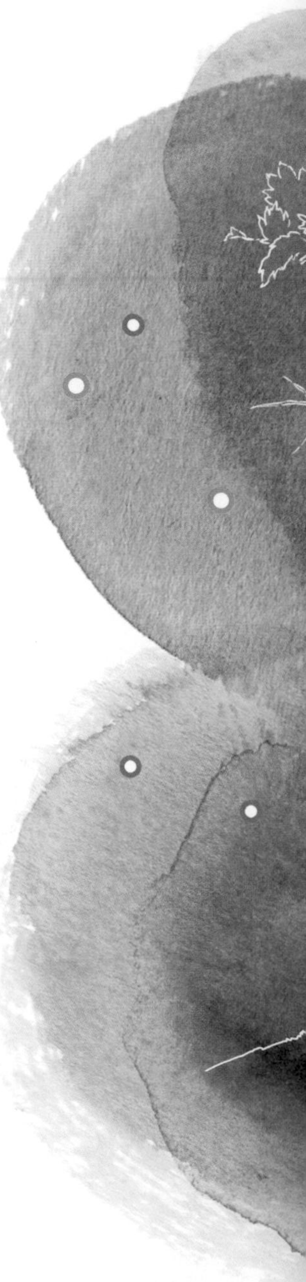

his daughter to study abroad and under the tutelage of other artists. When she complained of homesickness on a field trip to Transylvania, he replied by post: "If you really want to become an artist, you have to learn to surmount problems."[12]

At 22, Tina sold one of her first canvases – a painting of a kiln set against a forest sunset – to the Österreichischer Kunstverein (Austrian Art Association). She lived off the proceeds for the rest of the year, and sold an increasing number of canvases, nabbing solo shows and making a name for herself in Vienna and Munich. It wasn't easy. The prevailing attitude of the time held that women could be proficient at painting, but lacked the spark of creativity necessary for true genius. "A woman," sniffed the Austrian critic Arthur Roessler, "has no art of her own."[13]

Even one of Tina's old teachers, August Schaeffer, felt similarly. "Our painting ladies imagine that in their efforts they are more rousing and dashing than the men, they venture and take this position for all they're worth," he wrote. "Now the women are quite hard workers…they braid and weave away as if it were a matter of winning the world, as if they didn't already have this in their laps. But that's not enough anymore."[14]

In 1882, Tina finished her masterpiece *Spring at the Prater* and caused a sensation in Vienna. Thanks to her hours of plein-air painting at the Prater public gardens in the city, Tina rendered the panoramic park scene with consummate deftness; everyone in the picture, from women in petticoats taking the air to the housemaid babysitting her young wards, seemed touched by golden sunlight.

It was *too* bright, in fact, for the Künstlerhaus jury who were in charge of selecting work for its prestigious show – they thought it would distract from the darker pieces on show. The judges caved in only after a male painter appealed on Tina's behalf, and even then they hung the piece in an obscure corner of the gallery.

Tina had the last laugh. The painting showed up everybody else's work as hopelessly and unnaturally dreary. "It was a hole," one review went, "a hole in the wall, through which one believed one could see into open nature!"[15] When France's Minister of Fine Arts visited the exhibition, he said it was the highlight of the whole show; and upon visiting her studio, he encouraged her to submit the painting to the prestigious Paris Salon – she did so and was given an honourable mention.

Though Tina dedicated much of her later years to teaching aspiring female artists at her art school, she wanted her work to be viewed on its own, and refused to take part in group shows for women. Many of her paintings were lost when her family fled Austria with the advance of the Nazis. It was a miracle that Tina's work resurfaced at all, and it took years for her to reclaim her position in Austrian art history.

In all likelihood, she would have found this distressing but unsurprising."If I were not a woman," she once wrote in a letter, "my works would be viewed not only as independent, but also ahead of their time in Vienna, just as they were in Paris and Munich. I am valued by my colleagues, but nonetheless, when it really counts for me to be treated as an equal, to be honored and included because of the value of my work, I am always left out."[16]

JOSEPHINE HOPPER

veryone familiar with Edward Hopper's paintings knows the woman in them. She's the redhead in *Nighthawks*, hunched over a cup of diner coffee; the unaccompanied theatre usher in *New York Movie*; the contemplative woman in a cloche hat in *Automat*. Whatever the setting, his solitary female figure symbolizes something deeper than just a woman alone – she is a portal into the isolation that characterizes so much of his work. She's also based on a single person: his wife, muse and fellow painter Josephine Nivison Hopper (1883–1968).

Jo, as she was known to friends and family, was the woman behind Edward's career. She gave feedback on his sketches ("too much lipstick",[17] she said of the secretary in *Office at Night*), pushed him toward watercolours and a brighter colour palette, and even gave him the big break that led to his debut sell-out show. In the process, she gave up her own promising career in art.

Jo was born in New York to a Texan music teacher and a first-generation Irish immigrant, and she would later put her rebellious temper down to her Celtic blood. At her teacher-training college, she was listed as a "special artist" in her yearbook, and she published several drawings in the school newspaper.

After graduation, Jo initially turned her back on teaching in order to study painting at the New York School of Art. Her charisma and determination impressed her teacher, Robert Henri (*see also* page 98), who asked her to sit for a painting called *The Art Student*. In it, Jo stands rigid with a fistful of paintbrushes, looking fiercely at the viewer through a tangle of hair.

When she left art school, Jo had little intention of settling down – instead, she balanced a job as an elementary-school teacher with illustration commissions from newspapers like the *New-York Tribune* and bit parts in avant-garde plays. Art and culture, in all its various forms, became the driving force of her life.

By the time she married Edward Hopper, Jo was 41. They had both attended the New York School of Art, but their paths had rarely crossed until they encountered each other at the same Maine artists' colony one summer. He was quiet and stoical while she was chatty and outspoken, but the tall, skinny artist was exactly her type: "No one had ever called him handsome or distinguished when I married him," she wrote in her diary. "It was the 'long, lean & hungry' that got me."[18] Edward threw pebbles at the window of her boarding house to wake her up for their early-morning sketch sessions; she repaid the favour by nudging him toward her preferred medium of watercolour.

Jo was quickly establishing herself as an artist of note – her paintings hung next to those of Man Ray at exhibitions, and the *New York Times*'s exacting art critic Elisabeth Luther Cary highlighted her work above Georgia O'Keeffe's in a Brooklyn Museum group show. The show was also Edward's breakout moment, thanks to Jo. On her insistence, six of his watercolours were selected for exhibition, and critics were ecstatic about the discovery of this new artist. He even sold a painting for $100 – only his second-ever sale.

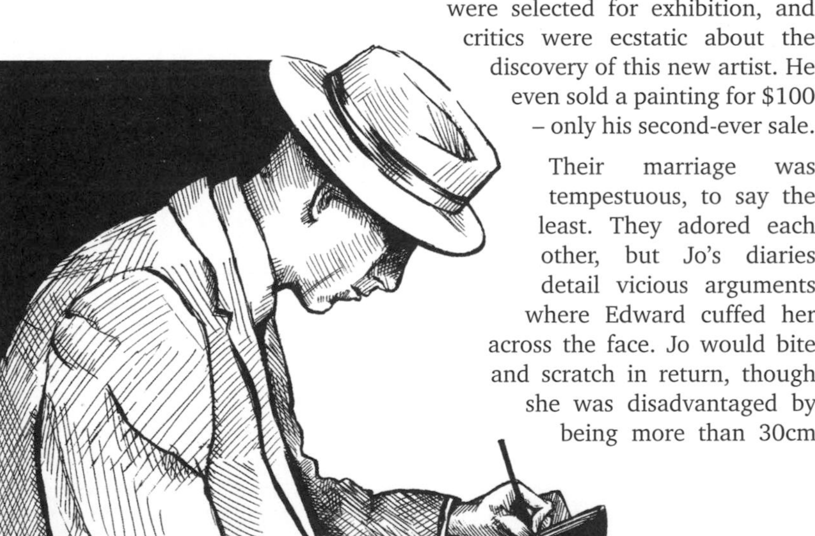

Their marriage was tempestuous, to say the least. They adored each other, but Jo's diaries detail vicious arguments where Edward cuffed her across the face. Jo would bite and scratch in return, though she was disadvantaged by being more than 30cm

(1ft) shorter. Jo was sanguine about the violence: "Swatting isn't as bad as meanness,"[19] she wrote; nevertheless Edward was also capable of plenty of meanness. He constantly complained about her inability to play the housewife – her idea of cooking extended as far as a can opener and a can of pea soup. "Isn't it nice to have a wife who paints?" she once asked. His reply: "It stinks."[20]

As Edward's star began to rise, Jo's began to sink. She became his assiduous record-keeper, tracking loans and sales of his work, dealing with his correspondence and archiving newspaper clips of his coverage. "Of course," she once wrote, "if there can be room for only one of us, it must undoubtedly be he. I can be glad and grateful for that."[21] Edward's paintings effectively became their children, though she grew resentful over her own declining career, even referring to her own works – which increasingly attracted bad reviews – as "poor little stillborn infants".[22]

Would her own career have soared if she hadn't married Edward? It is impossible to say. Though she bequeathed all her work to the Whitney Museum of American Art, most of it was dumped or destroyed, apart from 200 pieces recently discovered in its basement. But her mark is all over Edward's work. Until his death in 1967, Jo posed exclusively for Edward as model and muse – and it is her face, with its message of solitude and woe, that peeks out from his paintings. "It's such blessedness that Edward and I have each other," she once wrote. "Surely I'll be allowed to go when he does."[23] She died less than a year after he did.

ELISABETTA SIRANI

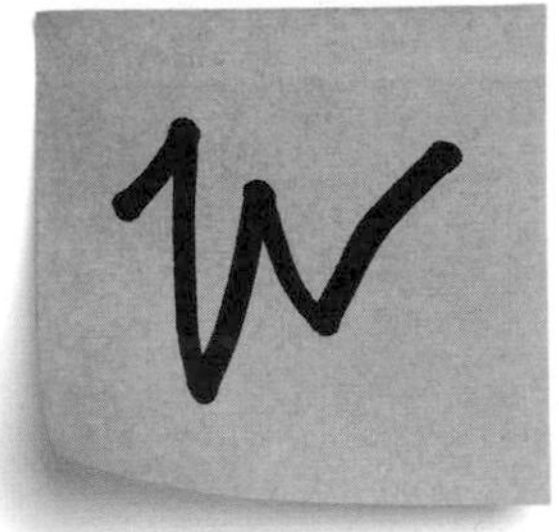

hen Elisabetta Sirani (1638–1665) died, she was honoured with the kind of public memorial service lavished on royalty. The city of Bologna, Italy, decked out the hallowed Basilica of San Domenico in fine black drapes, and a mass was specially composed for the occasion, with a life-sized effigy of the painter at her easel as the show-stopping centrepiece. "The entire City weeps having lost a Virtuosa and already have passed all the Women in the world she painted,"[24] lamented one of Elisabetta's patrons.

The young Italian painter did more than enough to merit such an outpouring of grief. At 27, Elisabetta had already worked as a professional artist for a decade, producing over 200 paintings for no less than 100 patrons from the highest echelons of Italian society. Her studio-salon hosted countless noble lords and ladies who visited to see Elisabetta in action and, more often than not, left with a commission of their own. In her "magisterial management of brushes", she was described by one admirer as the "the incomparable, immortal, and divine Paintress Signora Lisabetta Sirani".[25]

Elisabetta trained as a teenager under her father, Giovanni Andrea Sirani. His *bottega* (studio) in Bologna was one of the city's most successful, attracting a stream of regular patrons and apprentices. By the time Elisabetta was 17, various Italian cities had commissioned her to paint their public altarpieces, and at the age of 24 she inherited the workshop from her father when he fell ill. She quickly became renowned for the speed and ease with which she could sketch and complete a canvas. In her diary, she recounts the visit of a grand prince of Tuscany, who was so impressed that he immediately commissioned another work from her. "In the end he ordered a Blessed Virgin for himself, and I painted it immediately so it would be dry in time for his return to Florence,"[26] she notes.

Elisabetta's paintings are pure Baroque drama as seen through the eyes of a young woman, with historical heroines triumphing over wily men and the doubts of society. In *Timoclea of Thebes Throwing the Captain of Alexander's Army into a Well*, Elisabetta captures the Theban woman

mid-push as she shoves her rapist to his death, her face a mask of perfect determination. In *Portia Wounding Her Thigh*, Portia Catonis, the wife of Brutus, is shown stabbing herself to prove that she can keep the secret of Julius Caesar's assassination plot to herself.

Women were not just Elisabetta's subjects; they were also her apprentices and students. In her twenties, she set up Europe's first professional art academy for women. It attracted a steady supply of girls who wished to learn under the tutelage of Bologna's finest artist, many of whom then went on to become professional printmakers and painters themselves. Over the previous two centuries, researchers believe, there were only forty or so women artists in all of Italy, half of them cloistered nuns. To make a living from one's art – as Elisabetta and many of her disciples did – was in itself a revolutionary act.

Elisabetta knew that she was ahead of her time. Perhaps wise to the phenomenon of men claiming credit for, or throwing doubt on, women's work, she made sure she signed all her work in bold block letters. She even started weaving her name into the very texture of her paintings; you can spy her signature in the drape of a sleeve, or carved into the floorboards under a subject's feet. Her fame grew so quickly that she was noted as having notched up thirty commissions for paintings in the year before her death, while other, older and more established painters got by on three or so.

When Elisabetta died on an August evening not yet 28 years of age, she had already been incapacitated by a painful illness that nobody could quite diagnose. Her father accused a servant of poisoning her out of jealousy, but a subsequent autopsy found only ulcers and a few unexplained holes in her stomach lining; it is thought that the cause of her death may have been peritonitis following a burst ulcer.

The murder allegations elevated Elisabetta to the realm of legend; her death was reported on the front page of the city's newssheet. Her fame, however, had changed the way Italy looked at women artists. "She made us realize," said the 18th-century Bolognese painter and art critic Luigi Crespi, "that if from early adolescence Women, in addition to their talent and natural inclination, were also educated, as men are, equally like them they will succeed in every sort of science, profession and art."[27]

SYLVIA SLEIGH

hen Sylvia Sleigh (1916–2010) came across Jean-Auguste-Dominique Ingres's *The Turkish Bath*, she knew she had to respond to the 19th-century painting. "I wanted to show how I felt women should have been painted with dignity and individuality – not as sex objects,"[28] she said. The Welsh-born artist enlisted five men, including her husband, Lawrence Alloway, to pose naked in the place of Ingres's shamelessly objectified harem girls, rendering their 1970s quiffs and tan lines in exquisite detail. She explained her rationale:

I made a point of finding male models and I painted them as portraits, not as sex objects, but sympathetically as intelligent and admired people, not as women had so often been depicted as unindividuated houris. I had noted from my childhood that there were always pictures of beautiful women but very few pictures of handsome men so I thought that it would be truly fair to paint handsome men for women.[29]

Though she eventually became a naturalized US citizen, Sylvia carried the memory of her early days in British art with her. She remembered female students at the Brighton School of Art, where she had studied, being "treated in a second-rate fashion".[30] Apart from a one-off solo show at London's Kensington Art Gallery, she painted without much success and had to take a job in London in a Bond Street clothes shop on the side. "Every customer had a lady to look after them," Sylvia recalled. "It was very interesting. One of the most exciting things was undressing Vivien Leigh."[31] In Sylvia's paintings you can still see the influence of fashion in her attention to the domestic textiles and trappings of style, from a carefully placed Jorge Ferrari Hardoy butterfly chair to a pair of 1970s aviator sunglasses paired with a bandana.

Sylvia met Lawrence at an evening class on art history when he was only 17; she was 10 years older and already married. Over the course of a decade, they struck up a passionate friendship that blossomed into romance. "I love you, madly, intellectually, impulsively, constantly,"[32] he declared in one letter from 1949. Sylvia left her husband five years later and married Lawrence within the space of a few months. They relocated

to New York in 1961. Over the course of her career, she painted Lawrence over 40 times. She, in turn, is credited with introducing him to feminism and encouraging him, in his role as a curator and critic, to celebrate female artists.

Sylvia finally found her feet in New York. She became a key member of the Ad Hoc Women Artists' Committee, the activist group that famously protested against the Whitney Museum for selecting women for only five per cent of its annual show. She explained the situation:

It has always been difficult for women to do creative work or indeed to have any profession that endows prestige in our chauvinist patriarchal society. It was particularly hard for ambitious women painters who wished to paint the most highly regarded subjects – history pictures.[33]

Painting history pictures was precisely what Sylvia set out to do – with a feminist twist, of course. At a time when the art world was knee-deep in abstraction, she charted a course that recalled the portraiture of Velázquez and Titian. In her 1971 work *Philip Golub Reclining*, she flips the gender of Velázquez's famous *The Rokeby Venus*, in which a reclining nude woman stares at her reflection in the mirror. Instead, Sylvia's male model lies naked and stares at his mirrored self, while a fully clothed Sylvia is caught in a reflection, painting him with a look of utmost concentration.

"All our friends were abstract painters, and to be a 'realist' seemed rather beside the point," Sylvia once said. "I feel that what I want to express and communicate in my work can only be said in a figurative manner so I never defected from my course."[34]

And she flipped the script on her female sitters, too. Her *Goddess* series posed her female friends as religious deities like the Egyptian goddess Isis, and her group portraits of feminist collectives are almost documentary-like in their fidelity. Women are shown with their body hair, wrinkles around their eyes and sunburned elbows. In doing so, she cemented her reputation as a feminist artist, decades before it became a fashionable byline or label. She, in turn, always credited it with the making of her as an artist: "Feminism allowed me to express my thoughts freely. It gave me the freedom to show the beauty of the body – the most luminous parts equally."[35]

CAMILLE CLAUDEL

ne art critic called Camille Claudel (1864–1943) "the single female sculptor upon whose brow sparkles the sign of genius".[36] Another simply labelled her supernatural talent as "a revolt against nature".[37] The French artist sculpted several of the figures in Auguste Rodin's *Gates of Hell*, and her own work in plaster, marble and bronze communicated such intense power and grace that one of her pieces was described as "among one of the purest masterpieces of this century".[38] So how did a woman of such talent disappear into obscurity, condemned to spend the last 30 years of her life in a mental institution?

Camille was born into a comfortably well-off family in the French village of Fère-en-Tardenois. As an adolescent, she sculpted busts of her family for her own pleasure. A local sculptor, Alfred Boucher, was so struck by her work that he became her first champion and mentor, presenting her work to another sculptor at the École des Beaux-Arts. Women were not accepted at the prestigious art academy until the 1890s, but when her family moved to Paris, Camille got around the problem by founding her own studio and continuing to study under Boucher at the Académie Colarossi, one of the few art schools that did accept women.

Camille's work was compared to that of Rodin even before Boucher made the fatal introduction – a step that would propel the teenaged Camille into the most artistically enriching but destructive relationship of her life. She had barely turned 20 when she moved her practice entirely into Rodin's workshop and become his only female apprentice – he was 24 years her senior, and already had a partner, Rose Beuret, and a child. In his studio, Camille honed her already prodigious skills and quickly became his model, mistress and artistic collaborator. "I showed her where she would find gold," Rodin said of her, "but the gold she found is truly hers."[39]

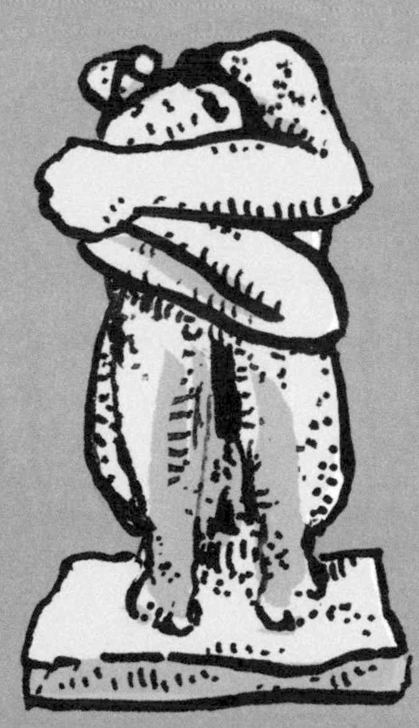

In Camille's hands, a cold hunk of marble could become two figures entwined in lustful surrender (*Sakountala*) or a triumphant Greek hero slaying a beast (*Perseus and the Gorgon*). She modelled women at every stage of their lives – from the contemplative and domestic (*Woman at Her Toilette*) to the aging and infirm (*Head of an Old Woman*). Her work was sensual, capturing intimate moments snatched at rest – like the group of women depicted mid-gossip in *The Gossips*. In 1903, the art critic Gabrielle Reval called her "the greatest French sculptor" alive.

A number of people, with the exception of his partner and her parents, knew about Camille's decade-long relationship with Rodin. But though he acted as her sponsor in the art world and helped to secure her commissions, their secret relationship grew to torment her. She realized that he would never leave Beuret for her, and that her reputation only suffered for her art's constant comparisons to Rodin. Camille ended the affair and set out on her own, but lacked the means or inclination to promote herself as a sculptor. As her commissions dried up, she worked herself to exhaustion attempting to create sculptures that would sell. Few of them did.

Her mental health began to deteriorate; she grew paranoid and imagined that Rodin – whom she now referred to as The Ferret – and his "gang" were intent on harming her. Convinced that they were trying to copy her work, she used a hammer to destroy her sculpture models and paid someone to bury them outside the city. Her sense of isolation intensified when her brother Paul, a doctor, moved away from Paris. "Her feeling of solitude," wrote one friend, "is such that she sometimes has the strange fear of having lost the use of speech."[40] She told police that two of Rodin's models had broken into her apartment to try to kill her, and she studded a broom with nails to fend off any trespassers.

Today, this would be described as a breakdown. In the early 20th century, however, her family saw no other option but to have her permanently institutionalized. "Camille Claudel suffers from systematized persecutory delusions," her admission notes read. "She believes she is the victim of criminal attacks by a celebrated sculptor…who has taken works she created and has tried to poison her, as he has done to many other people."[41]

Her doctors tried to encourage her to make more art, but she rejected all their attempts. She remained in psychiatric care for the rest of her life, though she constantly pleaded by letter with her family to set her free: "I haven't done all I have done just in order to end my life as a big shot in a mental institution, I've deserved other than that."[42] She died, still incarcerated, just shy of her 80th birthday; she had not worked in decades. "I live in a world so curious, so strange," she wrote from behind the walls of her prison. "Of the dream that has been my life, this is the nightmare."[43]

CATHARINA VAN HEMESSEN

In 1548, Catharina van Hemessen (1528–*c.*1587) sat down by a canvas in her father's Antwerp workshop and painted something truly remarkable. *Self-Portrait*, rendered in luminous oil paint on a wood panel, shows the 20-year-old at work by her easel. She clutches a fistful of brushes in one hand while balancing her palette against the base of her thumb. In her other hand, she holds a paintbrush, its bristles loaded with white paint and nudging gently against the canvas, where the faintest sketch of a face can be detected.

Catharina holds the viewer's gaze steadily; her expression has been described as forlorn, but it is more sober and dignified than it is sad. She looks older than her two decades, though the real-life Catharina took care to signpost her age and identity at the top left of the painting: "I Caterina van Hemessen have painted myself / 1548 / Here aged 20."[44]

What was so noteworthy about this self-portrait, other than the precocious skill of its subject and creator? It is the earliest-surviving example of a self-portrait of an artist – male or female – at work. Though other artists had made self-portraits in the past, Catharina's is believed to be the first to show one in the act of artistic production.

Sixteenth-century Antwerp was one of Europe's busiest centres for art and commerce, and Catharina was born into a family that took full advantage of the population's thirst for art. Her father, Jan van Hemessen, was an artist himself; influenced by the Italian Renaissance, he created sprawling genre paintings that updated religious or allegorical tales for contemporary times. As a child, Catharina was trained in his master workshop and often assisted him with his paintings, before finally being allowed to take on commissions of her own.

At the time, women were all but barred from training as artists – it was considered inappropriate for a woman to study the nude form or apprentice herself to a man. Catharina, however, found a way around this, thanks to her father and his workshop.

The children of artists were not required to report to their painters' guild, and their contributions to the work remained largely anonymous. Not so for Catharina, who learned to sign all her paintings and subsequently built a sizable income off commissions from wealthy Flemish and Dutch patrons.

Eschewing the crowd scenes and allegory of her father's work, she conducted a brisk trade in small but well-executed portraits not unlike the self-portrait she drew at the age of 20 – precisely detailed and unimpeachably solemn paintings that communicated something of the sitter's personality and elegance. In the 1551 painting *Portrait of a Lady*, Catharina depicts a woman of aristocratic birth in a transparent lace headdress and with the ever-fashionable accessory of a small dog tucked into the crook of her elbow.

Almost all of her surviving paintings date from 1548 to 1554, but her fame clearly spread beyond Antwerp. When she married the composer and organist Chretien de Morien in 1554, they sailed to Spain to attend court in Madrid as the guests of Queen Mary of Hungary, who was governor of the Netherlands. When Queen Mary died in 1558, she rewarded her loyal artist and musician with a substantial pension for the rest of their lives.

In the 1567 book *Description of the Low Countries*, the Italian writer Lodovico Guicciardini thought highly enough of Catharina to describe her as one of "the most outstanding women in this art [of painting] that are still alive today".[45] However, no works by Catharina from after 1554 exist, and some historians believe that she effectively stopped painting after her marriage. For now, all we have are ten or so signed paintings, stamped with the name of the woman believed to be the first artist in history to depict herself at work.

TIMARETE

hen you hear the words "Ancient Greek art", you probably think of Homer and sculptures of nude men with curiously small penises. So far, so male. But though men have been credited with some of the most famous pieces to survive antiquity, a lot less has been said about the women who were creating staggering works of art right next to their male counterparts – only for their work to be lost to the sands of time. Nowhere is that tragedy more self-evident than in the story of the painter Timarete (*fl.* c.5th–3rd century BC), sometimes known as Thamyris or Thamaris.

Everything we know about Timarete stems from the work of Pliny the Elder, a Roman historian from the 1st century AD. In his blockbuster encyclopedia *Naturalis Historiae* ("Natural History"), he sought to catalogue everything he knew about the world, including an entire book on the history of art, from its painting methods to its artists – men and women alike.

According to Pliny, Timarete was the daughter of an artist known as Micon, and she learned how to paint in his workshop. She was best known for a painting on wood of Artemis, the goddess of the hunt; Pliny had viewed the painting appreciatively at a temple in Ephesus. Such religious tablets would have been specially commissioned by the Ephesians and exhibited during festivals and rituals in honour of Artemis, meaning that Timarete was no artistic dilettante. Like her father, she was a working professional artist.

Timarete makes another appearance, 13 centuries on, in the work of Italian scholar Giovanni Boccaccio. Boccaccio wanted to put a female spin on Francesco Petrarch's biographical work *De Viris Illustribus* ("Lives of Famous Men"), and in the book *De Claris Mulieribus* ("On Famous Women"), published in 1374, Boccaccio wrote up

the lives of 104 exceptional women from ancient times to the then present day.

"In her own time Thamyris [Timarete] was a famous female painter, whose virtue, due to her living in antiquity, perhaps has been erased in large part from the memory of humankind," he notes. "Nonetheless, even until now it [time] has not been able to take away either her name nor her remarkable craftsmanship."[46] He writes that she was so talented that her portrait of Artemis was revered by the Greeks as "a rare and singular thing"[47] and that she "lived a long life"[48] and was able to pursue painting as she wished.

Boccaccio may have written a book all about women, but it didn't mean he was on their side. Of the female artists in *De Claris Mulieribus*, he writes: "I thought that these achievements merited some praise because the art of painting is mostly alien to the feminine mind and cannot be attained without that great intellectual concentration which women, as a rule, are very slow to acquire."

In 1405, Venetian intellectual Christine de Pizan also took up the challenge of documenting Timarete and other women of antiquity with *Le Livre de la Cité des Dames* ("The Book of the City of Ladies"), a book that recounted the lives of over a hundred praiseworthy women. She writes:

Should I also tell you whether a woman's nature is clever and quick enough to learn speculative sciences as well as to discover them, and likewise the manual arts? I assure you that women are equally well suited and skilled to carry them out and to put them to sophisticated use once they have learned them, just as is written concerning a woman named Thamaris [Timarete] who possessed such great subtlety in the art and science of painting that during her lifetime she was the most supreme painter known.[49]

She also notes that Timarete "abandoned all the usual tasks of women [and] pursued her father's art with subtlety of mind",[50] suggesting that – if nothing else – Timarete had the kind of dogged tenacity familiar to any woman who wants to make it in the art world.

"This painting," concluded de Pizan, "since it survived a long time, bore such great witness to the subtlety of this woman that even today her genius is still discussed."[51]

So, what exactly did Timarete's masterpiece look like? Here's the rub: nobody knows. Like many female painters from antiquity, all of

Timarete's work has been lost to time. On your next visit to a museum of antiquities, take a good hard look at the exhibit label next to a painting. You never know – it might be a long-forgotten Timarete.

MARJORIE CAMERON

ven among self-proclaimed sorcerers, rocket scientists and Scientologists, Marjorie Cameron (1922–1995) stood out. The Los Angeles occultist was known for her Surreal paintings that conjured up Jungian myth and aliens in coitus. In her old age, she took to practising t'ai chi with a sword and she drove around in a hearse. Neighbours called her a witch, an image she cultivated.

Born in small-town Iowa, the eldest of four daughters in a churchgoing family, she called herself just Cameron, as she hated her first name. At the age of seven, she produced a drawing in her second-grade class that was perhaps a precursor of things to come: "I was sitting in the back row and I drew a picture of somebody shitting," Cameron remembered. When her teacher demanded to see it, Cameron refused to hand it over, so the teacher "took me to the principal's office and I sat there all afternoon with that paper in my hand, refusing to give it up… I call that my first exhibit."[52] She left school as soon as she could, signing up to the navy and working as a mapmaker before moving to Pasadena, in the Los Angeles area, with her family.

She met her husband, Jack Parsons, at a raucous party in his 11-bedroom mansion in Pasadena. Jack was a leading Caltech rocket scientist and eccentric who also happened to be the leader of the California branch of Ordo Templi Orientis (OTO), Aleister Crowley's mystical organization. At the party, Jack and his friend, a pre-Scientology L Ron Hubbard, were fresh from casting a Crowley-inspired sex-magic ritual, which they called Babalon Working. The aim was to summon forth a spiritual being they dubbed The Scarlet Woman. Marjorie, with her red hair and imposing presence, more than fitted the bill.

Jack and his new flame hopped into bed with each other, stayed there for two weeks and were married a year later. Despite its magical beginnings, the marriage had its ups and downs. Cameron spent two years in Mexico alone after their open marriage faltered, fraternizing with artists and sleeping with bullfighters. They got back together again, but in 1952, Jack was blown up in a freak home-laboratory accident. They were meant to travel to Mexico the next day.

Cameron never stopped believing that Jack, who had been of interest to the FBI, had been assassinated. Racked by grief, she fled the intense press attention around her husband's death and his occult leanings and sought spiritual clarity and peace in isolated Beaumont, California. There she grew increasingly convinced that she was meant to carry out Jack's mystical vision. "The last year that my husband and I were together – all the time that we had been together – he had been preparing me for a public role, which he believed I was destined to fulfill,"[53] she said.

When she emerged from self-imposed seclusion, Cameron collaborated with artists like Kenneth Anger and Wallace Berman, seeing little distinction between being a muse and being an artist. "I call myself a catalyst and I'm a visionary," Cameron explained. "I don't confine myself to any one scene."[54] She singlehandedly stole the lead role from the American writer Anaïs Nin in Anger's art film *Inauguration of the Pleasure Dome* by simply walking on set and upstaging her. "Cameron blew in unannounced," the filmmaker remembered. "And there was this little shrunken creature which was Anaïs Nin in front of the majesty of Cameron, because Cameron wiped her out, you see."[55]

Her own work was nothing less than pure instinct, with her knowledge of magic and ritual providing rich inspiration and a never-ending cast of celestial beings and fairy-tale creatures. "Myths are not remote fables for entertainment, but the real archive of the human race,"[56] she wrote in 1953. Hallucinogenic drugs helped, too. After eating some peyote, she drew a picture of an ecstatic fork-tongued succubus having sex doggy style with an alien. The drawing scandalized the city when it was exhibited, with the Los Angeles vice squad shutting the whole show down and arresting its curator on obscenity charges.

In her later years, Cameron branched out into abstract art and created a group of paintings she titled the *Lion Path* series. Her eyesight was failing, but her lines of vivid blue and purple were just as electric as her earlier work. She never exhibited widely – she was known for tossing some of her work in the incinerator – but continued practising magic. Friends remembered her invoking a blessing every time she got behind the wheel of a car.

"Cameron's life was her art," her friend Scott Hobbs said after her death. "The way that she created magic, not only in her incredible paintings and poetry [...was] in the expressive way she lived."[57]

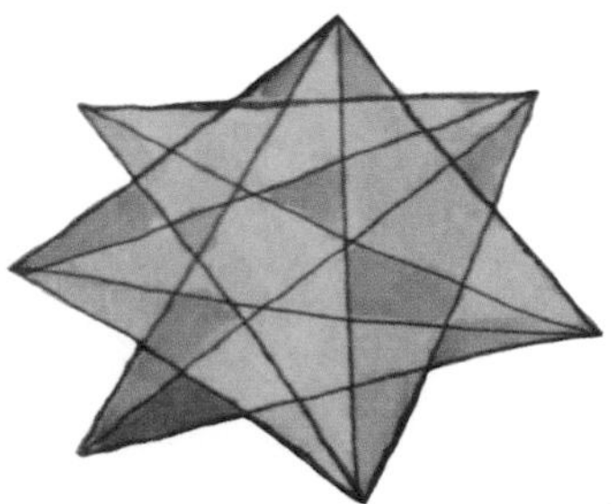

ANAXANDRA

he history of art is full of artistic families, from Elisabetta Sirani (*see* page 66) learning to wield the paintbrush in her father's *bottega* to Sofonisba Anguissola (*see* page 90) and her two painter sisters. But intriguing examples of women entering art through the family trade date back further than Renaissance Italy – in fact, all the way back to Ancient Greece.

Anaxandra (*fl. c.* 2nd century BC) was the daughter of a painter named Nealces (or Nealkes), and they lived in Sicyon, a city-state straddling the northern edge of the Peloponnese peninsula. With its flourishing lands of lush orchards and olive groves, it produced a host of artists and was called "the fatherland of painting",[58] drawing many an aspiring painter and sculptor to its streets.

The little that we know of Anaxandra comes mainly from Clement of Alexandria, a Christian scholar and theologian who is now venerated as an early Church Father. Writing sometime between AD 198 and 203, Clement mentions Anaxandra in his book *Stromateis* ("Miscellanies"), a wide-ranging text that covers everything from Greek culture and philosophy to their roles in the Christian faith.

In a chapter entitled "Women as well as Men Capable of Perfection", Anaxandra is one of only two female painters – the other being Irene, the daughter of a painter named Cratinus – that Clement deems worthy of inclusion in the section next to Sappho and the biblical heroine Judith. He adds that Anaxandra was taught everything she knew by her father and that Clement knew of her thanks to a since lost work by the Greek scholar Didymus.

Anaxandra was like Timarete (*see* page 79) in having learned how to paint from her father. One can imagine the two artistically gifted girls patiently grinding their fathers' paints or sweeping the floor of their workshops in exchange for being taught the marvellous skills of their trade. As Clement concludes: "Virtue, we have said, depends not on others, but on ourselves above all."[59]

The 17th-century Italian author and women's rights advocate Lucrezia Marinella also hails Anaxandra. In her masterpiece *The Nobility and Excellence of Women, and the Defects and Vices of Men*, she writes: "Both Clement

and Didymus of Alexandria praise Anaxandra for her remarkable knowledge of painting."[60] Little else is known about Anaxandra, but it is clear that her very existence as an early female artist is cause for celebration.

In 1994, the International Astronomical Union named a crater on Venus after Anaxandra, in keeping with their tradition of naming such geographical features after women who had made outstanding contributions in their field. She joins other artists like Georgia O'Keeffe, Frida Kahlo and Käthe Kollwitz on the surface of the distant planet. It is one way, at least, for the memory of a woman whose works have long disappeared in time to be etched into eternity.

"Faithful, chaste, wise and strong women have existed," Lucrezia Marinella writes poignantly in her book, "not only in Greece and Rome, but in every region where between the Indies and the Garden of the Hesperides the sun spreads its rays: their virtues are lost to fame so that from among a thousand hardly one is named."[61]

SOFONISBA ANGUISSOLA

enaissance Italy is best known for producing great masters like Michelangelo, Titian and Leonardo da Vinci. Less famous now – but no less esteemed back then – was Sofonisba Anguissola (*c.*1532–1625). Her extraordinarily lifelike paintings made her one of the first female artists to receive international acclaim; the King of Spain, Philip II, was so impressed that he sent for her to join his court. She was pronounced a *miracolo di natura*: a "miracle of nature".

Born into a noble family in the provincial northern city of Cremona, Sofonisba's class and gender would ordinarily condemn her to a lifetime of embroidery and feminine duty. But her father, Amilcare Anguissola, would have none of it. At the time, *The Book of the Courtier*, which praised the virtues of educating aristocratic women as well as men, was all the rage, and Amilcare took the book's lessons to heart. He supported all his children's artistic pursuits in the family *palazzo*, resulting in three of the Anguissola daughters – Lucia, Europa and Sofonisba – becoming painters.

It was Sofonisba who showed the greatest artistic potential. In fact, Amilcare became her Svengali, using his influence and power to champion his daughter. He allowed her to train under painters like Bernardino Campi and Bernardino Gatti, and sent Sofonisba's drawing of a laughing girl to Michelangelo to ask the most famous artist in Italy for his thoughts. Draw something more difficult, like someone crying, was the response. Sofonisba promptly sent back an impressively realistic picture of a smiling girl holding a crying boy. (The drawing still hangs in the Museo

SOFONISBA ANGVISSOLA
SOFONISBA ANGVISSOLA
SOFONISBA ANGVISSOLA
SOFONISBA ANGVISSOLA
SOFONISBA ANGVISSOLA
SOFONISBA ANGVISSOLA

Nazionale di Capodimonte in Naples today.) Michelangelo was impressed, and informally adopted her as a student of sorts; a letter from Amilcare dated 7 May 1557 thanks him for the "honourable and thoughtful affection that you have shown to Sofonisba, my daughter, to whom you introduced to practice the most honourable art of painting".[62]

Giorgio Vasari – the so-called "father of art history" – was stunned when he viewed her work at her father's house. Sofonisba's paintings of her sisters "appear truly alive", he declared, "and are wanting in nothing save speech". Another group family portrait was "executed so well that they appear to be breathing".[63]

The Chess Game, Sofonisba's 1555 painting of her three sisters huddled over a game of chess, is a case in point. It is an intimate female setting, fully realized by an artist who knows her subjects inside out – from the cheeky grin of a little sister who appears to have spotted an underhand manoeuvre to the poised hand of a player captured mid-move. Women were not allowed to use male models, so Sofonisba painted what was around her, including herself. In her early self-portraits, she is careful to depict herself as a woman of virtue. There are

no flashy dresses or jewellery; just Sofonisba in all black, sometimes paired with an object that emphasizes her virtuousness – reading a small book that opens onto a page on which is written "Sofonisba Anguissola, a virgin, made this herself in 1554", for example, or playing a harpsichord as an approving governess looks on.

There are also more experimental self-portraits that suggest Sofonisba was toying with the constraints placed on her as a woman artist. In a double portrait entitled *Bernardino Campi Painting Sofonisba Anguissola*, ostensibly a homage to her former teacher, she depicts Campi in the middle of finishing her self-portrait. A painted Sofonisba looms large in the canvas, dwarfing her old tutor as a small smile plays at the edge of her lips – as though she knows that the student has surpassed the master. All in all, she is believed to have produced more self-portraits than any other artist in her day, male or female.

Sofonisba's prodigious skill did not go unnoticed. In 1558, she left Italy to join the royal court of Philip II of Spain as a court painter and to attend his third wife, Isabel de Valois, as her lady-in-waiting. She gave the Queen drawing lessons and cemented her reputation as a portrait painter of extraordinary delicacy and skill. When Sofonisba died at the ripe old age of about 93, her husband left a loving tribute to her genius on her tombstone: "To Sofonisba, my wife, who is recorded among the illustrious women of the world, outstanding in portraying the images of man."[64]

CHARLOTTE SALOMON

he year 1943 should have marked the beginning of a new chapter in Charlotte Salomon's (1917–1943) life. She had finished her monumental work *Leben? oder Theater?* ("Life? or Theatre?") and had just married her close friend Alexander Nagler in the south of France. Instead, the summer would be Charlotte's last. In September, the police forced their way into their residence at the Villa L'Ermitage, arrested her and Alexander and sent them both to Auschwitz. Charlotte was gassed on arrival; she was five months pregnant. Alexander died the next year.

Even before the police came knocking, Charlotte, who initially fled Berlin in 1938, had realized the end was near. Just a few months prior to her capture, she sent the original proofs of *Leben? oder Theater?* to a friend and doctor who had counselled her through her depression. "Take good care of it," she begged, "it is my entire life."[65]

Death was never far from Charlotte's family, though she would only fully understand it in her twenties. She was named after her mother's youngest sister, who took her own life at the age of 18. Her mother killed herself when Charlotte was eight, though she was led as a child to believe that her mother had died of influenza. In a further operatic twist, a 35-page letter discovered in 2012 implies that Charlotte poisoned her own grandfather.

Born in Berlin in 1917, Charlotte grew up in the shadow of Hitler's rise to power. When she was 16, her Jewish father and her stepmother both lost their jobs. Perhaps unsurprisingly, Charlotte grew up to be a withdrawn and nervous young woman. She was one of the few Jews admitted into art school, partly because the admissions board judged her so "modest and reserved" that she would "present no danger to the Aryan male students".[66] But a deep well of intensity and feeling lay within Charlotte, and this repression found an extraordinary outlet in art.

MUSS BEMERKT
HIERZU
DASS SIE SICH NEI- WERDE
WER EX SCHEN
GES EINDE
DIE N ZEI
IM SEHR
BE -BE
SC ER
PA ARAU
NSE-
S DES
UR-
G SIC
AL-
MME
WAR
SCHE
TEN
DURFTE
ND EIL HITLER
S WAR NAME DE
GRÜNDER INDERES
FINDERS DIESER
PARTEI IM VOLKS
MUNDHIESSEN IHRE AAN
HÄNGER KURZ WEG
DIE NAZIS
WAR DAS

The semi-autobiographical series of 769 gouache paintings she titled *Leben? oder Theater?* traces the coming of age of a pseudonymous protagonist named Charlotte Kann, dated between 1913 and 1940. She described it as a *singspiel*, or a play with music. Music does figure hugely in it; there are multiple references to classical music and even choruses to accompany the action. She painted 340 transparent overlays of text to accompany certain paintings, sometimes painting the text and dialogue into the image itself. In some sections, Charlotte's work looks like it could be ripped from the pages of a contemporary graphic novel.

On its publication in 1963, *Leben? oder Theater?* was compared to *The Diary of Anne Frank*. Charlotte herself was a difficult and troubled teenager. When she was younger, she fell deeply in love with Alfred Wolfsohn, her stepmother's singing teacher. In Charlotte's work, he is wryly renamed "Amadeus Daberlohn" – a play on the phrase "Penniless Mozart". Despite being 21 years older, Alfred becomes the love of Charlotte Kann's life. In her work, Daberlohn was the first person to encourage Charlotte Kann's art, though he also damns her with faint praise: "In my opinion, you are destined to create something above average."[67]

In real life, Wolfsohn denied ever consummating their relationship, adding that he "had never come across a more withdrawn person"[68] than Charlotte. His approach to music, however, would prove revolutionary in Charlotte's own life. For Wolfsohn, creativity and death were inextricably linked. If an artist found a way to unlock their vocal range, they might conquer their fear of death and find a reason to live – and that is exactly what art did for Charlotte.

In 1938, Charlotte left Berlin for the Villa L'Ermitage, where her grandparents were staying with a wealthy American who housed refugees fleeing the war. Her grandfather and grandmother were stockpiling the barbiturate Veronal and morphine so that they could take their own lives if the German army ever came to their door. But when her grandmother grew increasingly convinced that death was near, she was denied access to her medication. She tried and failed to hang herself, throwing herself out of a window instead.

Suicide had stalked Charlotte's mother and her aunt, and now it had claimed her grandmother. When she was finally told the truth about her family, Charlotte channelled it all into *Leben? oder Theater?*. Paradoxically, the deaths only made her intent on living: "How beautiful life is, I believe in life!" her narrator cries. "I will live for them all!"[69] Charlotte Salomon resolved to do "something quite insanely extraordinary",[70] and checked herself into a hotel to work around the clock on her magnum opus.

In a letter only discovered in full this century, Charlotte admits to poisoning her grandfather's breakfast with Veronal and watching him die; in real life, her grandfather passed away after collapsing in the street in early 1943. Which is real and which is the lie? Or rather, which was life and which was theatre? Some argue that Charlotte had killed him, believing him to have abused the women in the Salomon family and driving them to death. Others argue that it was a mercy killing; and still others believe it was just one final artistic flourish from a woman who blended fact and fiction. Fittingly, the final image of Charlotte's masterpiece shows her heroine with her back to the viewer, paintbrush in hand. She took her secret to the grave.

CLARA TICE

Clara Tice (1888–1973), the "Queen of Greenwich Village",[71] loved three things in life: animals, art and scandal. Often spotted in public with her Russian wolfhound, the native New Yorker once declared that she was the first woman to bob her hair in all of America. In 1921, *Vanity Fair* proclaimed her – alongside writers Edna St Vincent Millay and Willa Cather – one of the "muses of New York's so-called Quartier Latin, who have achieved the highest distinction in the arts".[72] Clara designed the masthead of that issue for good measure.

Clara grew up on the top floor of a lodging house for homeless children, where her father was superintendent. Unlike her dad's unlucky wards, Clara was brought up in a warm and supportive family environment that encouraged her to pursue her creative interests. As a young woman, she found a mentor in the painter Robert Henri (*see also* page 62), who helped her exhibit and sell her first canvases. He instructed his pupils to stay true to their creative instincts, regardless of consequences: "It is all very fine to have your pictures hung," he once wrote, "but you are painting for yourself, not for the jury."[73]

Clara put that lesson to the test in 1915, when she had her first solo show at Polly's restaurant in Greenwich Village. Her graceful pictures of swooning Art Nouveau nudes – back rolls, chubby bellies and all – caught the attention of Anthony Comstock, the chief of New York's notorious Society for the Suppression of Vice. The state had given Comstock the power to police public obscenity, and Clara's sensuously feminine images were seen as perverse in the extreme. It was only through sheer good fortune that Clara's friends were tipped off about Comstock and managed to hide everything just before his vice squad raided the premises.

The failed bust ended up on the front page of the *New-York Tribune*, and Clara always maintained that the uproar was the making of her reputation. Offers of work poured in – her illustrations ran in *Vanity Fair*, the *New York Times*, the *Chicago Tribune* and the *Sun*, allowing her to inject a dose of art into otherwise staid newspapers. Clara even confronted her scandalous reputation head-on by staging her own mock trial, in which she was accused of murdering art.

A few months after the raid, she returned triumphantly with a new solo show, at Bruno's Garret, a well-known gallery and drinking hole in the Greenwich Village scene. She stuffed its walls with more than 250 watercolours of nudes, including scenes of interracial lesbian lovemaking. One art critic remarked that "a naturalness so unbridled is apt to frighten the citizens of the land of the free".[74] This time, Comstock stayed far away.

"Loved ones change, age does not always smooth away the cares and wrinkles, beauty becomes dumb, men impotent, women sterile; but my pictures can always bring back to me the original exaltation of creation, the freshness and aliveness of my models as I saw them in the perfection of movement," Clara once said. Her art had an intoxicating effect on all who viewed it – one restaurant patron, sitting underneath a commissioned mural of dancing sylphs, was moved to send back his beer after declaring, "Under that mural, I can drink only champagne."[75]

She became so famous that she was asked to play herself in a theatre production entitled *Greenwich Village Follies*. It was backstage at one of its runs where she was introduced to Patrick "Harry" Cunningham, the younger man who became her soulmate and life partner. Harry was also an artist, but quickly sidelined his own output to become Clara's full-time assistant, doing everything from stretching her canvases to cooking for her. When the Greenwich Village "it" girl tired of city life, she retired with her lover to the greener pastures of Connecticut, where they kept an ever-growing family of animals. From there, she continued to illustrate and paint, including *ABC Dogs*, an illustrated children's compendium of her favourite animal.

Clara returned to New York when Harry died in 1947, but was never quite able to scale the old heights of her Greenwich Village fame. Still, she always maintained that making art – whether or not it was appreciated or recognized – was more important than anything else: "There are two great joys of the artist which make him more self-sufficient than anyone else," she said. "They are the gruelling ecstasy of creation, and the realization that one's artistic productions will be a constant source of delight and pleasure, to the creator – if no one else."[76]

AMRITA SHER-GIL

hen she was 22, one of Amrita Sher-Gil's (1913–1941) many sexual partners made a wager with her: "I explained to Amrita how she was really a virgin, because she'd never experienced the spiritual equivalent of copulation; she'd had many lovers but they'd left no scar. 'I'll leave a scar,' I boasted. She laughed."[77] Whether he did make an impact or not, the young man – the English journalist Malcolm Muggeridge – was gone within a few months, though not before Amrita had painted a portrait of him.

Born in Budapest to a Hungarian opera singer and a Sikh aristocrat, Amrita Sher-Gil lived and painted with the blazing intensity of a shooting star. Despite dying at the age of 28 in mysterious circumstances, she left an indelible mark on India as its first great modern artist. With her combination of a Western art education and a deep and abiding love of India's traditional artistic forms, she is often described as the country's answer to Frida Kahlo. "How can one feel the beauty of a form, the intensity or the subtlety of a colour, the quality of a line," she once asked, "unless one is a sensualist of the eyes?"[78]

Always rebellious, Amrita spent her life in the pursuit of sensuality, much to the benefit of her art and the displeasure of her parents. As a 12-year-old, she painted a picture of an angry woman with her gown ripped away to reveal her breasts, a dagger in her hand. After her family left Budapest for Simla in India, she was thrown out of a convent school in Simla for declaring that she was an atheist. Her parents, however, were intelligent enough to realize that their daughter had been blessed with artistic talent – and were liberal enough to want to support it, so they uprooted the family in order that Amrita could study art in Paris.

In 1933, Amrita's oil painting *Young Girls* won a Gold Medal from the Grand Salon, a prestigious Paris art institute, which was an immense achievement for someone still training at the École des Beaux-Arts. The image shows Amrita's sister, Indira, sitting confidently in Western dress, training her frank gaze on Amrita's French friend, Denise, who slouches bare-breasted in a chair. It is an image of two women at rest; the nudity is incidental and entirely natural. In fact, Amrita painted herself nude many times, including a Gauguin-influenced image whose title, *Self-Portrait as Tahitian*, wryly poked fun at the French painter's exoticized oeuvre.

In the lively, cosmopolitan expat scene of Paris, Amrita's often remarked-upon beauty and charisma attracted countless men and women. But she felt one step removed from her European admirers, and grew close to Victor, her first cousin on her Hungarian mother's side – not least after Victor, a trained doctor, helped her get an abortion and cure a venereal disease she had picked up from a suitor. There was, however, still something missing: "Towards the end of 1933," she wrote, "I began to be haunted by an intense longing to return to India, feeling in some strange inexplicable way that there lay my destiny as a painter."[79]

Her Indian father feared that the return of his bohemian daughter to India would scandalize polite society, but Amrita would not be deterred. In a symbolic gesture, she binned all her Western clothes and replaced them with saris. Yet she credited her education in Europe for teaching her to appreciate the value of Indian art. "It seems paradoxical," she said, "but I know for certain that had we not come away to

Europe, I should perhaps never have realised that a fresco from Ajanta or a small piece of sculpture in the Musée Guimet is worth more than the whole Renaissance!"[80]

On her travels through the south of India, Amrita was shocked by the country's poverty, and she dramatically altered her painting in response. She started depicting the hustle and bustle of ordinary life, from villagers on their way to the market to the hill women of Simla, wanting to "interpret the life of Indians"[81] in her art. Nonetheless, she had little truck with sentimental cliché. "I hate cheap emotional appeal and I am not, therefore, a propagandist of the picture that tells a story,"[82] she said.

At 25, she announced her intention to marry Victor, which led her to fall out with her mother. Marrying first cousins was not the done thing in the Sher-Gil family. For years, her parents had predicted that she would end up alone and unloved on account of her "odious"[83] (read: independent) character. The marriage didn't last long, but not because Victor had an issue with her various affairs – in fact, he appeared to be relatively accepting of Amrita's sexual appetites.

Her premature death in December 1941 was entirely unexpected and remains unexplained – some believe that she contracted dysentery from some pakoras at a tea party, while others think she was the casualty of a botched abortion. Whatever the cause, Victor was unable to save her, and so the woman who grew up straddling India and the West died in the country that had made her an artist. "Europe belongs to Picasso, Matisse, Braque and many others," she once declared. "India belongs only to me."[84]

CLARA PEETERS

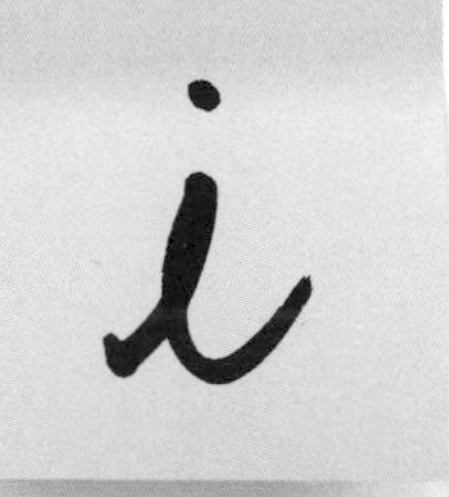

f you inch close to *Flowers with Ceramic Dish, Money, Drinking Goblets*, the 1612 still life by Clara Peeters (*fl. c.*1607–1621), you might be startled by the sight of several miniature faces peeking out of a gilded drinking cup. Meet Clara – these tiny, distorted reflections are images of the artist herself, palette in hand.

Clara Peeters is one of the great mysteries of art, albeit one who painted herself in plain sight. Little is known about her life. Born sometime in the late 16th century in Antwerp, Belgium, she somehow managed to jump all the usual barriers to women seeking a career in art to become one of the earliest pioneers of still life. If you have ever salivated over a menu or a smartphone photo of food, Clara's skill at culinary *mise en scène* will drive you wild with hunger. Nearly half a millennium after it was painted, you feel you can smell the ocean in *Still Life with Fish, Candle, Artichokes, Crabs and Shrimp*, each scale and fin depicted with absolute precision. She could paint the soft, doughy insides of a crusty pretzel with such painstaking brushwork that it's almost as if you can taste it in your mouth.

Dutch and Flemish painters were the first great masters of still life, and Clara was working in the early days of the genre. While others sought to inject allegories

of life and death into their art, Clara perfected an extraordinary realism matched by few of her peers. She could do big and blingy set pieces or small and modest spreads – her humble *ontbijtjes* (breakfast pieces) look plucked from the breakfast table of an average Flemish family, while the *banketjes* (banquet pieces) are fit to occupy pride of place in any royal household, with extravagant flowers, gleaming coins and exotic fruits from foreign climes. It was likely that Clara was permitted to apply her prodigious talent only to these domestic scenes, for women were barred from formal training, and there is no record of her by Antwerp's professional guild of painters.

"She's not allowed a big space so just decided to focus on a small one and does that really well," said Alejandro Vergara, the senior art curator who put on an exhibition of her work at Spain's Prado Museum in 2016 – the first time the venerable Madrid museum had ever given a woman a solo show. "And if you're painting in the realistic mode in Antwerp you're really being very different to everyone else working there."[85]

Clara is thought to have been a young woman – even a teenager – when she created her masterpieces. Some believe that she must have been born into an artistic family and received training at home; others hold that she was taught by Osias Beert, an Antwerp painter famed for his still lifes. Such paintings were collected by the Dutch and Flemish royal and aristocratic circles, and Clara's work was supported by the major artistic patrons of her time, an achievement that would have made her one of the few European women to live off her art. The dates for her birth, marriage and death vary or have been missed off the historical record completely; she is thought to have died sometime between 1621 and 1676.

Today, only 40 or so of her paintings have survived. The earliest one that bears her name is a 1607 painting of a candle flickering in dim light next to an inviting cup of wine. If it weren't for her tiny, miniaturized self-portraits, we would know even less about Clara than we already do. Luckily, she painted herself into several pieces – reflected in the shiny gilt of some of the objects she depicted – so that she would always, even in the smallest of places, be seen.

"That is a very unusual thing to do at the time. [It] seems to speak of someone who's discreet and modest, but really is seducing you into looking closely and carefully," Vergara told a reporter. "And when you do that, you find her. So she's really trying to be seen."[86]

META WARRICK FULLER

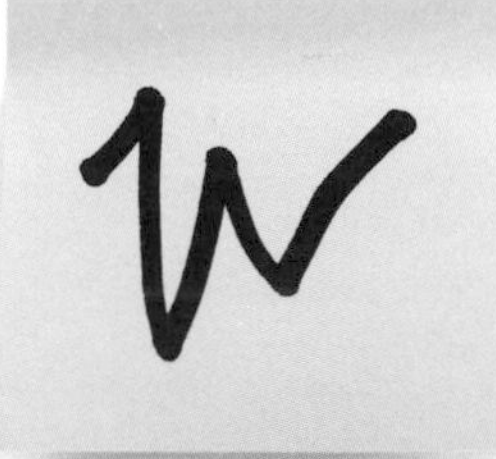

hat would you do if you lost all your work in a fire? After years of depression and angst, would you have the courage to start all over again? You would if you were Meta Warrick Fuller (1877–1968). After all, the African-American sculptor from Philadelphia was made of strong stuff. This was the woman who, when someone complained that her statue of the crucifixion of Christ was too gory, replied: "If the Saviour did not suffer, wherein lay the sacrifice?"[87]

Born to an affluent, middle-class family in Philadelphia, Meta spent her childhood visiting art exhibitions with her father and vacationing in Atlantic City during the summer. On graduating from high school, she won a prestigious three-year scholarship to the Pennsylvania Museum and School of Industrial Art, where she was one of the few black students on her course. Meta was an outstanding student, and her final-year metalwork sculpture, *Crucifixion of Christ in Agony*, was just one of her many student works to receive a coveted award.

On the advice of her teachers, Meta packed her bags for Paris in 1899 to study sculpture at the Académie Colarossi and attend lectures at the École des Beaux-Arts. On arrival, she went to the American Girls' Club, a boarding house for young American women where she had reserved lodgings, but was horrified to be turned away. The director justified this with the accusation, "You didn't tell me that you were not a white girl!"[88]

Fortunately, Meta found alternative accommodation, and she spent the next three years in a frenzy of activity. She attended drawing classes and anatomy lectures in the morning, worked in the afternoon on her own clay and wax models and spent the rest of her time wandering through Paris's wealth of museums. A friend at the Académie Colarossi even secured an invitation for her to meet Auguste Rodin – then the most famous sculptor in all of France (*see also* page 72).

Meta was hoping to study under Rodin, but he already had his own apprentices. He did, however, offer her crucial words of encouragement. As he examined her clay model depicting a tortured man eating his own heart, he exclaimed: "My child, you are a sculptor – you have a sense of form!"[89] With a single pronouncement, Rodin had legitimized all the hard work Meta had put into becoming an artist. Meta said that "with clenched fists, I determined to fulfill the fair promise he had bespoken for me".[90]

Meta's encounter with Rodin marked a turning point in her work. She began creating pieces that would see her dubbed the "delicate sculptor of horrors"[91] by the French press – works that combined sensuality and emotion with grotesque Impressionism. Her dark and utterly unique perspective captivated audiences in France. She held a solo show at Siegfried Bing's avant-garde gallery L'Art Nouveau in 1902, and two of her sculptures, *The Wretched* and *The Impertinent Thief*, were shown at the 1903 Paris Salon.

Meta returned to America with the words of W E B Du Bois (the African–American writer and activist whom she had met in Paris) ringing in her ears. "A word of advice from Dr. Du Bois before leaving was to the effect that I should make a speciality of negro types," she remembered. "I told him I did not believe I could so specialize but I considered the advice well meant."[92] His words would prove prophetic, however, for Meta would grow to devote the rest of her career to sculpting work that uplifted and celebrated black culture.

One of the first pieces she made on her return to the US was a plaque commemorating Emperor Menelik II, a heroic Ethiopian leader who had modernized his country and fought off Italian invaders. In 1907, Meta became the first black woman to receive an artistic commission from the government for her tableaux depicting African–American history at the Jamestown Tercentennial Exposition.

In 1909, she married the Liberia-born physician Solomon Carter Fuller, one of the first black men to practise psychiatry in America. But the next year, just a few months after she gave birth to their first son, tragedy struck: a fire ripped through the Philadelphia warehouse where she had stored over a decade's worth of sculpture.

Meta spent years grieving over the lost work, but she threw herself back into sculpting when Du Bois commissioned her in 1913 for her greatest work yet: a sculpture to commemorate the 50th anniversary of the Emancipation Proclamation. *The Spirit of Emancipation* is 2.4m (8ft) high and shows a black girl and boy standing proud and tall, looking off into the distance, while a third figure weeps. She described them as "suddenly freed children, who, beneath the gnarled fingers of Fate, step forth into the world, unafraid"[93] – and it marked the rebirth of her career as an artist. A 1999 bronze cast of the sculpture stands on Boston's Emancipation Trail as a testament to both the event that inspired it and the sculptor who created it.

Performance & Conceptual

BARONESS ELSA VON FREYTAG-LORINGHOVEN

hen Marcel Duchamp submitted a porcelain urinal signed "R. Mutt 1917" to New York's Society of Independent Artists, he created what is still regarded as one of the biggest artistic sensations of the 20th century. But what if Duchamp was getting away with a lot more than just the biggest prank in art history? What if *Fountain* wasn't his at all?

A couple of days before it was rejected by the society, Duchamp had written to his sister, "One of my female friends, under the masculine pseudonym, Richard Mutt, sent in a porcelain urinal as a sculpture."[1] Historian Irene Gammel argues that this provides the most solid proof yet that *Fountain* was actually the work of someone else – namely, the revolutionary artist and poet Baroness Elsa von Freytag-Loringhoven (1874–1927), heralded by her peers as the living embodiment of Dadaism. As Duchamp himself put it: "She's not a futurist; she is the future."[2]

Before Elsa married into aristocracy, she was born plain old Elsa Plötz in a provincial city on the Baltic Sea. When her mother died, 18-year-old Elsa ran away to Berlin and enjoyed several years performing, modelling and sleeping her way around the city's erotic vaudeville circuit. "Now I began to know what 'life' meant, every night another man," she declared. "I was intoxicated."[3] When she ended up in hospital with syphilis, she merely rolled her eyes at other patients who went to extreme lengths to cover up the cause of their illness: "Since syphilis was a fact – why flim flam about it? I felt interesting – not dishonored."[4]

"The Baroness", as her friends called her, had the title in name but little else. At the age of 39, she wed a penniless German aristocrat in New York, but he quickly decamped to Germany to fight in the war. (Elsa was not overly bothered; this was already her third marriage.) Instead, she was content to stage a one-woman cultural revolution from her shabby two-room tenement apartment. To Elsa, art and life were one

CORONATION
1WHITE
2 SILENCE
SHEATHES SHEATHES
DADA
39 ELSE-BARONESS
40 VON FREYTAG
42 LORINGHOVEN
!
34 HUDSON
35 DEEP
36 ASLEEP
37 IN
38 ICE

and the same, and she committed to both with a fierceness that terrified and intimidated others. Her ex-lover, the poet William Carlos Williams, both adored and hated her. "She was courageous to an insane degree," he once said. "I found myself drinking pure water from her spirit."[5] Another poet, Wallace Stevens, was afraid to venture past 14th Street lest he run into her. Jane Heap, the influential literary editor of *The Little Review*, championed her as "the only one living anywhere who dresses dada, loves dada, lives dada".[6]

As Duchamp and Picasso were making assemblages and readymades, Elsa turned her own body into a work of junk art. She made a bra out of cans of tomatoes and accessorized a velvet hat with ice-cream spoons; her idea of makeup was painting her lips black and pasting a two-cent stamp on her face. Accompanied by her pet dogs, she would sally forth in Manhattan with a coal pail on her head and a birdcage containing a live canary slung around her neck. Her apartment was a mess of found objects and stolen goods; she regularly escaped the police with such graceful aplomb that any attending officers were inclined to let her go.

"I have all possibilities," she wrote in a letter to a friend. "I am Teutonic and female and alive…I have my full power – I am amazone."[7] When her love affair with William Carlos Williams ended, she shaved her head and painted it red, explaining: "Shaving one's head is like having a new love experience."[8] She turned Duchamp's rebuff of her advances into howlingly radical poetry and got it published as the ultimate put-down. "How can you who have had the honour of printing Yeats open your pages to the work of the Baroness von Freytag-Loringhoven?"[9] wrote one reader to *The Little Review*. "We do intend to drop the Baroness," came Jane Heap's reply, "right into the middle of the history of American poetry."[10]

Elsa never let rejection put her off for long – her art and her appetite always came first, or, as she put it in her poem "A Dozen Cocktails – Please": "No spinsterlollypop for me – yes – we have / No bananas I got lusting palate – I / Always eat them"[11]. In the two surviving frames of a 1921 Duchamp and Man Ray film entitled *Elsa, Baroness von Freytag-Loringhoven, Shaving Her Pubic Hair*, she is shown dancing in the nude, ecstatic and entirely self-possessed. Like Duchamp, she created readymade sculptures, though only a photo remains of her best-known work, *God*, consisting of a cast-iron plumbing trap pointing toward the sky.

"Art [is] no infirmary for emotion-starved – passion-crippled – soul-injured males,"[12] she once declared. New York, too, was no infirmary for a woman of such progressive passion. When she returned to Germany, she found that Europe offered no such refuge either. At the age of 53, the Baroness suffocated to death as a result of a gas leak in her flat. Nobody knew if it was suicide or accident. For years, she was consigned to the margins of history as an eccentric sideshow in Dadaist art, though she is now slowly being rediscovered as one of its most forward-thinking figures. She was, said *The Little Review* founder Margaret Anderson, "perhaps the only figure of our generation who deserves the epithet extraordinary".[13]

GINA PANE

Gina Pane (1939–1990) walked over fire. She climbed a ladder studded with metal shards, barefoot. She plucked the thorns from roses and used them to cut open her arms. She forced raw meat down her throat. She sliced into her lips and sawed at her hands with razor blades. Disliking the theatrical implications of the word "performance", Gina called these sessions of ritualistic violence "actions". In the process, she created some of the bloodiest and most transgressive art of the 1970s and 1980s.

Born in the French seaside town of Biarritz, Gina attended the École des Beaux-Arts in Paris from 1960 to 1965 but, on graduation, shunned conventional sculpture and painting. An early work involved digging a hole in the ground and using a mirror to refract sunlight into it, and then simply walking off. Her artistic approach of self-inflicted violence was born of the May 1968 protests, one of the greatest upheavals in 20th-century France. As students in Paris took to the barricades and faced down tear gas and riot police, ten million workers downed tools and walked out of their factories in solidarity with the demonstrators. The country ground to a near-halt, leaving nobody unaffected – Gina included.

"Before May 68, all living forces in Paris were working intensely to be able to get beyond the 'Social Criticism Theory' in order to be at peace with 'real life'," she said. "In this broken, upset environment, creativity was emerging everywhere. The confrontation of mine with the post-1968 public benefitted from a relationship that I could define as 'Active' and my work was not only looked at but lived."[14]

By the 1970s, Gina was producing work that expressed just what she meant by the word "active". She turned her body into an instrument that bled and burned, hoping to shock her audiences into emotion or action. The violence was never glamorized or turned into spectacle; Gina always wore a plain uniform and sometimes sunglasses, casting herself in the position of Everywoman. Each action was meticulously executed and controlled, down to the lighting and sound, and even its audience. She documented the actions in photography and on videotape, assembling them into independent artworks that she described as *constats* (statements or reports).

In doing so, she pushed herself to the very limits of human endurance, pioneering a form of art that became known as *art corporel* or body art. "I wound myself but I never mutilate myself," she once said. "The wound? It lies at the centre of a process of identifying, recording and locating a certain malaise."[15] If her suffering was like that of a martyr – and Gina's work frequently referenced Christianity – it was that of a coolly composed saint, transposed beyond individual suffering and projected into the service of something greater.

As a queer woman, Gina's work could also be deeply sensual, even romantic. In 1973 – at a time when lesbians were still regarded as freaks and perverts – she performed *Azione Sentimentale* ("Sentimental Action") in all white for an all-female audience. Holding a bouquet of roses, she pierced her arms with their thorns and then used a razor blade to cut her palms to a recording of two women – one French and one Italian – reading love letters to each other.

Gina never saw her self-inflicted violence as gratuitous, though audience members with a weak stomach might be forgiven for feeling faint. That was the point, more or less. Amid the televised spectacle of the Vietnam War, Gina wanted to shock people into feeling something, whether it was empathy, horror or fear. In *Nourriture/Actualités télévisées/Feu* ("Food/TV News/Fire"), Gina invited audiences to view her shoving 600g (more than 1¼lb) of raw ground beef into her mouth and then spitting it out, before watching the news on TV through the glare of a light bulb. For the climax of the action, she extinguished fires with her bare hands and feet.

"Nobody said anything – the silence was terrifying,"[16] she said of the third act. "At the end of the 20 minutes, everyone there remarked: 'It's strange, we never felt or heard the news before. There's actually a war going on in Vietnam, unemployment everywhere.'...Until this moment, they were anesthetized in the face of world news."[17] In her 1974 text *Lettre à un(e) inconnu(e)* (unofficially translated as "Letter to a Stranger"), she addresses her audience members directly to lay bare the reason for her self-inflicted suffering: "When I open up my 'body', so that you can see your own blood there, I do it out of love for you, love for the other. P.S. That is why your presence is so important to me during my actions."[18]

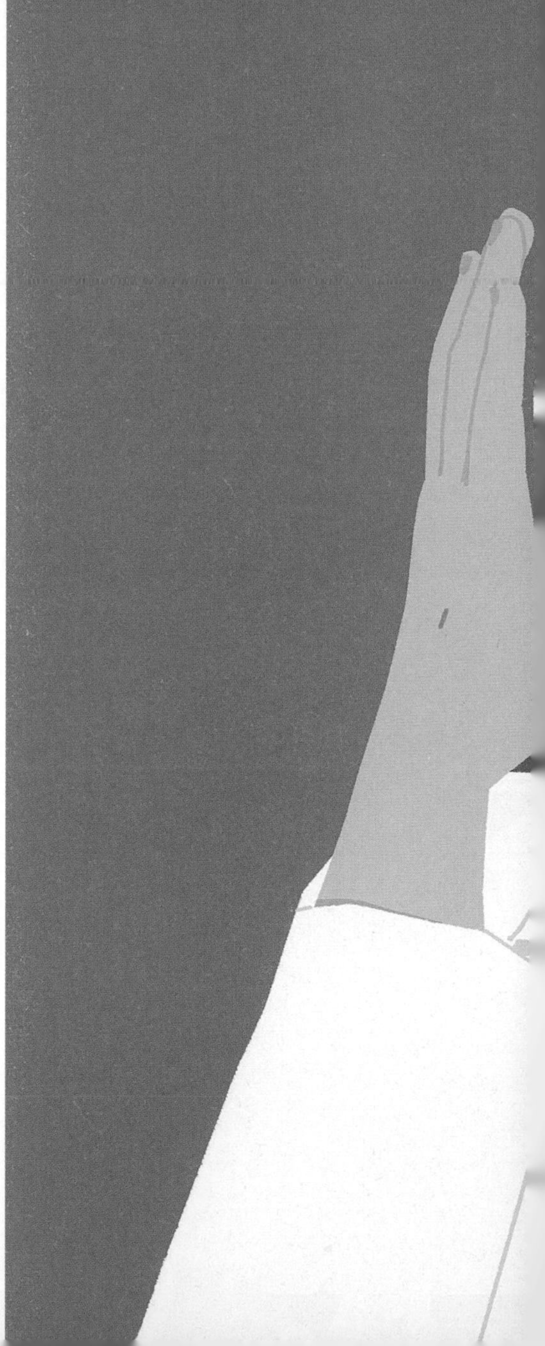

EMMY HENNINGS

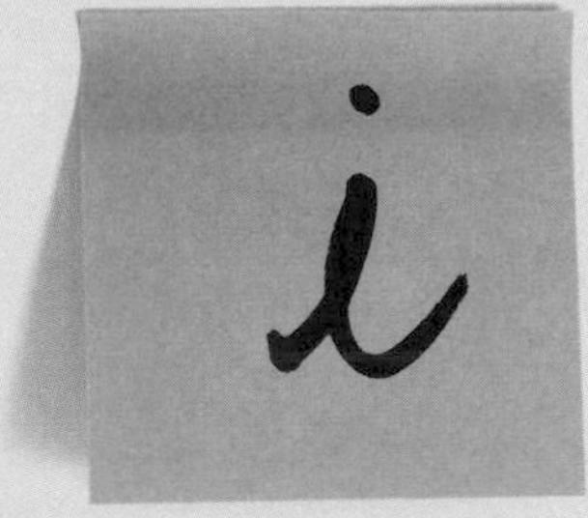

n 1916, at a time when Europe was halfway through the misery and destruction of World War I, something truly strange and new was happening in the back room of a seedy tavern in Switzerland. With Emmy Hennings (1885–1948) as its co-founder and her soon-to-be husband, Hugo Ball, by her side, Cabaret Voltaire was thrust onto an unsuspecting world. Zurich had never seen anything like it.

Just a few days earlier, Hugo had placed an advert in a Swiss newspaper announcing its launch: "Cabaret Voltaire," he declared. "Under this name a group of young artists and writers has formed in the hall of the 'Meirei' at Spiegelgasse 1 with the object of becoming a centre for artistic entertainment and intellectual exchange. The Cabaret Voltaire will be run on the principle of daily meetings where visiting artists will perform their music and poetry. The young artists of Zurich, whatever their orientation, are invited to bring along their ideas and contributions."[19]

Named after the 18th-century French wit and Enlightenment philosopher, Cabaret Voltaire ran for only a few months but launched a brand-new art movement: Dada. In its short-lived but remarkable run, artistic exiles and draft dodgers from various European countries reacted to the horror of the war by questioning everything and pushing art to its very limits. As founding member Hans Arp wrote of the time: "Revolted by the butchery of the 1914 World War, we in Zurich devoted ourselves to the arts. While the guns rumbled in the distance, we sang, painted, made collages and wrote poems with all our might."[20] And the undisputed star of Cabaret Voltaire, as one reviewer in the *Zürcher Post* described her? Emmy Hennings.

Born in Flensburg on the northern German coast, Emmy described herself as a "seaman's child"[21] and had the wanderlust to match. By the time she turned 24, she had separated from her first husband and suffered the death of their infant son. After having another baby – unceremoniously depositing it with her mother back in Flensburg – Emmy embarked on the itinerant life of a travelling performer, roaming variety halls and theatres from Budapest to Berlin as a singer and actress.

The life of a jobbing performer didn't pay much, and Emmy supplemented her income with sex work, occasionally getting hauled to jail for stealing from her clients. She had a magnetic effect on the opposite sex, and battled a drug habit. "I have been addicted to ether for some time and really going to the dogs," she wrote in a letter to a friend in 1912. "I am in a state of eternal agitation, spiritually of course (not sexually, which perhaps would be better)."[22] One of her former lovers wrote in his diary: "The poor girl gets too little sleep. Everybody wants to sleep with her, and since she is so accommodating, she never gets any rest."[23] An artist's sketch of Emmy from 1914 shows her hunched over a syringe, appearing to shoot up.

In 1913, Emmy met Hugo at the avant-garde literary cabaret Café Simplicissimus in Munich, where she had scored a regular gig as a singer. Hugo was a theatre director; they shared a love of performance but a frustration with its limitations. "We believe in the proven truth of illusion,"[24] Emmy said scathingly of theatre. When it seemed increasingly likely that Hugo would be called up for the German army, the couple fled together to the sanctuary of politically neutral Switzerland.

At Cabaret Voltaire, Emmy was able to bring her decade of experience in theatre to the stage and invent something startling and new. She read poetry (her own, as well as other people's) and danced and sang – old love ballads, archly satirical songs and folk numbers from her youth – making them all strange and new with outlandish costumes, dramatic intensity and physical movement. Decades before the term "performance art" was coined, Emmy electrified audiences with her genre-bending soup of art, literature and theatre. "Emmy has the greatest success," Hugo wrote in a letter to his sister. "They translate her verses for Bucharest. She has a whole colony of friends there. The French are kissing her hand. They love her beyond words."[25]

None of this, however, translated into financial success. Emmy was left flogging hand-bound booklets of her verse to audiences during the interval, and slowly became disenchanted by Dada. In July of that year, Emmy and Hugo left Zurich and, four years later, married. Emmy converted to Catholicism and attacked that with all the zeal of her Cabaret Voltaire performances – but in the process, completely renounced her Dadaist past. Instead, she became a poet and an author, as well as the editor and publisher of her husband's work. "About this time I occasionally made notes, which I soon destroyed for the most part," she wrote of the time preceding and during Cabaret Voltaire. "I wanted to forget, to bury what had been."[26]

LETÍCIA PARENTE

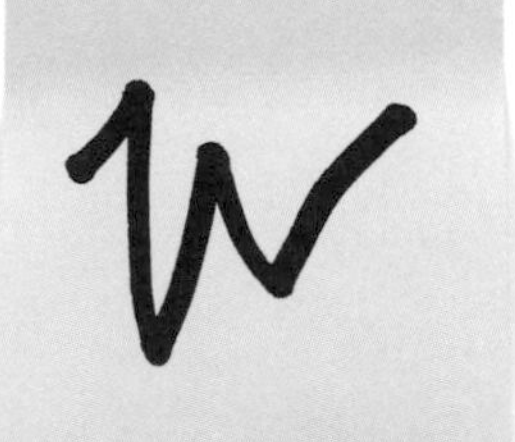

orried about making it as an artist before you hit 30? Take comfort from Letícia Parente (1930–1991), who only started making art in her 40s, after she had married and had five kids. The trailblazing multimedia artist has been compared to Andy Warhol and Bruce Nauman in her native Brazil, presenting, as they did, a radically new way of interacting with a then-emerging technology: the humble VHS tape.

Born in Bahia, Letícia originally trained as a scientist and worked as a chemistry professor, becoming one of the first women appointed to the Brazilian Academy of Sciences. In 1971, the mother of five spontaneously decided to attend some workshops run by artists Ilo Krugli and Pedro Dominguez. Upon her graduation into the world of art, she joined a group of other pioneering Brazilian video artists and began making the kind of art that could easily get her thrown into prison under her country's military dictatorship.

At the time, her government was engaged in the systematic torture of hundreds of individuals deemed to be leftist enemies of the state; one interrogation tactic involved the application of electric shocks to victims' ears and feet. In the 1975 work *Marca registrada* ("Registered Trademark"), Letícia films herself slowly and methodically sewing the words "Made in Brasil" into the sole of her bare foot. "It's an agony! It's afflicting, because the needle goes in, hurts my foot – it could only be my own foot,"[27] she said of the work.

Though Letícia had a thriving career outside the home – she wrote scientific textbooks, taught classes at high school and university and worked as a director for a rural public education system – most of her work was filmed in the confines of her Rio de Janeiro apartment. Another film, *In*, shows Letícia attempting to hang a blouse in her closet while still wearing it, painfully contorting herself in an attempt to insert the clothes hanger. In *Tarefa I* ("Task 1"), she climbs onto an ironing board in all her clothes and lies perfectly still as another woman irons her.

The old adage, "the personal is political", carries a lot more weight when your beliefs can see you spirited away to a torture chamber and killed in the night. In Letícia's world, domestic drudgery entails discomfort – even violence – on both an intimate and national level. A photographic work, *Série 158*, saw Letícia cut out images of women from fashion magazines and distort their features, warping them beyond recognition. In other works, she pushed safety pins through the eyes and mouth of a woman from a glossy magazine spread, and she defaced illustrations of women by stitching through their faces. "I was concerned with things being questioned in several ways," she once said, "because I was interested in the answers."[28] Tellingly, one of her videos shows Letícia injecting herself with a series of vaccines, one after the other; they are labelled anti-cultural colonialism, anti-racism, anti-political mystification and anti-mystification of art.

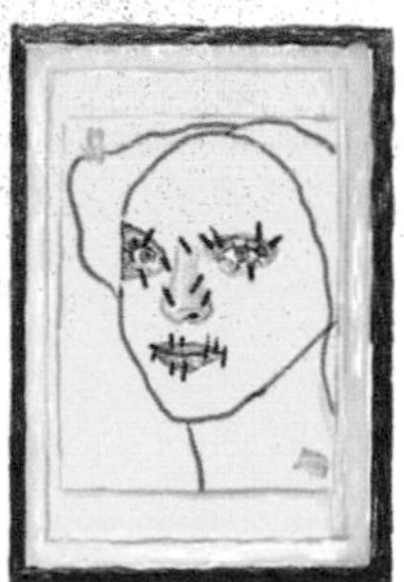

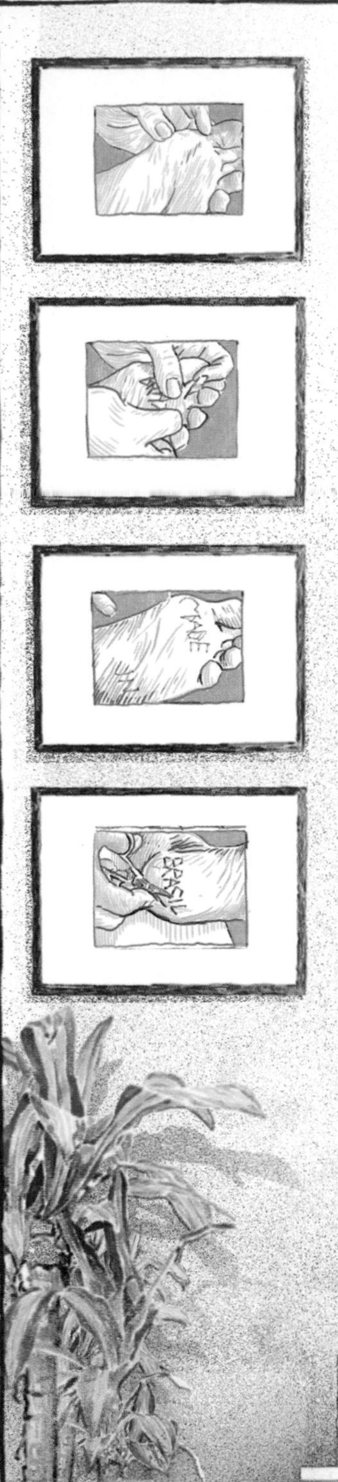

Letícia sometimes struggled to reconcile the seemingly contradictory halves of her life in science and art, before she realized that the former could benefit her artistic practice. "For some time I found it difficult to carry the burden of appearing as a professional scientist in an 'opposite' professional area," she wrote. "I had the impression that art professionals did not accept that condition. However, little by little that impression was gone."[29]

"In some works, the method of approach may be enriched with a perspective or view that is used in scientific subjects. It is the destruction of another taboo. The rationality it requires, however, does not intend to put the logic on a pedestal – it also becomes subject to criticism and denunciation."[30]

The large-scale installation *Medidas* ("Measures") for her first solo show in the Modern Art Museum of Rio was hailed as the first in the country to fuse art and science to dazzling effect. Audience members were asked to visit so-called stations in the piece to record their body measurements on card; visitors were thus distilled down to their body metrics – height, blood type, face shape, even lung capacity.

Letícia lived to see Brazil shake off military rule in 1985, but over a third of her video work from the time of the regime has been lost. Her reliance on now-obsolete technology and the carelessness of art institutions have been cited as reasons for their disappearance. Her remaining work survives as a testament to the power of critique – not just in the service of protesting against an oppressive state, but to challenge wider, unquestioned social norms. "There's always this attempt, on the part of society, to tell you how to dress, how to carry yourself," explained her son, André Parente, "and this is what Letícia confronts."[31]

Craft

TOKUYAMA GYOKURAN

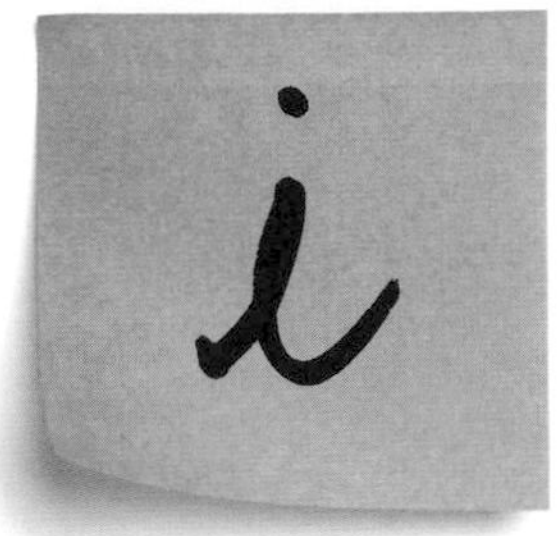

n Japan's Edo period (1603–1868), the illegitimate children of samurai rarely became celebrated artists. Then again, Tokuyama Gyokuran (1727/8–1784) was an uncommon woman for her time. When the Japanese calligrapher, painter and poet got married, she flouted convention by refusing to shave her eyebrows. She was a successful businesswoman, running a bustling teahouse named the Matsuya near a popular Shinto shrine in Kyoto. Once, she visited a noble family's household bearing a bucket of fish as a gift. In short, Gyokuran was delightfully and stubbornly immune to the social niceties and expectations of others.

Gyokuran was initially named Machi and was the result of a decade-long affair between her mother, Yuri, a noted poet and the original proprietor of the Matsuya, and a high-ranking retainer of the ruling Tokugawa shogun. Though he later abandoned Yuri to take up his duties in Edo, she never let their daughter forget her roots. "Your father was a samurai," she told her. "You must respect yourself as a woman – never look down on yourself!"[1] Little wonder that Machi grew up to pursue a life of fiercely idiosyncratic and artistic independence.

Like her mother, Machi composed *waka* poetry, but it was in painting and calligraphy that she truly excelled. As a young woman, she studied under the noted artist Yanagisawa Kien, who was among the first to incorporate Chinese brushwork into Japanese art. It was from Kien that she derived the name Gyokuran ("Jewel Waves"), an artistic moniker that she went under for the rest of her days.

At some point, when Gyokuran was in her late teens or early twenties, Yuri turned her attention to finding a good husband for her daughter. Gyokuran shared her teacher with

an impoverished artist called Ike Taiga, who scraped a meagre living from his paintings and calligraphy. "Others regarded him of no consequence," recalled the 18th-century biographer Rai San'yō, "but Yuri quite on her own made up her mind that he had great promise and in the end gave him her daughter in marriage."[2]

Gyokuran (who today is often known by her married name, Ike Gyokuran) and Taiga were blessed with perfect compatibility, and both embarked on parallel but complementary careers. Like their artistic mentor Kien, they were active proponents of *nanga*, a style of Chinese-inspired painting characterized by an admiration of nature and the use of poetic inscriptions. Gyokuran ran the Matsuya from their modest, straw-thatched hut near Kyoto's Gion Park, continuing her studies in painting under Taiga and directing his education in Japanese poetry herself.

Taiga's work leaned toward the big and bold in the form of screens and sliding doors, but Gyokuran flourished in small and exquisite spaces. At least half of her surviving work exists on ornamental fans. Every single one is a perfectly balanced composition of text and image. Works like *Akashi Bay* conjure up the image of a lonely fishing village with just a few graceful strokes and washes of black ink. In *Bamboo Fan with Inscription by Yuri*, Gyokuran also paid homage to her own literary heritage, painting an elegant tangle of bamboo next to a poem by her mother:

I repeat my vow

in unchanging colors of

the ageless bamboo –

which still creates ten thousand

generations of shadows.[3]

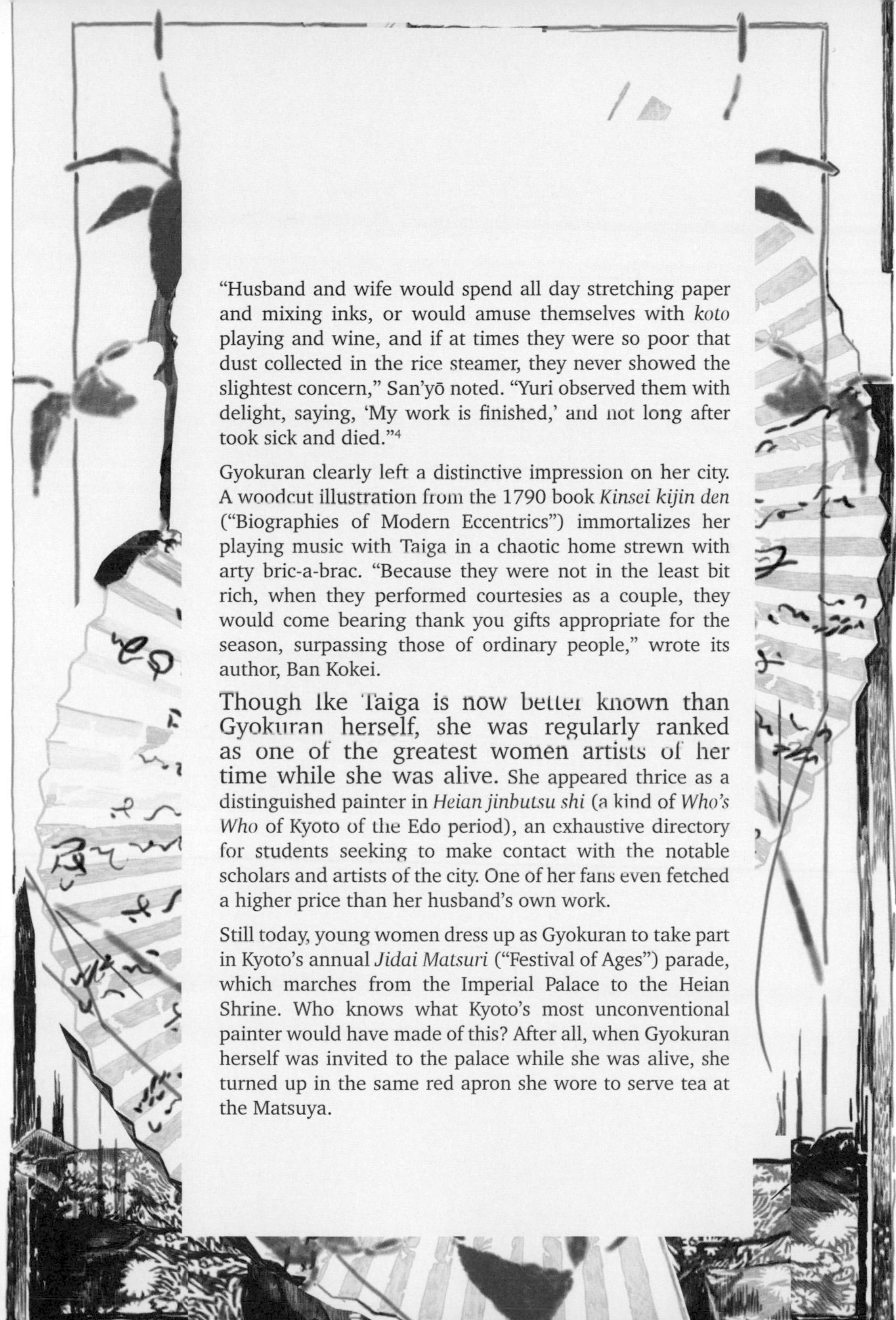

"Husband and wife would spend all day stretching paper and mixing inks, or would amuse themselves with *koto* playing and wine, and if at times they were so poor that dust collected in the rice steamer, they never showed the slightest concern," San'yō noted. "Yuri observed them with delight, saying, 'My work is finished,' and not long after took sick and died."[4]

Gyokuran clearly left a distinctive impression on her city. A woodcut illustration from the 1790 book *Kinsei kijin den* ("Biographies of Modern Eccentrics") immortalizes her playing music with Taiga in a chaotic home strewn with arty bric-a-brac. "Because they were not in the least bit rich, when they performed courtesies as a couple, they would come bearing thank you gifts appropriate for the season, surpassing those of ordinary people," wrote its author, Ban Kokei.

Though Ike Taiga is now better known than Gyokuran herself, she was regularly ranked as one of the greatest women artists of her time while she was alive. She appeared thrice as a distinguished painter in *Heian jinbutsu shi* (a kind of *Who's Who* of Kyoto of the Edo period), an exhaustive directory for students seeking to make contact with the notable scholars and artists of the city. One of her fans even fetched a higher price than her husband's own work.

Still today, young women dress up as Gyokuran to take part in Kyoto's annual *Jidai Matsuri* ("Festival of Ages") parade, which marches from the Imperial Palace to the Heian Shrine. Who knows what Kyoto's most unconventional painter would have made of this? After all, when Gyokuran herself was invited to the palace while she was alive, she turned up in the same red apron she wore to serve tea at the Matsuya.

HANNAH RYGGEN

n 1937, Pablo Picasso debuted *Guernica* at the Paris Expo in the Spanish Pavilion. Directly adjacent to it was the Norwegian Pavilion, which exhibited a work of similar intensity and passionate anti-war feeling: *Ethiopia*, a tapestry by the textile artist Hannah Ryggen (1894–1970). Unlike the initially lukewarm reception that *Guernica* received, *Ethiopia* caused a sensation.

In the space of a few patterned frames, Ryggen attacks the colonial imperialism of Italy's invasion of Ethiopia, Africa's oldest independent country, and shows an Ethiopian soldier triumphantly waving Mussolini's decapitated head. When the tapestry went on display in Paris, the offending part was folded down, to spare Italian visitors any embarrassment.

Ryggen's raw, no-holds-barred political sensibility and her breathtaking technical skill were a study in contrasts. She turned the decorative medium of tapestry into a vehicle to communicate her disgust at a world of increasing upheaval and violence; Hitler, Winston Churchill and the atrocities of the Vietnam War all figure in her work. "I always weave in a certain rhythm from beginning to end," she wrote in a 1946 letter. "I prefer to collect myself and then let loose with explosive effect."[5]

Born in Malmö, Sweden, Ryggen trained as a painter before marrying the Norwegian artist Hans Ryggen. The couple moved to an isolated farm in Ørlandet, Norway, five hours by steamboat from the nearest city of Trondheim. Decades before the term "off-grid" was coined, Ryggen and her husband lived off the land and their livestock. He built her a loom, and Ryggen taught herself how to weave. Their flock of sheep provided her with the wool, and she extracted dyes from foraged lichen and other local vegetation, which she fermented in human urine using traditional folk techniques. (Guests at the farm were instructed to help with chamberpot donations.)

The scale of a tapestry, and the labour required, usually makes its weaving a group endeavour; Ryggen, however, was all on her own. And she didn't make things easier on herself when she dispensed altogether with preparatory sketches, creating each piece off the cuff, with images springing straight from her mind's eye and onto the loom. She once said that working on each piece made her feel like "an ant carrying one pine needle at a time, stubbornly intent on its goal".[6]

The remoteness of Ryggen's living situation proved no barrier to her political activism or keenly developed sense of justice. "Right from my first arrival at Ørlandet, we received *Dagbladet* [a Norwegian left-wing newspaper] – for more than 30 years – and thanks to that we could follow what was going on in the world, which I at least was interested in," she said. "Even as a child I was a red revolutionary."[7] Her views are crystallized in a comment she made in 1942:

...every man and woman, whether rich or poor, ought to be raised capable of two things: producing their own food and supporting themselves. It is an indignity that some serve others. Everyone should work, no one should be above another. Equality for all mankind. We are all flesh and blood, just the same.[8]

Ryggen's work was a sharp critique of the fascism that swept Europe in the first half of the 20th century. The tapestries *Death of Dreams* and *Liselotte Herrmann*, which she created within three years of each other, depict the German pacifist Carl von Ossietzky, who won the 1935 Nobel Peace Prize, and the German Communist Liselotte Herrmann, both imprisoned and executed by the Nazis for treason.

In 1940, the horrors of Nazism came knocking on Ryggen's door with the German invasion of Norway. Ørlandet was turned into a Nazi military base, and over seven thousand German troops were stationed in the region. Ten prominent members of the local community were rounded up and shot; her husband was interned in a prison camp as a political dissident.

Ryggen was undeterred – she displayed her anti-fascist tapestries on her washing line, in full sight of the Nazis walking past. A year after martial law was imposed on Trondheim, she finished her tapestry *6 October 1942* to commemorate the tragic day itself. It shows the German execution of local theatre director Henry Gleditsch, overseen by a spectral vision of Hitler, who flies through the air like a grotesque phantom. Ryggen and her family float uneasily in a nearby boat.

After World War II, she took on issues like nuclear proliferation and American intervention in Vietnam, turning US President Lyndon Johnson into a lurid cowboy in the tapestry *Blood in the Grass*. In *Mr Atom*, she personified nuclear weaponry as the sinister "Atom King", floating cross-legged in the air. "I base my images on life itself," she said. "The difficulty is shaping my experience so that it defers to the weave, yet is as strong as possible about what is on my mind."[9]

Ryggen, a card-carrying member of the Communist Party, refused to sell her work to private collectors and bequeathed most of it to public museums and art galleries. To this dyed-in-the-wool revolutionary, life, politics and art were indistinguishable parts of a whole.

ESTHER INGLIS

igger doesn't always mean better – at least not in the world of Esther Inglis (1571–1624), the Scottish miniaturist who crafted tiny calligraphy books adorned with seed pearls and gold embroidery. Working about a hundred years or so after the dawn of the printing press, Esther excelled in the space between printed word and art, and she spent her life seeking wealth and success using her talent for creating precious, jewel-like *objets d'art*.

"Blessed is the man that findeth wisdome, and the man that getteth understanding," one of the pages in her manuscripts goes. "For the merchandise therof is better then merchandise of silver."[10] For Esther, raised in Scotland and born to two French Huguenot refugees, education promised a route out of the grinding poverty that saw her family survive off poor relief. Thanks to her schoolmaster father and calligrapher mother, Esther was one of the few working-class girls in Edinburgh to learn to read and write.

Renaissance women were barred from studying the nude form, and many with artistic inclinations turned toward self-portraits and copying instead. Esther did both. In her books, she copied out devotional poetry and Bible verses in dozens of fiendishly difficult scripts. Many of them, like French secretary hand or mirror writing, are obsolete today. They retain all their exquisiteness and charm in Esther's hand, but you may need a magnifying glass to look at them. Some of her lines from Psalms or Ecclesiastes stand at less than 1mm (3/64in) tall; her smallest book clocks in at about 4 × 5cm (1½ × 2in).

Esther
INC

To assert her authorship of each work, Esther signed the manuscript and drew self-portraits to insert between the pages. In one delightful frontispiece, she wears a black dress with a white ruffle and surrounds herself with animal motifs, from a vividly green flock of parakeets to a squirrel clutching a nut. As in many of her miniaturized self-portraits, she poses by her writing desk with the implements of her trade. Perhaps sensing that female self-promotion might strike others as unseemly, Esther always makes sure to assert her humility in her portraits. She described her first two books, which she dedicated to Elizabeth I, as "a portrait of the Christian Religion, that I have drawn with the pen, which I send to your Majesty to honour the small knowledge that God has given me in the art of writing and portraying".[11] Many of her self-portraits carry the inscription "From the Lord goodness, from myself nothing".[12]

In 1596, Esther married Bartholomew Kello. Both found employment under King James VI of Scotland as scriveners, a now-defunct profession that involved reading and writing official documents on behalf of royalty, nobles and public institutions. It appears to have been an unconventional marriage. Esther retained her father's surname, and Bartholomew became an assistant of sorts to his wife, ferrying her books to their intended recipients and helping her to translate texts. Even in a portrait commissioned to commemorate her marriage to Bartholomew, Esther is the very image of the working woman – clasping a small book, possibly one of her own, to her chest.

Aside from Bartholomew's assistance, Esther was an unusually independent artist in her chosen medium. Since medieval times, hand-wrought manuscripts like hers were the products of a workshop full of people (usually men). Her books, however, were all crafted by her own hand, right down to the illustrations, the minuscule binding and the sumptuous embroidered velvet covers. Esther wasn't producing any of these works on commission. Her tactic consisted of dedicating a book to a member of the ruling classes – like the Queen or the Countess of Bedford – and sending it out on spec in the hope that she would receive some money from its new owner in return. In a dedicatory verse, she hails her own entrepreneurial "Amazonian spirit"[13] in this regard.

Esther's manuscripts were widely admired by a range of patrons who treasured them as inventive collectibles and miniature works of art. In one work dedicated to Queen Elizabeth I, Esther writes that she hopes "this little present, written by my hand, in a foreign land, might obtain a place in some retired corner of your cabinet".[14] An anonymous writer named S.G.D. praises her in one dedicatory sonnet as the "Matchles Mistresse of the golden pen".[15]

Despite Esther's talent and royal patronage, she died in debt at the age of 53. Remarkably, however, almost 60 of her tiny manuscripts have survived the centuries. There is no other women of the Renaissance period whose signed manuscripts live on in such quantities – a testament to Esther herself, and to the devotion her small but significant artworks inspired in others.

IAIA OF CYZICUS

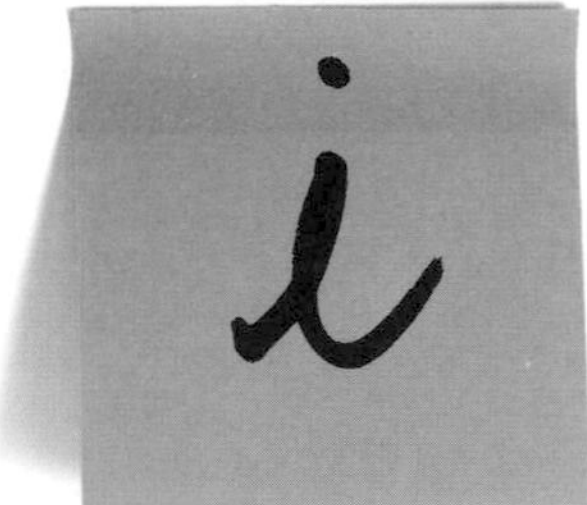

In 2017, a group of researchers from the University of Luxembourg embarked on an ambitious study to quantify just how little women artists were paid in comparison with men. After crunching 1.5 million auction results from 45 countries, they found that a painting by a woman would typically sell for 47.6 per cent of the price of a work by a man. "Women's art," the scientists concluded, "appears to sell for less because it is made by women."[16] That year, a painting by Leonardo da Vinci sold for $450 million, eclipsing all other auction records – including the $44.4 million record set by Georgia O'Keeffe's *Jimson Weed/White Flower No. 1* as the highest price ever fetched for a piece of art by a woman.

Some men have sneered at the idea that women's art even deserves to be paid as much as men. "Women simply don't pass the [market] test," German artist Georg Baselitz told a *Der Spiegel* reporter in 2013. "Women don't paint very well. It's a fact."[17]

But you don't have to peer into the distant future to see a time when a woman artist gets paid the same as a man. All you have to do is look at the ancient past, at the case of Iaia of Cyzicus (*fl. c.*100 BC). Like Timarete (*see* page 79), Iaia – who was also known as Lala, Laia or Marcia – is mentioned by Pliny the Elder in his encyclopedia *Naturalis historia* ("Natural History"), and subsequently by Giovanni Boccaccio in *De claris mulieribus* ("Concerning Famous Women").

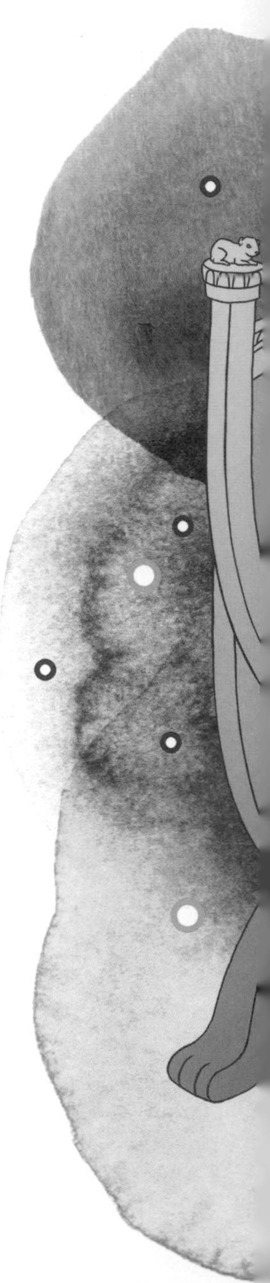

In fact, of the handful of female artists recorded by Pliny the Elder as working in the Greco-Roman Empire, Iaia is the one he singles out as the most impressive. "No artist worked more rapidly than she did," he writes, "and her pictures had such merit that they sold for higher prices than those of Sopolis and Dionysios, well-known contemporary painters, whose works fill our galleries."[18]

So who was Iaia, the woman whose work outpriced not one but two acclaimed male painters? We know that she was born in the town of Cyzicus in what is now present-day northwest Turkey, but worked and lived in Rome. We know that she painted on ivory and wood, and Boccaccio records that she also carved ivory, or, according to one translation, marble. Her artistic lineage is unclear – Pliny is silent on where or how Iaia acquired such remarkable skills, such as whether she had an artist father who passed on his knowledge. He does, however, give a brief rundown of her work: "She painted chiefly portraits of women, and also a large picture of an old woman at Naples, and a portrait of herself, executed with the help of a mirror."[19] Pliny notes, too, that Iaia remained single all her life.

Boccaccio, in slightly more overheated Italian prose, describes Iaia as an "eternal virgin of Rome"[20] and puts her habit of painting predominantly women down to the demands of "chaste modesty"[21]. "The preservation of her virginity merits being exalted with more surprising and sublime praises,"[22] he declares, though he adds that he cannot find any record of Iaia taking a vow of chastity to any goddess or priestesshood. As sex-obsessed as *De claris mulieribus* gets over the question of Iaia's purity, the illuminated book from 1374 does give us the oldest retrospective portrait of the artist in question. Iaia is depicted in her workshop, gazing at her reflection in a mirror while attending to her self-portrait. Two other portraits lie in the background of the painting, standing tall next to some marble sculptures – all of women.

Of course, this depiction of a medieval atelier would be far from the reality of a painter and sculptor living during the time of Augustus Caesar, the first Roman emperor. Unfortunately, nothing of Iaia's work has survived the ages, and we will never get to see the work that so moved Pliny the Elder and the art buyers of Ancient Rome. But if you ever meet someone who claims that women's art hasn't ever sold and can never sell well, you'll know which artist to point him to.

WEI SHUO

n China, the expression *wenfang sibao* is used to refer to a quartet of specific objects: brush, ink, paper and inkstone. Its translation? The four treasures of the study. As a civilization that prizes calligraphy – not painting or sculpture – as its greatest visual art, there could be no other way to describe its tools. And nobody was more devoted to it than Wei Shuo (AD 272–349), more commonly known as Lady Wei – China's earliest-recorded female calligrapher and one of the pioneers of the art form.

Born during the Jin dynasty in present-day Shanxi, Wei Shuo belonged to an illustrious family of calligraphers and scholars. Her uncle and cousin were both well-respected calligraphers who had mastered the many different schools of the art; Wei Hang, her cousin, had written a book, entitled *Si ti shu shi* ("The Trend Toward Four Styles of Calligraphy"), which later landed him a mention in the official *History of the Jin Dynasty*.

In ancient China, one's deftness with a brush indicated more than just expertise – it was considered a powerful expression of your innermost thoughts and spirit. Later on, in the Qing dynasty (1644–1912), the scholar Liu Xizai believed that it could communicate everything from the artist's own private ambitions to their intellect and learning. But this was an art form that was dominated by men; few women were expected to learn to put brush to paper.

For Wei Shuo, however, calligraphy held the promise of creation itself. "A horizontal line has the momentum of clouds stretching in an unbroken chain for thousands of miles; a dot, a stone falling from a lofty peak; a vertical stroke, a withered vine thousands of years old; a hooked dot, hundreds of arrows shot at one time,"[23] she once said. With just a few well-formed characters, an especially skilful calligrapher like Wei Shuo could sketch nothing less than the entire world.

It is said that she displayed an interest in calligraphy even as a young girl, when she was permitted to observe the men in her family at work. On a good day, she might be graciously allowed to grind ink for their inkstone. Once she was alone, Wei Shuo would practise the brushstrokes from memory, and it was only after her uncle accidentally saw her work that she was finally allowed to learn calligraphy.

None of her work has survived, but her artistic legacy lives on. Just like her cousin, Wei Shuo wrote a celebrated treatise that established some of the foundational rules of calligraphy and dramatically influenced its aesthetic philosophy. *Bizhen tu* ("Illustrated Formation of the Writing Brush") is no obscure philosophical tract either. Think of it as Wei Shuo's battle cry for the art form, as this extract from it illustrates:

Paper is battle ground. Brush is sword and shield; ink is armor; inkstone is a city wall and a moat; the heart's intent is the general; technical skills are lower-ranking generals; and structure is the strategy. Lifting the brush heralds life or death; moving the brush executes a military order; and whatever comes under the brush is killed![24]

The original thousand-word treatise may have once included illustrations, but its text is now all that remains. Wei Shuo also provided clear, to-the-point instructions for beginners who wished to learn calligraphy, incorporating everything from how to hold a brush to what kind of ink to use – essential tenets of the art that were later followed for centuries.

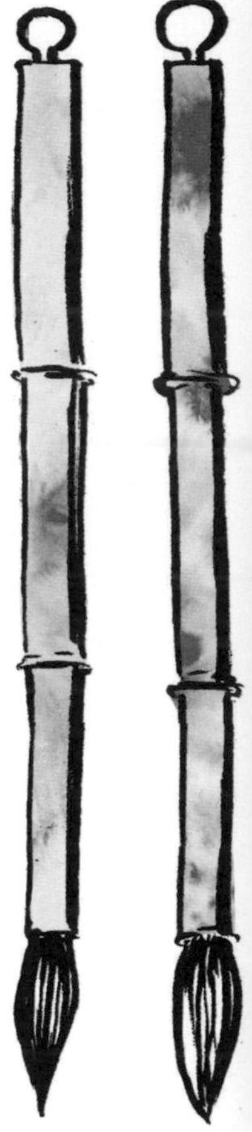

For Wei Shuo, calligraphy required nothing less than total and utter commitment and determination. It required careful preparation, too. The idea of thoughtlessly committing ink to paper horrified her. "Those in whom the mental conception follows while the brush leads, they will be defeated," she wrote. "Those in whom the mental conception precedes and the brush follows, will be victorious."[25] These principles served Wei Shuo and her students well – her most famous disciple, Wang Zixi, became known as the Sage of Calligraphy and is one of the most revered calligraphers in Chinese history.

Wei Shuo herself was never able to reach the same heights as Wang Zixi. Her son, Li Chong, notes in his biography of her that the family struggled financially after the death of Wei Shuo's husband, a regional inspector – so much so that Li Chong had to plead with his bosses for a promotion in order to help his mother out with money. For all her love of the brush, Wei Shuo never lived to reap the rewards of her craft. But her influence is plain to see in the still-thriving art form and the foundations on which she built calligraphy.

HARRIET POWERS

hat is the difference between craft and art? Critics have wrestled with the question for years. Craft, with its implications of domestic use and women's work, has long been dismissed as a lesser form of art – if it even qualifies as art at all. Only recently have traditional crafts like pottery and quilting been considered worthy artistic mediums. Long before contemporary artists like Tracey Emin took up the needle and thread, however, there was Harriet Powers (1837–1910) – a former slave from the USA's Deep South.

Harriet was born into slavery near Athens, Georgia, and married her husband, Armstead Powers, at the age of 18. After the end of the Civil War and the Emancipation Proclamation freed slaves in the South, the couple were able to buy a small farm. They had nine children, only three of whom survived. In between eking out a modest living off the land and raising her children, Harriet found time to make cotton quilts of remarkable power and deep symbolism.

The first record of the Powers quilts comes courtesy of a white artist and teacher named Jennie Smith, who spotted what is now called the *Bible Quilt* at a cotton fair in Athens – a carnival-esque county fair that included a Wild West show, a circus and various craft exhibitions. "I have spent my whole life in the South, and am perfectly familiar with thirty patterns of quilts, but I had never seen an original design, and never a living creature portrayed in patchwork, until the year 1886,"[26] Jennie wrote in her diary. That is, until she spotted Harriet's remarkable quilt. "[A]fter much difficulty," Jennie went on to say, "I found the owner, a negro woman, who lives in the country on a little farm whereon she and her husband make a respectable living."[27]

Jennie offered to buy the quilt, but Harriet wouldn't budge. The piece was not for sale. Four years later, however, the Powers family had fallen on hard times and were looking for ways to make ends meet. Harriet sent word to Jennie that the quilt was now available. Harriet and Armstead pulled up in front of Jennie's house in an ox-cart, with the precious quarry wrapped for protection in a clean flour sack inside a crocus sack. "She offered it for ten dollars – but – I only had five to give,"[28] Jennie wrote in her records.

Harriet reluctantly took the money and parted ways with the quilt, but only after explaining the allegorical meaning of the work to Jennie. Each of the 11 panels, she informed Jennie, told a story from the Scriptures, beginning with Adam and Eve naming the animals in Eden and ending with Christ's crucifixion and a depiction of the Holy Family. The quilt measures roughly the length and width of a small bed, with appliqué used for the motifs and both hand- and machine-stitching.

The *Bible Quilt* and a second work, known as the *Pictorial Quilt*, are all that survive of her work. Neither quilt is a straightforward biblical narrative, however. Contemporary scholars have pointed to the remarkable similarities between Harriet's quilting style and the tapestries of the Fon people in western Africa, which extensively utilize appliqué and animal symbols. There are other indications that Harriet's inspirations extended far beyond those of a pious churchgoer. Several of the 15 rectangles in the *Pictorial Quilt* depict scenes from African–American folk history and memory – like the Leonid Meteor Shower of November 1833, which made people fear that the end of the world was nigh. In weaving together West African symbols, Old and New Testament scripture and African–American folk history, Harriet created something radically new.

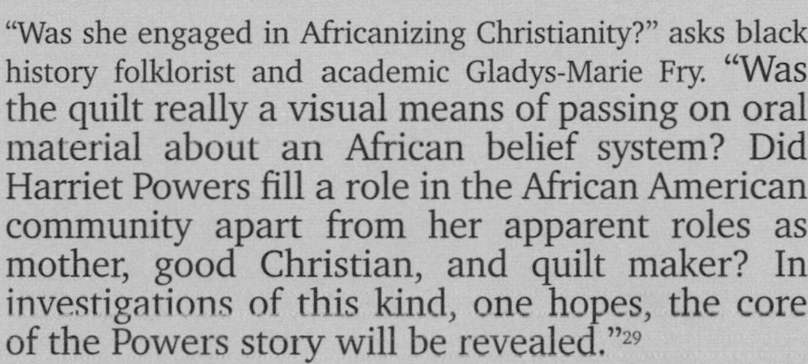

"Was she engaged in Africanizing Christianity?" asks black history folklorist and academic Gladys-Marie Fry. "Was the quilt really a visual means of passing on oral material about an African belief system? Did Harriet Powers fill a role in the African American community apart from her apparent roles as mother, good Christian, and quilt maker? In investigations of this kind, one hopes, the core of the Powers story will be revealed."[29]

There is still much to discover about the creator of these quilts. In 2009, historian Kyra E Hicks discovered a long-lost letter from Harriet that put paid to many assumptions about the quilter, including that she was illiterate. "I am the mother of 9 children — 6 dead and 3 living. I am 58 years old,"[30] Harriet wrote, adding that she had made at least four quilts that had been exhibited in the South and had won awards. Along with the letter, Hicks made a second discovery: a photo of Harriet herself. The woman now known as the "mother of African–American quilting"[31] is posed in an apron adorned with the same heavenly bodies she depicted in her own work, the moon and the stars – proof that women have been blurring the line between the domestic and art for years.

BONNIE NTSHALINTSHALI

In 1993, the Venice Biennale opened its doors to South Africa. Thanks to the long-standing cultural boycott of South Africa's apartheid regime, artists from the country had not exhibited at the event for 25 years. After the release of Nelson Mandela in 1990, however, Biennale artistic director Achille Bonito Oliva decided that the time had come to re-embrace South African art – beginning with two sculptures from the young ceramicist Bonnie Ntshalintshali (1967–1999).

Bonnie grew up in rural KwaZulu-Natal, a long way from the vaporetto rides and champagne receptions of the world's most famous art fair. Born to a housekeeper on a farm named Ardmore near Winterton, a small town in the shadow of the Drakensberg mountains, she fought off polio as a child and had a deformed foot to show for it. After graduating from high school, 18-year-old Bonnie was hired to pick tomatoes, but her disability meant she couldn't move around as easily as the other farmhands.

Janet, her mother, had a plan. Fée Halsted, a Zimbabwean ceramicist from the University of Natal, had moved to Ardmore after being laid off from her job as an art teacher. Her boyfriend, James Berning, had bought the farm with his family and offered her the use of a thatched hut to start a studio. Fée was looking for apprentices, and Janet knew just the person for the job.

"When I met this charming, unassuming young woman, I knew without hesitation that I wanted to work with her,"[32] Fée wrote in her memoirs. "Bonnie was a gifted artist and I felt privileged to work with her and bring out her potential." Their relationship laid the foundations for Ardmore Ceramics, founded in 1985. "Ardmore became a success," Fée later said, "because of Bonny's [*sic*] craftsmanship, skill and meticulous attention to detail."[33]

At first, Bonnie and Fée used commercial plaster moulds to produce small decorative objects, like little ducks that they sold to tourists for two rand each (the equivalent of about $4.50 at that time). However, once Bonnie had learned basic ceramic techniques from Fée, she quickly developed her own inimitable style. Individually sculpting figures in clay and building them into a tableau, Bonnie would fire the pieces at 1,200°C (2,200°F) and paint them in thick, opaque Plaka paint. Her sculptures explode with exuberant colour and pattern, often incorporating intricate details of the bountiful nature surrounding the farm. People teeter on obelisks carved out of columns of cattle and wild beasts or on plinths crawling with crickets and frogs. Even a rare autobiographical work has Bonnie at her desk examining a miniature stack of animal sculptures.

Bonnie was raised as a Catholic, and the Bible exerted a strong pull on her imagination. Her work dramatically reinterprets the traditional gospels through a South African lens. In *The Last Supper*, she puts a Zulu twist on Leonardo da Vinci's famous work: although Bonnie's Christ is white, most of his disciples are black, and they are gathered around a traditional feast of sour porridge and goat. "It has turned out to be just as I had imagined," she said after finishing the work. "The goat's head on the table is a traditional dish, eaten especially by the Zulus at a funeral. No forks have been laid because we eat only with knife and fingers."[34] In *God is Angry Because His Animals Are Being Killed (or Last Judgement)*, she depicts God as a black man – or to be specific, a Zulu chief wrapped in the traditional royal attire of leopard pelts. "People have to respect nature and learn to deal with animal life as well," Bonnie explained. "They also are created by God and adorn his heaven, too. Because man is so rapacious in his hunting and is finishing off the whole animal world, God is angry."[35]

In 1990, Bonnie and Fée were jointly awarded the Standard Bank Young Artist Award for Fine Art, one of most prestigious art prizes in South Africa. It was the first time that it had been awarded to a black artist, or to a pair working jointly.

An exhibition of their work went on to tour the country, even though Bonnie was refused entry at a guesthouse en route to the inaugural exhibition. (In Fée's words: "Apartheid was still alive and kicking."[36])

As Ardmore Ceramics grew in renown, more women began asking to learn how to throw a pot or paint a glaze, and Bonnie and Fée happily obliged. Eventually, the studio grew to encompass a hundred working sculptors, both male and female.

Not everyone appreciated Bonnie's work. South African art critic and artist Kendell Geers sneered that her sculptures were "charming visual distractions, commanding only momentary glances" and criticized her naive style as stilted. "Lacking any such [conceptual] training, Ntshalintshali relies on the charming quaintness of her 'ethnic licence' for applause,"[37] he wrote.

If Bonnie's work did have a conceptual or political message, it was one that went largely unnoticed at the time. Instead, people wondered if her work idealized South Africa to the detriment of acknowledging its racial inequalities. They also asked whether Fée – though she ran the studio as a cooperative – was exploiting the black sculptors who worked at Ardmore.

Bonnie's rebuttal lay in the success of her own work. At the 1993 Venice Biennale, she was the only South African artist picked for the Aperto, devoted to emerging international artists. Achille Bonito Oliva wrote of Bonnie's work: "Her narrative flows richly…there are still many stories to be told."[38]

Sadly, Bonnie never got to tell those stories. Six years on, she fell victim to the HIV epidemic that ravaged South Africa, and died in a hospital which was so overwhelmed by patients that people were expiring in the reception lounge. In her honour, Ardmore Ceramics built the Bonnie Ntshalintshali Museum, South Africa's first museum dedicated to a black artist.

ENDE

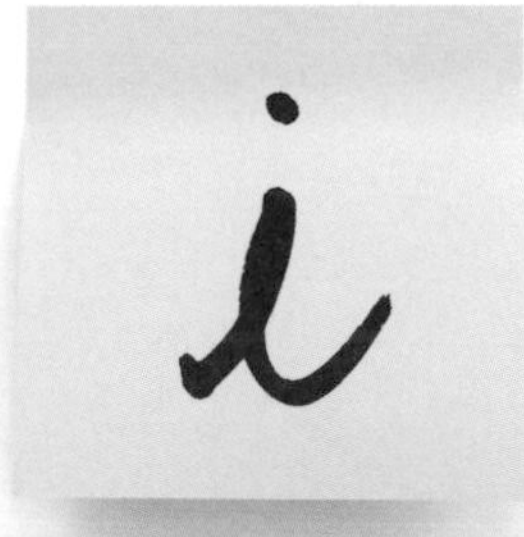

t wasn't just the approach of the second millennium, with its fears of the Y2K bug wiping out computers, that created doomsday paranoia around the world – people have been panicking over the end of the world for centuries. In the 10th century, Christians all over Europe were terrified that the advent of the first millennium would bring with it hellfire and damnation. But what would that fiery Armageddon look like? Enter Ende (*fl. c.* AD 975), the Spanish nun who quite literally painted the Apocalypse, and has the distinction of being one of the earliest-documented women artists in Western Europe.

Frustratingly little is known about Ende. Her origins and family background, along with the dates of her birth and death, are a mystery. Some scholars even disagree over the name Ende and argue that she was called En, though this is not a common Spanish name. All we have to go on is the illuminated manuscript that she illustrated in AD 975 – a masterpiece known as the *Beatus of Girona* (or the "Gerona Apocalypse"), which contains *Commentary on the Apocalypse*, a text written by the Spanish monk Beatus of Liébana.

With no less than 184 miniatures illustrating Beatus's words, the manuscript has been described by New York's Metropolitan Museum of Art as "one of the most richly decorated of the Beatus Commentaries, and one of the best documented".[39] But the *Beatus of Girona* is no sombre holy text. More than a thousand years later, its colours remain exuberantly sumptuous, and its figures writhing in eternal damnation are as unsettling as they must have been in the Middle Ages.

There are 26 surviving illuminated manuscripts of *Commentary on the Apocalypse*, but only one – the *Beatus of Girona* – contains the work of a woman. And Ende wasn't shy about making sure she was properly credited. Along with the name of a male colleague, Emeterius, her name is inscribed in the manuscript colophon (inscription): "*En depintrix* [or *Ende pintrix*] *et Dei aiutrix*"[40] ("Ende, paintress and helper of God"). Tellingly, Ende's name appears ahead of Emeterius's in the colophon, which goes on to note: "The book was successfully completed on Tuesday, July 6. In those days Fredenando Flaginiz was at Villas, the Toledan town, fighting the Moors. The year was 975."[41]

So what can we say about Ende? Historians believe that she was probably a nun, and nuns at that time could lead fulfilling lives that went far beyond the austerity we now associate with women of the cloth. Convents in Europe had the distinction of being among the few places where women could pursue an intellectual life that would have otherwise been cut short by the demands of marriage and family. It was not unusual for nuns to learn to read, write or paint, as long as their talents were used in the service of God. The *Beatus of Girona*, believed to have been produced in the monastery of Tábara in León, northwest Spain, would certainly have fitted that bill.

Scholars over the ages have tried to differentiate the hand of Ende from that of her male co-creator Emeterius. Previous attempts have seen people resort to sexist cliché to distinguish between the two – arguing, for instance, that the daintier and more feminine images could be ascribed to Ende, or that a misspelled word or a grammatical error was the work of someone belonging to a supposedly less intelligent gender.

But if you really want to separate out Ende's work from Emeterius's, you only have to look at an earlier version of the *Beatus of Girona* that was completed by Emeterius in AD 970. Less than ten of these earlier miniatures have survived, and it is clear that the later *Beatus of Girona* is a far superior piece of art; in the words of medievalist Annemarie Weyl Carr, the earlier one has "none of the crisp elegance"[42] of the later version. With its ornate, highly decorated illustrations that hark back to Islamic iconography, and its unique twists on biblical imagery, the *Beatus of Girona* contains a thoughtful depth and expressiveness lacking in its predecessor. The snake in its illustration of the Garden of Eden, for example, sinuously wraps its length around a palm tree; as if to underline the Mediterranean feel, a nervous-looking Adam and Eve clutch a frond to hide their privates.

Ende was not the only painter–nun in the Middle Ages; more would follow in the centuries after her, including the 13th-century German nun Gisela of Kerzenbroeck. But Ende's greatest success can be traced in the longevity of the *Beatus of Girona*, which remains pored over as one of the singular artistic achievements of the Middle Ages. For something that was made in the "End Times", that is pretty impressive work.

Photography

VIVIAN MAIER

ivian Maier (1926–2009) was a mystery, even to those who lived with her. Born in New York City, she nevertheless maintained that she was a Frenchwoman, and she spoke with an indeterminate European accent. When she worked as a nanny, she could swing between kind-hearted and warm, and curiously cold. She forbade her charges from entering her room in the family household, and she asked for locks to guarantee her privacy. When one child trespassed in her attic room, he found reams of newspapers stacked taller than he was. "I'm sort of a spy,"[1] Vivian once declared.

Vivian was a photographer, but she was unlike any the world had seen before. For one thing, she refused to seek any kind of fame or success, though her work more than merited it. She doled out false names to her film processors, and despite helping to raise several children of the various Chicagoan families that hired her as a nanny, she slipped out of their lives like a pat of hot butter once they were fully grown. None of her employers knew the extent of her obsession with photography, and she never married or left behind a family of her own to guard her legacy. "It's *Miss* Maier, and I'm proud of it,"[2] she would tell people.

Her secret artistic life only emerged when a real estate agent and garage sale enthusiast named John Maloof paid $400 for a box of photographic junk at a thrift auction house in Chicago in 2007. It contained over thirty thousand negatives – every single one of them Vivian's. When John began scanning in the images, he was stunned.

Maloof ended up devoting his life to hunting down more of Vivian's work, and finding out as much as he could about the enigmatic woman. "I owe Vivian an honest effort to get her recognized as one of the great photographers of her time," he said. "She was a singular person, extremely intelligent, and her talent was extraordinary."[3]

Vivian took photographs from Egypt to Italy to Thailand, but she is best known for her images of America. Nothing escaped her eye, from the birthmark on the back of a child's spindly leg to the lantern jaws of tough guys hanging around a parked car. Today, her black-and-white photos of street life in all its raucous drama and urban grit rank alongside those by Diane Arbus and Robert Frank.

It turned out that Vivian was born to a French woman, named Jaussaud Maier, and had spent most of her childhood in France – hence the accent. In 1951, 25-year-old Vivian got on a ship from Le Havre and returned to America, where she picked up steady work as a live-in nanny on the West Side of Chicago. None of her employers remembered her discussing family or friends; instead, she would say: "I have to tell you that I come with my life, and my life is in boxes."[4]

At one interview, she turned up with a large carpet bag and an old-fashioned long coat; one of the children she cared for described her as a Mary Poppins-type figure, albeit with a twin-lens Rolleiflex constantly slung around her neck. Armed with her trusty camera, Vivian would walk for hours around Chicago taking photos, dragging her young charges along for the ride.

"I don't think she liked kids at all really," says Joe Matthews, whom Vivian looked after in the 1980s. "I think she liked images. When she saw an image she had to capture it. I think it was the same compulsive behaviour that made her hoard newspapers."[5]

In her twilight years, Vivian wound up homeless and was only rescued when two of her former charges paid the rent on a studio apartment for her. In November 2008, she was admitted to hospital after slipping on some ice, and died a few months after. She was survived by over 150,000 images and hundreds of rolls of film, which were auctioned off by creditors when she failed to pay up for her storage locker. Her work languished in obscurity until its unlikely rescue by John Maloof.

"I suppose nothing is meant to last forever," Maier once said. "We have to make room for other people. It's a wheel – you get on, you go to the end, and someone else has the same opportunity to go to the end, and so on, and somebody else takes their place. There's nothing new under the sun."[6]

What would Vivian have made of her latter-day fame? Her self-enforced solitude has led some to see her as a tragic heroine. Others see a woman who carefully cultivated her own company and relished her freedom; who took photos not for the praise or adulation of others, but for the private joy of documenting life as she witnessed it.

"Many of her subjects I recognize," Joe Matthews's sister Sarah said. "The one that sticks in my head is the picture she took of a man whose face was burned off, whom we often saw. I remember seeing him as a child and wondering if I should look or not. I remember thinking about that. She truly did look at people in a different way and was not afraid to look."[7]

LOLA ÁLVAREZ BRAVO

ola Álvarez Bravo (1903–1993) often said that she had led three lives: the first started when her father died, the second when she married the photographer Manuel Álvarez Bravo and the third when she left him to begin her own career as an artist. In the process, she would become one of Mexico's first female photographers, and her images of her homeland and its artists would eventually be acknowledged as some of her country's most iconic.

Born in Lagos de Moreno, Lola was sent to live with her rich father in Mexico City as a little girl. The 28-room mansion was a child's fantasy brought to life, complete with its own theatre and ballroom. When she turned 13, however, her father died, and she found herself sharing a shabby tenement flat with her older half-brother and his wife. Despite her precipitous fall in fortune, her change in address allowed her to spend more time with Manuel Álvarez Bravo, a childhood friend turned neighbour. He romanced her on the roof terrace of the apartment block, and they married in 1925.

Manuel had taken photographs since he was a teenager, and Lola also developed a love of the medium. "At the beginning, photography was for me, a kind of contagion from Manuel Álvarez Bravo,"[8] she once explained. When they moved to Oaxaca for Manuel's job at the Treasury Department, they converted their kitchen into a darkroom and washed negatives in cooking pots. At first, Lola's involvement was as a loyal assistant: "Manuel would take the photographs, but I would suggest scenes and things. I participated, although only marginally. Then we would go home to work in the darkroom."[9]

On their return to Mexico City, Manuel became ill and Lola took on the task of developing his photos. In 1934, Manuel and Lola separated, but she never forgot how being in a darkroom made her feel. "A pure desire," she said of photography, "turned into an occupation."[10]

Lola may have been born into privilege and wealth, but she was no dilettante. At a time when women were largely regarded in Mexico as muses or models, Lola was determined to make a living from photography. After stints as a primary school art teacher and an archivist, she finally secured, in the mid-1930s, her first professional photographic commission – for *El Maestro Rural* ("The Rural Teacher"), a government publication for teachers. It was followed by more commissions from the many magazines that flourished in post-revolution Mexico. On her assignments, Lola travelled up and down the country, photographing everything from architecture to local folk art.

"My photography is a search: the great question, when I go to the streets or to the country, is what I am going to encounter," she said. "The photography I like has a sense of mystery, of surprise, of expectation."[11] The decade of the 1930s saw the international avant-garde flocking to Mexico, and Lola soaked up their influences and styles. She photographed everyone from the poet Octavio Paz to the novelist Carlos Fuentes, and took some of the most intimate – if not the most iconic – images of Frida Kahlo, whom she photographed at the painter's residence, the now famous Casa Azul, between 1944 and 1945. Lola's skill at composition and mastery of light and shadow saw her dubbed "the best painter in Mexico" by the painter Alfonso Michel.[12]

But Lola's greatest contribution to art came in the form of her raw, unvarnished photos of Mexican life itself. With her technical skill and razor-sharp eye, Lola sought to highlight the grinding poverty and hardship of the country's indigenous peoples and its working classes. In *El sueño de los pobres 2* ("The Dream of the Poor 2"), Lola photographed a malnourished-looking child asleep in a pile of filthy shoes; in another, *Por culpas ajenas* ("By the Fault of Others"), a blind young woman begging on the street stares blankly down the lens. Her photos were deeply compassionate but never sentimental. "I believe that I am obligated to expose a reality for which we are all at fault,"[13] Lola said.

Other photographs showed a profound respect for the indigenous traditions that were dying out in a fast-modernizing Mexico. When Lola travelled to the rural highlands, she photographed a funeral procession of Zapotec villagers etherally shrouded in ceremonial white. She named it *Entierro en Yalalag* ("Burial in Yalalag") and felt it was one of her best pictures.

For most of her life, Lola's art was eclipsed by that of Manuel, who later became one of Latin America's most acclaimed photographers.But she continued taking photographs until her deteriorating eyesight

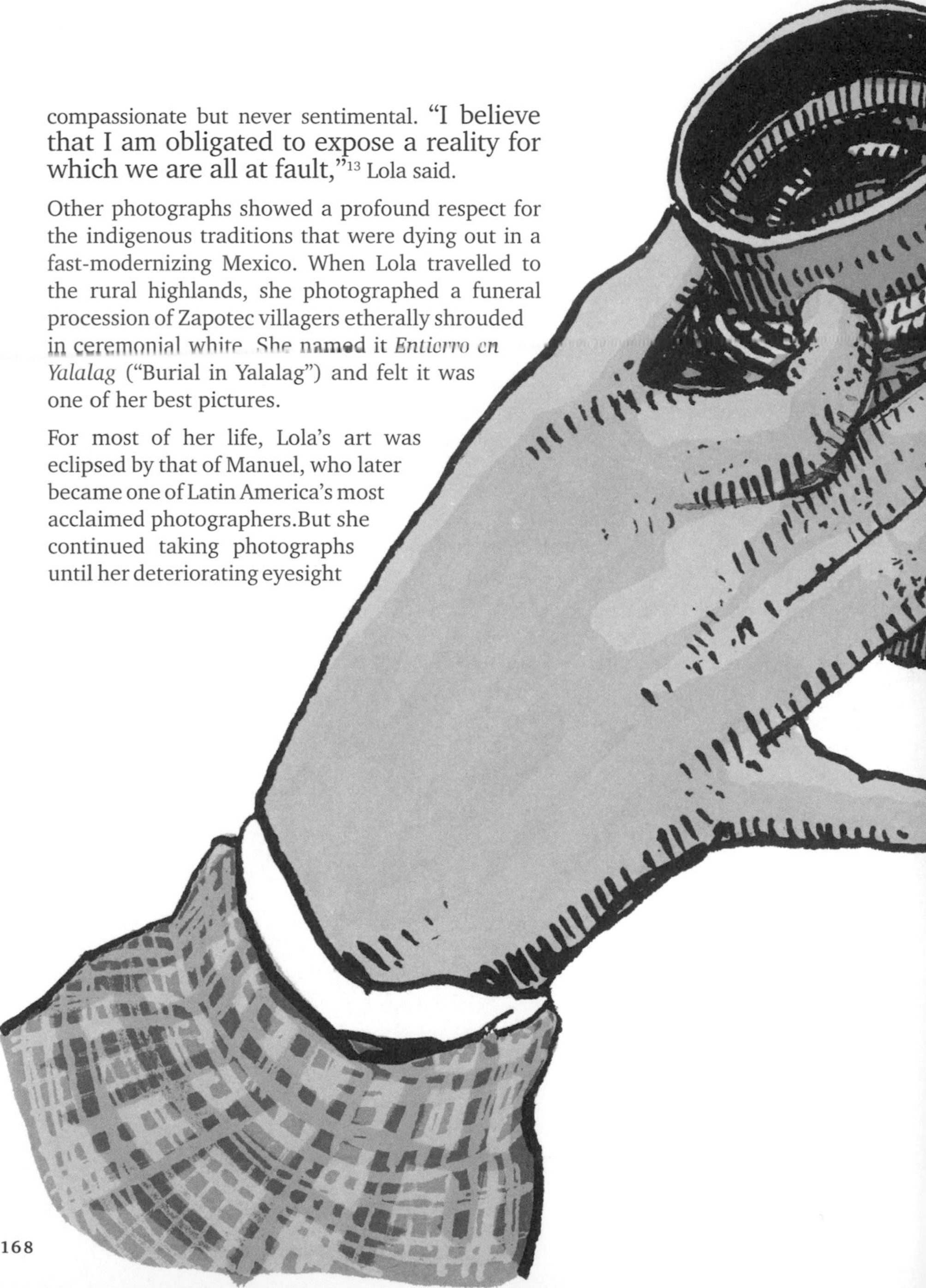

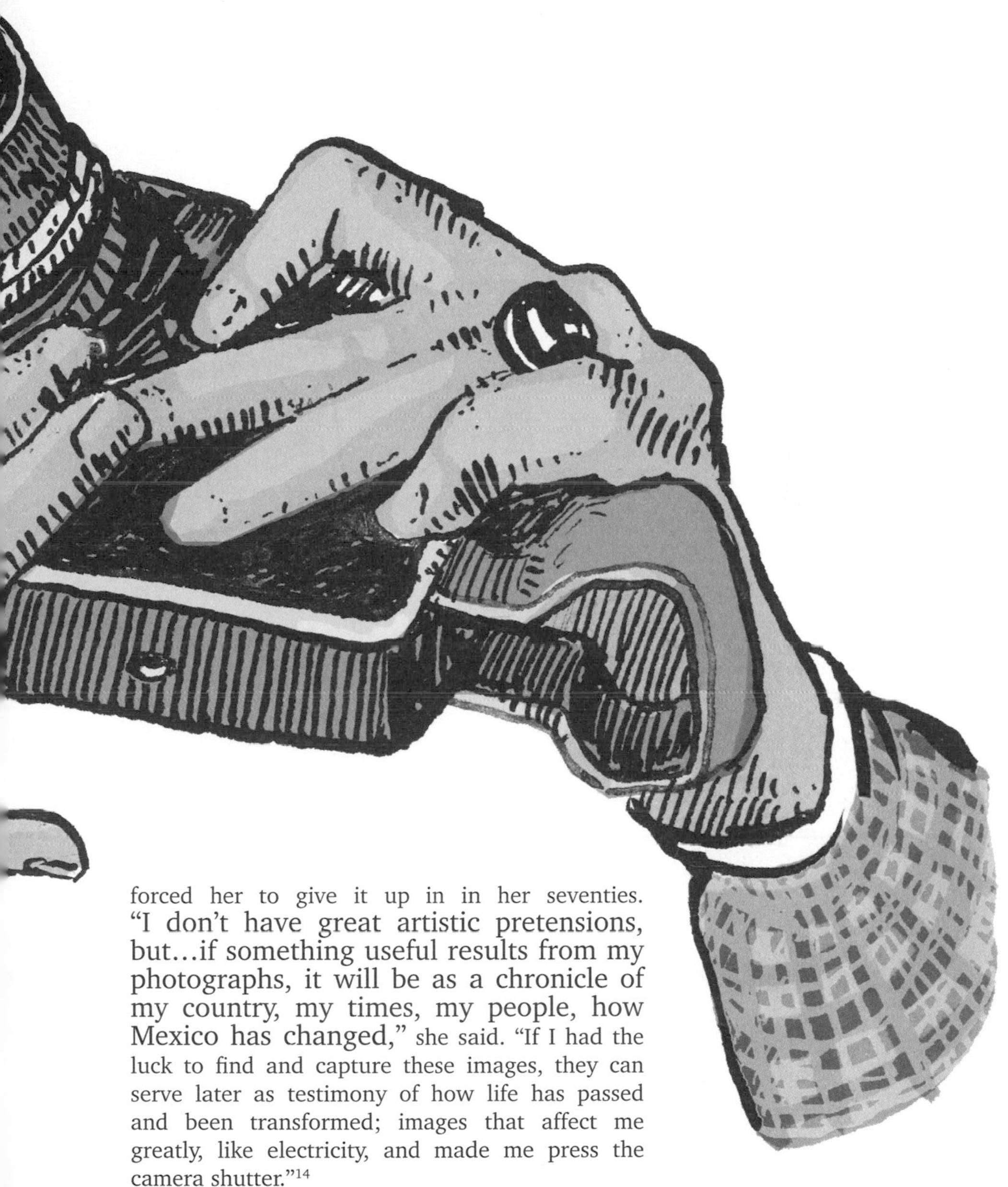

forced her to give it up in in her seventies. "I don't have great artistic pretensions, but…if something useful results from my photographs, it will be as a chronicle of my country, my times, my people, how Mexico has changed," she said. "If I had the luck to find and capture these images, they can serve later as testimony of how life has passed and been transformed; images that affect me greatly, like electricity, and made me press the camera shutter."[14]

MARIANNE BRESLAUER

hen Marianne Breslauer (1909–2001) was 15 years old, she made a visit to an art gallery that changed her life: "I saw a photo exhibition at the Flechtheim Gallery: portraits of the photographer [Frieda] Riess, and as I liked them so much I decided to study photography."[15] It is not known if Marianne ever crossed paths with the German portrait photographer who set her on this course, but Reiss's influence is clear in Marianne's captivating images of the New Woman, the liberated generation of women in the Weimar Republic who were fiercely bohemian and determined to explore life on their own terms.

Born in Berlin to liberal and artistic parents, Marianne trained at the Lette-Verein, a famed school for women that had run photography courses since 1890. After completing an apprenticeship at Berlin's Handwerkskammer (Chamber of Crafts), Marianne left Germany for the bright lights of Paris. Armed with an introduction from a family friend, she approached Man Ray in the hope of studying under him. The photographer told his would-be apprentice that she could use his studio as she pleased – but that she should discover her own path without him.

As rejections went, this one proved to be the making of Marianne. Instead of training as someone else's pupil, she embarked on an exploration of her new city and honed her photographic eye. This was the age of Brassaï and the great heyday of Parisian street photography, and Marianne was just as in love with the city as the Hungarian–French pioneer of photography. But she wasn't attracted by its grand boulevards or affluent clientele. "What interested me was reality, more precisely, the unimportant reality, the reality most people overlooked,"[16] she explained. The street performer in the park; the homeless vagrant by the Seine – Marianne captured everyday life at the

margins of society with consummate sensitivity and empathy.

Back in Berlin, Marianne worked for two years as a photojournalist for Ullstein, a German publishing house. But she lacked "the swift eye for a sensation and the audacity required of a photo-reporter"[17] and swiftly quit to work as a freelance photographer. She was already taking her best photos on the side anyway. Her portraits of her female friends must rank among the most sensual and stylish evidence of a radical new attitude and lifestyle taking hold in Germany. For the New Woman, all norms of gender and sexual identity were to be playfully tossed out the window. Marianne – who married the art dealer Walter Feilchenfeldt in 1936 – once explained, "We were all very similarly dressed, masculine, with short hair, got up 'in the lesbian' [*auf lesbisch*] so to speak, but in no way really so!"[18]

Marianne never explicitly identified as bisexual or queer, but she made a muse out of Swiss photojournalist and gay writer Annemarie Schwarzenbach, and travelled through the Pyrenees with her. In Marianne's deeply intimate images, Annemarie cuts a strikingly androgynous and charismatic figure. "She had the same effect on me as she had on everybody: this strange mixture of man and woman," Marianne once explained. "She corresponded to my image of the Angel Gabriel in paradise."[19]

But the libertine days of the Weimar Republic soon came to an end with the rise of National Socialism. In the 1930s, Marianne returned home from overseas assignments to find that she was *persona non grata* in Nazi Germany. As a Jew, she was barred from publishing her work in German magazines and papers; she had to resort to publishing under pseudonyms. As the political climate became increasingly dangerous, she and Walter decided to leave Berlin in 1936 and head for the relative safety of Amsterdam, where they married.

By 1937, Marianne had given up her photography to join Walter as an art dealer and raise their children. In any case, she had grown increasingly weary of her chosen medium. "Had I continued to work in that field," she later explained, "I would have turned to film. I was finished with photography."[20] In 1939, they travelled to Switzerland and were forced to remain there due to the outbreak of war in Europe. Marianne lived in Zurich for the rest of her life.

"Neither technical perfection nor striking subject matter are decisive [in a good image]," she once said. "What matters is the power of the image, the expression – the secret of the moment captured."[21] Though she took an estimated one hundred thousand images over the course of her brief but significant career, most of her work has been lost, and only a few hundred negatives and prints remain. We may never see all the moments of fleeting beauty that Marianne Breslauer captured.

ALICE GUY-BLACHÉ

lthough she used her lens for moving pictures rather than photography, Alice Guy-Blanché warrants a special mention for blazing a trail through what remains one of the most male-dominated industries on the planet, over a century ago. She became the world's first female filmmaker and studio head, making over a thousand films and receiving critical acclaim for establishing the concept of narrative film.

The year was 1895. The woman who was to become Alice Guy-Blaché (1873–1968) had been born in France, of Chilean parents, and she was working for the studio pioneer Léon Gaumont, who had just acquired the 60mm motion picture camera from its inventor, Georges Demenÿ. When Alice attended a screening held by the Lumière brothers, she was captivated by the possibilities of the brand-new medium – and, in her words, "I thought I could do better."[22]

When she nervously asked Gaumont if she could use his camera, he regarded her request as "a young girl's thing"[23] and Alice secretly rolled her eyes, noting in her memoirs, "My youth, my lack of experience, my sex all conspired against me."[24] Nevertheless, she was able to lay her hands on his newly christened Bioscope and set about writing, producing and directing a one-minute silent film entitled *La Fée aux Choux* (French for "The Cabbage Fairy"), based on a French fairy tale. At a time when people were still figuring out exactly what the medium should be for – the Lumière brothers, for instance, were filming people leaving their factory at the end of a day – Alice's debut was pure cinematic magic. "My first film," she said, "thus saw the light."[25]

Just two years after joining Gaumont's studio, she became head of production. When she married a fellow Gaumont employee, Herbert Blaché, the couple

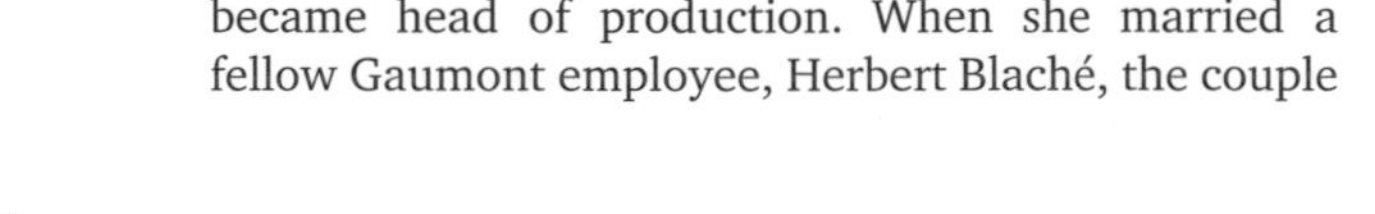

moved to America and in 1910 founded Solax Studios in New York. Over the course of her career, Alice directed everything from detective stories and romantic comedies to westerns, action films and dramas, and she passed milestone after milestone with consummate ease.

Her longest film, *La Vie du Christ* (English title: *The Birth, the Death and the Life of Christ*), from 1906, clocked in at a then-epic 34 minutes and featured a cast of hundreds and multiple elaborate sets. Her 1912 film *A Fool and His Money* was the first with an all-black cast. She experimented with innovations and special effects like double exposures and synchronized sound. And she championed women in film, writing scripts that called for strong female leads, and, in the case of the 1912 sci-fi movie *In the Year 2000*, even imagining a world ruled entirely by women. She recognized the prejudice against women in a 1914 article for *Moving Picture World*, and argued, "[there] is nothing connected with the staging of a motion picture that a woman cannot do as easily as a man, and there is no reason why she cannot completely master every technicality of the art."[26]

But Solax suffered a decline in fortunes once the centre of film production left the East Coast for the sunnier climes of Hollywood. Alice was forced to sell the business, and when her husband founded his own studio in 1914, her career was slowly subsumed by his. Herbert demoted her to assistant-directing duties on his own films – and cheated on her with an actress in her twenties.

Alice divorced Herbert in 1922, but struggled to find her feet in the fast-changing industry. She returned to France and worked as a film lecturer and writer yet never made another movie. In 1927, she visited the Library of Congress to look up her old films; they had none.

Though Alice died believing that decades of work had disappeared into the ether, film archivists and historians have since rescued and preserved over a hundred of her films. In 2010, the Whitney Museum in New York broadcast all of them in tribute to the "key but unsung figure of the early years of cinema".[27] A year later, she was posthumously inducted into the Directors Guild of America as a member. In a speech, Martin Scorsese hailed her achievements, mourned the loss of her full oeuvre and quoted Alice in her own words from almost a hundred years prior: "I have a right to be who I am."[28]

Design

LADY ELIZABETH WILBRAHAM

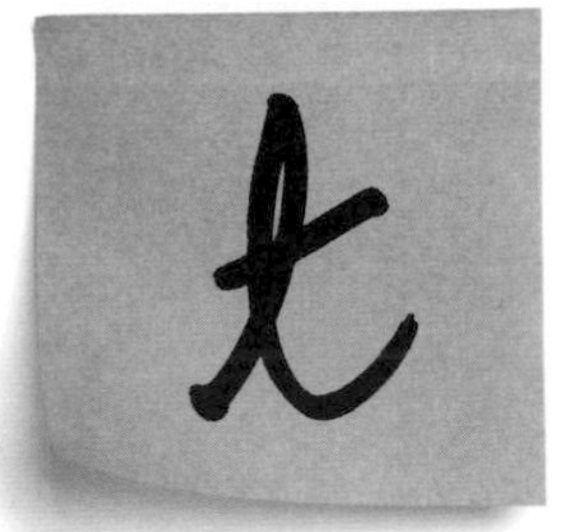

he stately home of Wotton House in Buckinghamshire, UK, is a stunning example of early 18th-century English Baroque architecture. With its elegant sash windows and expansive pleasure gardens, it bears a striking resemblance to Buckingham House – the building that was to form the basis for Buckingham Palace itself. But while the provenance of the latter is well established, the original architect of Wotton House remains unknown.

In 2007, the current owner of the estate organized a conference in its grounds and challenged scholars to uncover the real creator of Wotton House. The historian John Millar suggested that the mystery figure was no gentleman architect like Buckingham House designer William Winde – it was Lady Elizabeth Wilbraham (1632–1705), a little-known aristocrat who is hailed by some as Britain's first female architect.

Millar went one step farther, proposing that she actually taught the great Christopher Wren himself, and was the real architect behind 18 of the 52 churches he built after the Great Fire of London. "There is no smoking gun," Millar cautioned, but added: "Wren had no time to learn architecture until he was 33. Of all the people who could have taught him – and there were very few architects in the UK in the early 1660s – Wilbraham's style is by far the closest to his, based on her documented buildings."[1]

At the age of 19, Elizabeth Mytton married Thomas Wilbraham, the impossibly rich heir to the baronetcy of Wilbraham. Even at a young age, Elizabeth demonstrated a clear passion for architecture. She is thought to have spent

her honeymoon studying the great buildings of Italy and the Netherlands, and arranged a meeting with Pieter Post, the pioneer of Dutch Baroque architecture.

The Wilbrahams marked 1671 with the completion of the grand Weston Park mansion in Shropshire, England. Though Elizabeth did not leave behind many records, there is some evidence to suggest that she was the designer behind the couple's new residence, including her well-worn copy of Andrea Palladio's *The First Book of Architecture*, complete with annotations about raw material costs. She also designed and built a chapel at her husband's family estate in Woodhey, Cheshire.

It would have been considered extremely unseemly in the 17th century for women to practise architecture. That meant that Elizabeth would have had to operate with a degree of subterfuge, employing men to supervise the construction of her designs and never taking the credit she fully deserved. She was better known as an architectural patron, rather than as an architect in her own right. Even when her contributions were well documented, people were reluctant to give Elizabeth her rightful credit – and this continued well into the 20th century.

In Nikolaus Pevsner's 1974 book series *The Buildings of England*, the scholar offhandedly mentions that Elizabeth was "credited with the design"[2] of Weston Park, and describes one of her other buildings as "an enterprise of Lady Wilbraham".[3] As the architectural historian Cynthia Hammond points out: "No other work of architecture has these awkward designations. In the vast majority of cases in Pevsner's encyclopedic survey of English architecture, a building is 'by' the architect, with no other qualifications."[4]

Millar, on the other hand, believes that Elizabeth could have designed up to eight projects a year, including private homes and churches, and he traces her influence in up to 350 buildings. Unfortunately, with only 28 architectural drawings and 5 models surviving, we may never know the true extent of Elizabeth's architectural practice.

In 2008, historians unearthed a cache of Elizabeth's letters that discussed potential suitors for her children, offering a brief insight into the mind of a remarkable woman. As a spokesperson for the Weston Park Foundation put it: "We don't know a great deal about Lady Elizabeth so this sheds a lot of light on her approach to the marriages of her children. The letters explain the importance of a suitable match within the aristocracy of the day. She was certainly a very strong lady and knew what she wanted and how to get it."[5]

LINA BO BARDI

nce described as “the most underrated architect of the 20th century”,[6] Lina Bo Bardi (1914–1992) built fewer than 20 of her architectural designs and spent over a decade out of work – but it didn’t stop the Brazilian designer from leaving an immense stamp on her beloved country.

Born Achillina Bo in Rome, Italy, Lina added many strings to her bow over the years: she was a designer of furniture and also of stage sets, a magazine editor and a scholar, on top of being an architect. She was just 28 when she founded her own architectural practice – only to watch it get bombed to pieces during World War II. In 1946, she married fellow journalist and art dealer Pietro Maria Bardi, and moved with him to São Paulo when he was offered a job there.

“I wasn’t born here,” Lina once said of her adopted homeland. “I chose to live in this place. That’s why Brazil is my country twice over.”[7] She fell deeply in love with its people and culture, and became a naturalized citizen in 1951. Lina marked the occasion with her first solo project: the couple’s new home on the outskirts of São Paulo. Casa de Vidro (“Glass House”), with its tranquil glass-fronted Modernist exterior, still stands on its distinctive stilts, surrounded by tropical greenery and vegetation.

In 1945, before Lina had moved to Brazil, *Domus* magazine had commissioned her to document the sites of World War II bombings in Italy. Her socialist politics were forged in the wake of the destruction she witnessed. She extended that to her architectural practice, taking on few private clients and choosing to develop her career in the service of the Brazilian people. “I work for public power,” Lina explained. “I have designed only two or three houses for friends, for people very close to me. If someone with money were to ask me to design a house for him or her I would refuse.”[8]

Wheras most mid-century Brazilian architects looked toward Europe, Lina continually emphasized the importance of Brazilian culture and geography in her work. While living in

Bahia, in northern Brazil, she was commissioned to design a museum in an abandoned sugar plantation. She spoke of her desire to build a place that was the opposite of "a place in ruins, where antique curios are stacked up and where dust prevails like in the catacombs".[9]

The year 1964 proved disastrous. The military coup in Brazil installed a dictatorship that shut down her museum and forced the rising architect into the wilderness. Rather than flee the country as other artists and intellectuals were doing, Lina chose to stay in Brazil, and her career suffered as a result. Architectural commissions dried up, and she busied herself with other artistic projects, including designing stage sets for experimental plays.

Happily, the 1980s brought better fortune. As the dictatorship loosened its grip on power, she received a commission for what was to be one of her greatest and most beloved projects: the SESC Pompéia (Pompéia Factory Leisure Centre), a multistorey community space carved out of an abandoned oil drum factory. For someone who once described architecture as "an adventure in which people are called to intimately participate as actors",[10] there could be no better project.

The hulking remains of the factory had already been commandeered by locals for purposes that included everything from barbecues and amateur dramatics to dance clubs and soccer matches. Lina, whose work thrived at the intersection of human interaction and public space, quickly saw what needed to be done: "What we want is precisely to maintain and amplify what we've found here, nothing more."[11]

Instead of demolishing the factory, Lina listened carefully to those already using the space for community purposes and then she incorporated their ideas into the final design, with a swimming pool, a sunbathing deck, a theatre, soccer fields and a freshwater stream that was replenished by the São Paulo rains. The SESC Pompéia is now a treasured landmark of the city, hosting innumerable shows, exhibitions and festivals.

As with all of Lina's public buildings, it is intimately linked to its social purpose, its environment and all those who pass through it – a vision of architecture at its most democratic and accessible. "When we design, even as a student, it is important that a building serves a purpose and that it has the connotation of use," Lina once declared. "It is necessary that the work does not fall from the sky over its inhabitants, but rather expresses a need."[12]

GUNNBORGA THE GOOD

hen you imagine the Vikings, you probably think of feared warriors and illiterate savages who wouldn't think twice about robbing, looting and killing anybody who got in their way. But a visit to the Swedish municipality of Nordanstig, in Hälsingland, might be enough to change your mind.

Better known for its elaborately painted farmhouses and soaring pine forests, the region is also home to something far smaller yet no less historic. The Hälsingland Rune Inscription 21 is a clunkily named but impressive rough-hewn boulder, about 2m (6ft 6in) in height, carved with runic inscriptions. The carved runes are by Gunnborga the Good (*fl. c.* 11th century), the only known female Viking runemaster in history.

The Old Norse word for rune can mean anything from "secret knowledge" to "sign used in magic". Nobody knows exactly how or where the runic script came from, but rune stones were erected across Scandinavia, with the vast majority of them located in Sweden, like Gunnborga's. In ancient Norse mythology, runes were a hard-won gift from the god Odin to his people. The epic poem *Hávamál* describes how the god sacrificed himself to learn the secret script:

I know that I hung on a windswept tree for nine whole days, wounded by a spear and given to Odin, myself given to myself, on the tree of which no one knows from which roots it grows. I was given neither bread nor drink from a horn, I peered down; I took up runes, shouting I took them, I fell down afterwards.[13]

Runes may conjure up the idea of magic and sorcery, but scholars today dispute the supernatural qualities that have commonly been ascribed to the script. Though some grave-bound rune stones warn of curses and supernatural threats, many were simply erected to commemorate fallen kinsmen, to hail the living or to lay claim to one's inheritance. In the Viking Age version of someone bragging about themselves on social media, they were also commissioned by others to celebrate their achievements – one rune stone in Denmark was commissioned by a man who built a nearby bridge and wanted people to know it was by him.

Gunnborga is among the hundred or so identified runemasters from Sweden. Along with their unidentified contemporaries, they carved and hoisted aloft no less than 1,700 rune stones. As the only female runemaster in the region, Gunnborga would have occupied a unique position in her society. Viking Age women – though able to enjoy relative freedoms, like the power to divorce and the ability to own and inherit property – have not commonly been recorded in history with a chisel and hammer in hand, and while the runic script was widely used and understood, making a rune stone would have required artistry and specialist knowledge of stonemasonry.

In Viking myth, however, women were sometimes associated with intimate knowledge of runes – so much so that it is a fearsome Valkyrie in the Old Norse poetic text *Sigrdrífumál* who instructs the legendary warrior Sigurd in how to carve runes for battle:

Victory-runes you shall carve
if you want to have victory,
and carve them on your sword-hilt;
some on the blade-ridges,
some on the straps,
and name Tyr twice.[14]

For now, we know little of Gunnborga or the circumstances that led to her becoming her land's only female runemaster – but suffice to say, she would have been in good company with the Valkyries.

DAHL COLLINGS

nybody who has ever visited a shopping centre in the week before Christmas knows that department stores are usually where hope goes to die. But for multidisciplinary artist and graphic designer Dahl Collings (1909–1987), one emporium in central London gifted her with her biggest break – and the most formative learning opportunities of her career.

Simpson's of Piccadilly is now home to a bookshop, but in 1936 it encompassed the most modern 1,000 square metres (11,000 square feet) of shop floor in the UK, complete with its own computerized check-out system and golf range. For Dahl, an Australian émigré who had decamped to London just one year earlier with her husband, Geoffrey Collings, the store was where she learned to be an artist – thanks in no small part to László Moholy-Nagy. A former professor at Germany's influential Bauhaus art school, he had fled the Nazis and wound up in charge of visual merchandising at Simpson's instead.

Born Dulcie Wilmott in Adelaide, Dahl had trained at various art schools and won a scholarship from the Society of Artists. At 18, she landed a job as an illustrator at a big Australian department store and freelanced for other shops and publications. For *The Home,* a forward-thinking Australian magazine inspired by lifestyle publications like *Vogue*, Dahl created hand-coloured covers made of collage figures from cut-out fabric, string, feathers and raffia. But it was only after her move to London in search of glamorous new opportunities that she began to truly develop her style and her artistic philosophy.

At Simpson's, Dahl was encouraged to consider every step of the design process and to treat it as part of a bigger whole. "We're not just going to have the tablecloths yellow and order yellow tablecloths," László would instruct. "We're going to think about it."[15]

"Moholy wouldn't tell me what to do, I had to tell him what could be done," Dahl recalled. "And so I began experimenting. With

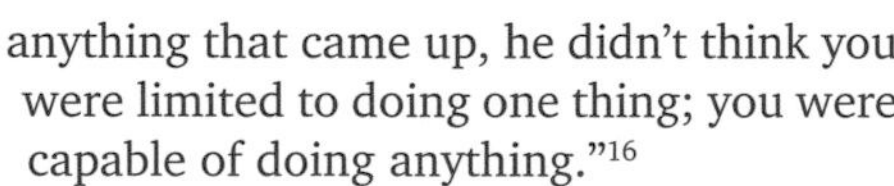

anything that came up, he didn't think you were limited to doing one thing; you were capable of doing anything."[16]

Inspired to experiment, Dahl channelled striking colour and Bauhaus design principles into the shop's restaurant menus, window displays, silverware, furnishings and in-store graphics. Her approach was direct but never unsophisticated – in fact, it was why she was hired by Simpson's in the first place. "[László] saw that I had used watercolour, fabrics, and other materials in a way he hadn't seen before,"[17] Dahl explained.

Her husband Geoffrey, who had given her the affectionate nickname Dahl, was also an artist. They worked together collaboratively as a pair for most of their lives, producing everything from advertisements for cruises to exhibitions of contemporary Australian art and design. The artist and graphic designer E McKnight Kauffer, best known for his posters of the London Underground, wrote of their show *Three Australians:* "We must get rid of the idea from our minds that Australia only stands for Sheep Farming, the Life of the Open Air, and Sports – especially cricket. Slowly and surely there are influences at work introducing other aspects of what might be called intellectual life."[18]

Dahl embarked on contributing to her country's "intellectual life" when she and Geoffrey returned to Sydney in 1939. Buoyed by their experiences in London, they sought to introduce modern design to the Australian art scene. They helped to design the Australian Pavilion at the 1939 New York World's Fair, they made a film in Tahiti and they co-founded Sydney's Design Centre, an industrial and commercial design studio. In 1953, they even set up their own film studio – Collings Productions. Produced and directed by Dahl, *The Dreaming*, a film about Aboriginal art, went on to receive an award at the Venice Biennale Festival of Art Films.

As she progressed as an artist, Dahl never forgot what she had learned at Simpson's. The free-spiritedness and sense of boundless possibility she developed there never left her art or her life, and it led her to experiment widely and promiscuously. Later on, she designed costumes and sets for Australian period dramas, produced illustrations for *Harper's Bazaar* magazine and the cosmetics company Elizabeth Arden, created fabrics as well as posters for ocean liners and painted the mural of a local kindergarten.

"They have made illustrations, posters and folders, designed window displays and made photographs without number for concerns whose name is legion," said Design Centre co-founder Richard Haughton James of Dahl and her husband. "As plain producers of 'useful art', these people are the designers of our world."[19]

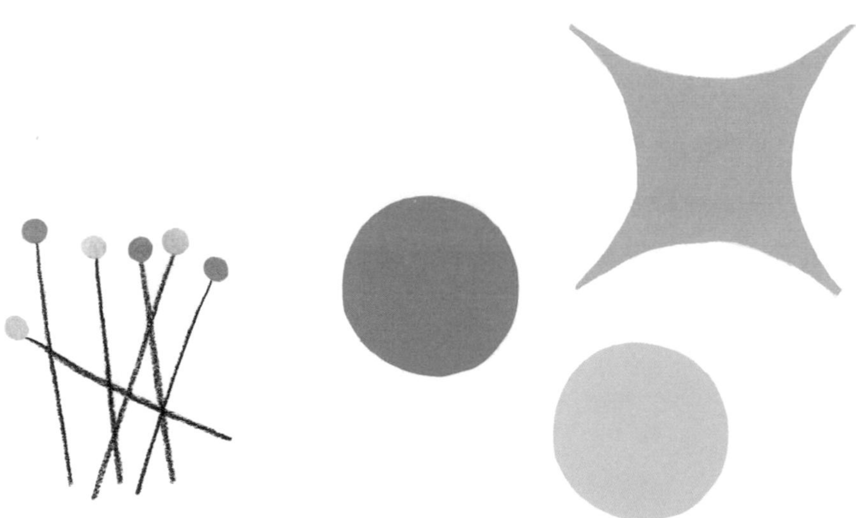

ALERO OLYMPIO

lero Olympio (1959–2005) built her career on bricks – laterite bricks, to be precise. The visionary Ghanaian architect's distinctive bricks were made by hand and compressed manually with a powerful hydraulic press, their distinctive red colour the result of its natural iron-oxide properties. Laterite is everywhere in the West African country, where it is primarily used to make roads. But Alero saw its potential for something more: the building blocks for a radical school of architectural design, no less.

"I wanted to be able to do experiments and try things that people hadn't done before in Ghana," she explained, "and I think I wanted to devise a form of construction that would be labor-intensive and that would develop handcrafting skills and produce a real contemporary African style of architecture."[20]

Alero was born in Ghana's capital Accra in 1959, two years after Ghana became the first sub-Saharan African colony to gain its independence. Her family was a deeply political one; her grandfather, Sylvanus Olympio, led neighbouring Togo to independence in 1960 and served as its first president, while her mother, Cecile McHardy, left Jamaica to live and work in Ghana, wooed by Kwame Nkrumah's call to build the first truly pan-African nation.

Alero inherited from her family an intense patriotic feeling for Ghana – a sense of pride and loyalty that also extended farther afield to encompass the continent of Africa itself. Even when she travelled to Scotland to attend school and study architecture at the University of Dundee, she never forgot her homeland. In fact, it was stints of practising architecture in Scotland and France that made her decide she had to come home, as she explained:

I think the West was actually responsible for making me look elsewhere, because I realized that in the Western world everything had already been done. And I realized that they had a whole history of developing their art and architecture that has resulted in quite a variety of really extraordinary technologies and forms and spaces and light, and I thought that it would be a great challenge to try and pursue that in Africa and try and also develop an architecture, and create a studio – a Bauhaus equivalent – where you explore developing a vernacular for Africa.[21]

Plus, Alero wanted to get her hands dirty. She was disappointed to find that architects in Europe were simply desk-bound planners whose finished sketches would be passed on to be built by someone else. That didn't satisfy Alero, who believed that construction and design were two sides of the same coin. "I liked the idea of building; I wanted to become a builder," she said. "And I couldn't do that here, easily. So I decided to go back to Ghana to do it."[22]

Back home, she was aghast to find that a rapidly developing Accra was slashing away at its natural greenery and becoming increasingly reliant on imported construction materials like concrete. The expanding middle classes were splashing out on sprawling houses with little to no regard for the natural environment or sustainability. "Certainly, you're paying for space," Alero explained. "You're not necessarily paying for good design. So, what I try to encourage is to be able to use the environment, to use the outside space, for instance, which is practically free."[23]

That didn't just mean using laterite bricks. It also meant channelling traditional African influences and materials into her ideas, sometimes even relying on local villagers to pitch into construction. Her adobe-style buildings incorporate courtyards that recall Ashanti village compounds; an Alero house near the ocean might use seashells sourced from the local beach.

"I tried to make sure that the material provides the beauty of the building," she said. "I try to make sure that I'm not using any European classical symbols… Ionic columns and Italian capitals and bases to the friezes and cornices and so on."[24]

One of her finest projects, the Kokrobitey Institute, was built by a beach according to the beautiful proportions of a traditional Ashanti courtyard. It still stands today, and its design centre has been renamed in Alero's honour. The institute's founder, Renée Neblett, said:

What impressed me with Alero after I started to deluge her with reports on all the advice I had received, was that she listened patiently, and then asked, 'But what do you want to have happen there?' She was the first person who made me realize, in the most fundamental way, that building the site was not just about the nuts and bolts – it was as spiritual as it was physical.[25]

CORITA KENT

he term "religious art" brings to mind illuminated manuscripts, gloomily painted medieval allegories and Baroque canvases of Christ being flayed on the cross. It doesn't usually suggest Pop Art. But the exuberant, bright canvases of Corita Kent (1918–1986), formerly known as Sister Mary Corita, show that faith can dwell in the most unlikely places.

Born Frances Elizabeth Kent in Fort Dodge, Iowa, USA, Corita grew up in a Catholic family and took her vows at the Order of the Immaculate Heart of Mary in Los Angeles after graduating from high school. As Sister Mary Corita (she dropped the Mary and was known to all as Corita), she ran the art department of Immaculate Heart College and nurtured it into an improbable centre for the LA art scene, with visits to the designer Ray Eames's studio and guests like the inventor Buckminster Fuller.

Corita ran her department by a set of ten self-imposed rules. "Nothing is a mistake," read one. "There's no win and no fail. There's only make."[26] Another instructed: "Be happy whenever you can manage it. Enjoy yourself. It's lighter than you think."[27] Corita, who managed to combine the seriousness of her faith with the joy of art, was a walking exemplar of all of her ten commandments.

Desiring to make her art accessible and affordable, Corita chose to specialize in the process of silkscreen printing, also known as serigraphy, in which stencils are used to transfer ink onto a print surface. In 1962, she came across a series of paintings of soup cans from a then obscure young artist named Andy Warhol at the nearby Ferus Gallery on La Cienega Boulevard. Shortly after, Sister Corita became a fully paid-up member of the Pop Art movement.

Where Andy Warhol sought to use screen printing to signal the commercialization and mass culture of the age, Corita saw the potential for divinity in the advertising jingles of Madison

Avenue. She plucked slogans from Wonder Bread and General Electric to use on her colourful prints, combining them with lines from Gertrude Stein, Martin Luther King, Jr and the Beatles. Corita sprinkled this with a dash of religiosity, with quotes from Psalms and other Bible verses, or mischievious statements like "Mary mother is the juiciest tomato of all".[28] (The fruity reference was courtesy of the Del Monte Foods slogan.)

The Catholic sister with an artistic habit soon became famous, with a *Newsweek* cover in 1967 titled "The Nun: Going Modern".[29] As the Vietnam War lurched on, her art became increasingly political. "Love is here to stay," implored *look*, a piece created in 1965, the year that America began bombing Vietnam with napalm. "And that's enough."[30]

As an artist, Corita had been encouraged by the decrees of the Second Vatican Council, which called for Catholicism to modernize itself for an increasingly irreligious world. "Art does not come from thinking," she once said, "but from responding."[31] The Los Angeles archdiocese, however, disagreed – and they had the Order of the Immaculate Heart of Mary in their sights. Its cardinal, James McIntyre, criticized the sisterhood for being too progressive and described Corita's art as "particularly troubling".[32] Feeling the pressures of her rising celebrity and the Church's wrath, Sister Corita hung up her veil and left the Order in 1968. "Cardinal McIntyre… thought they were going too far, too fast," said Doris Donnelly, another teacher at the Immaculate Heart College. "I was in my office and one of my colleagues came in and she sat down and she said, 'Corita's leaving.' It was a total surprise and it was a sad day."[33]

In *news of the week*, made a year after her departure from the Order, Corita quotes a Walt Whitman poem: "Agonies are one of my changes of garments."[34] She laid the text next to

magazine covers of bloodied and weary-looking soldiers from the US Army and the Viet Cong.

Despite the censure of her own archdiocese, Corita never lost her faith and remained close to her sisters. Many followed Corita out of religious life, and the Order split from the Church and reformed as a lay community two years after her departure.

Freed from religious life, Corita embarked on some of her biggest works yet, including a commission from the US Post Office that resulted in the "Love" stamp, which went on to sell over seven hundred million copies. In 1971, the Boston Gas

Company asked her to turn a hulking and unloved gas tank into what would later become the largest copyrighted artwork in the world: *Rainbow Swash*, which transformed the 43-m (140-ft) tall monument with playful swatches of colour.

Through it all, Corita never lost sight of her roots as a teacher. Even in the middle of a long battle with cancer, she was hard at work on a book entitled *Learning by Heart: Teachings to Free the Creative Spirit*. "We can all talk, we can all write, and if the blocks are removed, we can all draw and paint and make things,"[35] she wrote. The book was published posthumously in 1992.

Endnotes

INTRODUCTION

1 Quoted in Loreck, Janice. "Just name three female artists: !Women Art Revolution on screen", The Conversation, 20 Oct 2014. Accessed 7 May 2018 https://theconversation.com/just-name-three-female-artists-women-art-revolution-on-screen-32744
2 Accessed 7 May 2018. http://freelandsfoundation.co.uk/research/representation-of-female-artists-in-britain
3 Accessed 2 May 2018. https://nmwa.org/advocate/get-facts
4 Nochlin, Linda. "Why Have There Been No Great Women Artists?" *The Feminism and Visual Culture Reader* (1971), pp 229–33. Accessed 2 May 2018. https://deyoung.famsf.org/files/whynogreatwomenartists_4.pdf
5 Accessed 2 May 2018. http://www.tate.org.uk/art/artworks/guerrilla-girls-guerrilla-girls-pop-quiz-p78815
6 Halperin, Julia. "'It Is an Unusual and Radical Act': Why the Baltimore Museum Is Selling Blue-Chip Art to Buy Work by Underrepresented Artists", *Artnet News*, 30 Apr 2018. Accessed 2 May 2018. https://news.artnet.com/market/baltimore-museum-deaccession-1274996
7 Ibid.

ABSTRACT

1 Levin, Gail. "Janet Sobel: Primitivist, Surrealist, and Abstract Expressionist", *Woman's Art Journal*, vol. 26, no. 1 (2005), p.10. JSTOR, https://www.jstor.org/stable/3566528
2 "Palette Packin' Grandma to Open One-Man Show", *Brooklyn Eagle*, 24 Apr 1944. Quoted in Seaberg, Libby. *Will the Real Janet Sobel Please Stand Up?* Accessed 20 Jan 2018. http://www.janetsobel.com/SiteJuly24/1.html
3 McBride, Henry. "Janet Sobel", *New York Sun*, 1994. Cited in Levin, Gail. "Janet Sobel: Primitivist, Surrealist, and Abstract Expressionist", *Woman's Art Journal*, vol. 26, no. 1 (2005), p.11. JSTOR, https://www.jstor.org/stable/3566528.
4 Levin, Gail. "Janet Sobel: Primitivist, Surrealist, and Abstract Expressionist", *Woman's Art Journal*, vol. 26, no. 1 (2005), p.10. JSTOR, https://www.jstor.org/stable/3566528
5 Ibid., p.8.
6 "Services Held for Mrs. Sobel", *Courier News*, 12 Nov 1968.
7 Neale, Margo. "Emily Kame Kngwarreye: The Impossible Modernist", *Artlink*, vol. 37, no. 2 (June 2017), p.42.
8 Skelton, Russell. "Japan Takes Emily to Heart", *Sydney Morning Herald*, 31 May 2008. Accessed 13 Jan 2018. http://www.smh.com.au/news/arts/japan-takes-emily-to-heart/2008/05/30/1211654305476.html
9 Green, Jenny. "Holding the Country: Art from Utopia and the Sandover", Hetti Perkins (ed.), *One Sun One Moon: Aboriginal Art in Australia*. Art Gallery of New South Wales, 2007, p.205.
10 Kngwarreye, Emily, in interview with R Gooch at Soakage Bore, 1990, trans. Petyarr, K, quoted in Hodges, C, "Alhalkere" in Neale, M (ed.), *Emily Kame Kngwarreye, Alhalkere: Paintings from Utopia.* Queensland Art Gallery, Brisbane, 1998, p.33.
11 Schwartzkoff, Louise. "Stroke of Genius as Unseen Emilys Go on Display", *Sydney Morning Herald,* 20 Dec 2007. Accessed 14 Jan 2018. http://www.smh.com.au/news/arts/stroke-of-genius-as-unseen-emilys-go-on-display/2007/12/19/1197740378161.html
12 Myers, Fred R. *Painting Culture: The Making of an Aboriginal High Art*. Duke University Press Books, 2002, p.324.
13 Sylvester, Rachel. "Conmen Make a Killing on Aboriginal Art Market", *Sunday Telegraph*, 17 Sept 1995. Accessed 18 Feb 2018. https://www.rebeccahossack.com/usr/documents/press/download_url/539/the-sunday-telegraph-17-sept-1995-.pdf
14 Green, Jenny. "World of Dreamings: Traditional and Modern Art of Australia", National Gallery of Australia. Accessed 14 Jan 2018. https://nga.gov.au/Dreaming/Index.cfm?Refrnc=Ch6
15 Higgie, Jennifer. "Longing for Light: The Art of Hilma af Klint" in *Hilma af Klint: Painting the Unseen.* Serpentine Sackler Galleries, 2015, p.16.
16 Ibid., p.17.
17 Voss, Julia. "The First Abstract Artist? (And It's Not Kandinsky)", *Tate Etc.*, issue 27 (Spring 2013). Accessed 14 Jan 2018. http://www.tate.org.uk/context-comment/articles/first-abstract-artist-and-its-not-kandinsky
18 Quoted in Clayton, Eleanor. "Seeking 'A Blazing Reality': Nasreen Mohamedi's Photographs". Accessed 13 Jan 2018 http://www.tate.org.uk/whats-on/tate-liverpool/exhibition/nasreen-mohamedi/blazing-reality
19 Quoted in Pundir, Pallavi. "A life on the lines: Celebrating three decades of Nasreen Mohamedi's work", *Indian Express*, 22 Nov 2015. Accessed 13 Jan 2018 http://indianexpress.com/article/lifestyle/art-and-culture/a-life-on-the-lines-celebrating-three-decades-of-nasreen-mohamedis-work/
20 Quoted in Spence, Rachel. "Nasreen Mohamedi, Tate Liverpool, UK – review", *Financial Times*, 30 June 2014. Accessed 13 Jan 2018. https://www.ft.com/content/6715ad90-f2ea-11e3-a3f8-00144feabdc0
21 Pundir, Pallavi. "A life on the lines: Celebrating three decades of Nasreen Mohamedi's work", *Indian Express*, 22 Nov 2015. Accessed 13 Jan 2018 http://indianexpress.com/article/lifestyle/art-and-culture/a-life-on-the-lines-celebrating-three-decades-of-nasreen-mohamedis-work/
22 Ibid.
23 Singh, Kishore. "Celebrating minimalism with Nasreen Mohamedi", *Forbes India*, 5 July 2016. Accessed 13 Jan 2018. http://www.forbesindia.com/article/think/celebrating-minimalism-with-nasreen-mohamedi/43697/1
24 Kapur, Geeta. "Elegy for an Unclaimed Beloved: Nasreen Mohamedi 1937–1990". Accessed 13 Jan 2018 http://www.tate.org.uk/whats-on/tate-liverpool/exhibition/nasreen-mohamedi/elegy-for-unclaimed-beloved
25 Ibid.
26 Budick, Ariella. "Alma Thomas Defied Gravity and Reached for the Stars", *Financial Times*, 19 Aug 2016. Accessed 20 Jan 2018. https://www.ft.com/content/45ac0118-645d-11e6-8310-ecf0bddad227
27 Accessed 20 Jan 2018. https://nmwa.org/explore/artist-profiles/alma-woodsey-thomas
28 Johnson, Ken. "Alma Thomas, an Incandescent Pioneer", *New York Times*, 4 Aug 2016. Accessed 20 Jan 2018. https://www.nytimes.com/2016/08/05/arts/design/alma-thomas-an-incandescent-pioneer.html
29 Ibid.
30 Ibid.
31 Embuscado, Rain. "Celebrate Alma Thomas's 125th Birthday With Five Remarkable Facts", *Artnet*, 22 Sept 2016. Accessed 20 Jan 2018. https://news.artnet.com/exhibitions/alma-thomas-birthday-facts-660602
32 Budick, Ariella. "Alma Thomas Defied Gravity and Reached for the Stars", *Financial Times*, 19 Aug 2016. Accessed 20 Jan 2018. https://www.ft.com/content/45ac0118-645d-11e6-8310-ecf0bddad227
33 Kalina, Richard. "Through Color", *Art in America*, 20 July 2016. Accessed 20 Jan 2018. http://www.artinamericamagazine.com/news-features/magazines/through-color/
34 Schjeldahl, Peter. "Alma Thomas's Late Blooms". *New Yorker*, 25 July 2016. Accessed 20 Jan 2018. https://www.newyorker.com/magazine/2016/07/25/alma-thomas-and-sports-photography
35 Grandas, Teresa. "The Rest Can Go to Hell. Other Possible Tales of Carol Rama and Turin" in Anne Dressen, Teresa, and Beatriz Preciado (eds), *The Passio Grandasn according to Carol Rama*. Museu d'Art Contemporani de Barcelona (MACBA), 2015, p.54.
36 Ibid., p.49.
37 Ibid., p.50.
38 Lloyd, Ann Wilson. "ART/ARCHITECTURE: Brushwork with a Certain Fine Madness", *New York Times,* 1 Nov 1998. Accssed 14 Jan 2018. http://www.nytimes.com/1998/11/01/arts/art-artchitecture-brushwork-with-a-certain-fine-madness.html
39 Ibid.
40 Ibid.
41 Budick, Ariella. "Carol Rama – Her Dark Materials", *Financial Times*, 30 June 2017. Accessed 14 Jan 2018. https://www.ft.com/content/7abfe792-461c-11e7-8d27-59b4dd6296b8
42 Fossati, Filippo, and Levi, Corrado. "An Interview with Carol Rama",

Accessed 14 Jan 2018. https://zoltanjokay.de/zoltanblog/2013/09/carol-rama-half-3/

43 Charlotte Posenenske. "Statement", *Art International*, no. 5 (May 1968). Accessed 13 Jan 2018. http://artistsspace.org/exhibitions/charlotte-posenenske

44 Judah, Hettie. "Don't Look Now: The Artists Who Turn their Backs on the World", *Guardian*, 20 Apr 2017. Accessed 13 Jan 2018. https://www.theguardian.com/artanddesign/2017/apr/20/tell-them-i-said-no-artists-who-turn-backs-on-world-martin-herbert

45 Charlotte Posenenske. "Statement", *Art International*, no. 5 (May 1968). Accessed 13 Jan 2018. http://artistsspace.org/exhibitions/charlotte-posenenske

46 "Charlotte Posenenske an einen Bauunternehmer", *EgoIst*, vol. 1, no. 17 (1970). Quoted in Mehring, Christine. "Public Options", *Art Forum*, Sept 2010. Accessed 13 Jan 2018. https://www.artforum.com/inprint/issue=201007&id=26163

47 Gauntlett, Suzy. "The Painter Princess", *Tate Etc.*, 7 June 2017. Accessed 21 Jan 2018. http://www.tate.org.uk/art/artists/fahrelnissa-zeid-22764/tate-etc/fahrelnissa-zeid-the-painter-princess

48 "Fahrelnissa Zeid in Four Key Works". Accessed 21 Jan 2018. http://www.tate.org.uk/art/artists/fahrelnissa-zeid-22764/lists/four-key-works

49 Accessed 21 Jan 2018. http://www.tate.org.uk/art/artists/fahrelnissa-zeid-22764/room-guide

50 "Fahrelnissa Zeid in Four Key Works." Accessed 21 Jan 2018. http://www.tate.org.uk/art/artists/fahrelnissa-zeid-22764/lists/four-key-works

51 Ibid.

52 "Fahrelnissa Zeid: City by City." Accessed 21 Jan 2018. http://www.tate.org.uk/art/artists/fahrelnissa-zeid-22764/quick-read/city-by-city

53 Ellis-Petersen, Hannah. "Fahrelnissa Zeid: Tate Modern Resurrects Artist Forgotten by History", *Guardian*, 12 June 2017. Accessed 21 Jan 2018. https://www.theguardian.com/artanddesign/2017/jun/12/fahrelnissa-zeid-tate-modern-resurrects-artist-forgotten-by-history

54 Moss, M, trans. from Dutch, quoted from memory by Nijhoff, A H, in exhibition catalogue *Marlow Moss*, Amsterdam, Stedelijk Museum, 1962. Cited in Howarth, Lucy. "Marlow Moss: Dress Address Name" in Kane, Nina, and Woods, Jude (eds). *Reflections on Female and Trans* Masculinities and Other Queer Crossings*, p.12.

55 Howarth, Lucy. "Marlow Moss (1889–1958)". Diss., University of Plymouth, 2008, p.70.

56 Accessed 19 Jan 2018. http://www.tate.org.uk/art/art-terms/n/neo-plasticism

57 Cited in Howarth, Lucy. "Marlow Moss: Space, Movement, Light". Accessed 19 Jan 2018. http://www.tate.org.uk/whats-on/tate-britain/display/bp-spotlight-marlow-moss/essay

58 de Sabloniere, Margit. "Bij Het Heengaan Van Martow Moss", *Museumjournaal Series 4*, nos 5–6 (1958). Cited in Howarth, Lucy. "Marlow Moss (1889–1958)". Diss., University of Plymouth, 2008, p.101.

59 Howarth, Lucy. "Marlow Moss (1889–1958)". Diss., University of Plymouth, 2008, p.89.

60 "Exhibition Review for Marlow Moss at the Hanover Gallery", *New Statesman*, 5 Apr 1958. Quoted in Howarth, Lucy. "Marlow Moss (1889–1958)". Diss., University of Plymouth, 2008, p.41.

61 Bibeb. "A H Nijhoff: Ik Voel Er Absoluut Niet Voor Alle Woelingen in Mijzelf Op Tafel Te Gooien", 1967. Cited in Howarth, Lucy. "Marlow Moss (1889–1958)". Diss., University of Plymouth, 2008, p.98.

FIGURATIVE

1 Corbett, Rachel. "A Journey Deep Inside Spain's Temple of Cave Art", BBC, 19 Nov 2014. Accessed 21 Jan 2018. http://www.bbc.com/travel/story/20141027-a-journey-deep-inside-spains-temple-of-cave-art

2 Hughes, Virginia. "Were the First Artists Mostly Women?", *National Geographic*, 9 Oct 2013. Accessed 21 Jan 2018. https://news.nationalgeographic.com/news/2013/10/131008-women-handprints-oldest-neolithic-cave-art/

3 Ibid.

4 Penn State, "Women Leave Their Handprints on the Cave Wall", *ScienceDaily*, 15 Oct 2013. Accessed 21 Jan 2018. https://www.sciencedaily.com/releases/2013/10/131015113909.htm

5 Snow, Dean R. "Sexual Dimorphism in European Upper Paleolithic Cave Art", *American Antiquity*, vol. 78, no. 4 (Oct 2013), p.758.

6 Ibid., p.760.

7 Ibid.

8 Weidner, Martha. *Views from Jade Terrace: Chinese Women Artists, 1300–1912*. Indianapolis Museum of Art, 1988, p.117.

9 Weidner, Martha. "The Conventional Success of Ch'en Shu", *Flowering in the Shadows: Women in the History of Chinese and Japanese Painting*. University of Hawaii Press, 1990, p.125.

10 Lee, Lily Xiao Hong Lee; Lau, Clara; and Stefanowsky, A D. *Biographical Dictionary of Chinese Women: V. 1: The Qing Period, 1644–1911* Routledge, 1998, p.19.

11 Johnson, Julie M. "Writing, Erasing, Silencing: Tina Blau and the (Woman) Artist's Biography", *Nineteenth Century Art Worldwide*, vol. 4, no. 3 (autumn 2005). Accessed 31 Jan 2018. http://www.19thc-artworldwide.org/index.php/autumn05/208-writing-erasing-silencing-tina-blau-and-the-woman-artists-biography

12 Ben-Eli, Birgit. "Tina Blau: 1845–1916", *Jewish Women's Archive*. Accessed 31 Jan 2018. https://jwa.org/encyclopedia/article/blau-tina

13 Harriman, Helga H. "Olga Wisinger-Florian and Tina Blau: Painters in 'Fin de Siècle' Vienna", *Woman's Art Journal*, vol. 10, no. 2 (1989), p.23. JSTOR, http://www.jstor.org/stable/1358208

14 Johnson, Julie M. "Writing, Erasing, Silencing: Tina Blau and the (Woman) Artist's Biography", *Nineteenth Century Art Worldwide*, vol. 4, no. 3 (Autumn 2005). Accessed 31 Jan 2018. http://www.19thc-artworldwide.org/index.php/autumn05/208-writing-erasing-silencing-tina-blau-and-the-woman-artists-biography

15 Ibid.

16 Ibid.

17 http://www.telegraph.co.uk/culture/art/10157460/Edward-Hoppers-art-through-his-wifes-eyes.html. Accessed 17 Aug 2017.

18 Levin, Gail. *Edward Hopper: An Intimate Biography*. University of California Press, 1998, p.167.

19 Ibid., p.340.

20 Ibid., p.343.

21 Ibid., p.409.

22 Ibid., p.351.

23 Ibid., p.563.

24 Modesti, Adelina. *Elisabetta Sirani "Virtuosa": Women's Cultural Production in Early Modern Bologna*. Brepolis, 2014, p.50.

25 Ibid., p.25.

26 Ibid., p.189.

27 Ibid., p.25.

28 Latimer, Quinn. "A Step Out of Time", *Frieze*, 7 Mar 2013. Accessed 23 Jan 2018. https://frieze.com/article/step-out-time

29 Artist statement at Elizabeth A Sackler Center for Feminist Art. https://www.brooklynmuseum.org/eascfa/feminist_art_base/sylvia-sleigh. Accessed 11 Apr 2018.

30 Accessed 23 Jan 2018. http://www.tate.org.uk/whats-on/tate-liverpool/exhibition/sylvia-sleigh

31 Grimes, William. "Sylvia Sleigh, Provocative Portraitist and Feminist Artist, Dies at 94", *New York Times*, 25 Oct 2010. Accessed 23 Jan 2018. http://www.nytimes.com/2010/10/26/arts/design/26sleigh.html

32 Hughes, Maggie. "Sylvia Sleigh and Lawrence Alloway, Mutual Muses", *The Iris*, 21 June 2012. Accessed 23 Jan 2018. http://blogs.getty.edu/iris/treasures-from-the-vault-sylvia-sleigh-and-lawrence-alloway-mutual-muses/

33 Accessed 24 Jan 2018. http://arts.brighton.ac.uk/alumni-arts/sylvia-sleigh

34 Latimer, Quinn. "A Step Out of Time", *Frieze*, 7 Mar 2013. Accessed 23 Jan 2018. https://frieze.com/article/step-out-time

35 Accessed 24 Jan 2018. http://arts.brighton.ac.uk/alumni-arts/sylvia-sleigh

36 Witherell, Louise R. "Camille Claudel Rediscovered", *Woman's Art Journal*, vol. 6, no. 1 (1985), p.6. JSTOR, https://www.jstor.org/stable/1358057

37 "The Triumph of Tragedy", *Economist*, 5 Jan 2006. Accessed 4 Feb 2018. http://www.economist.com/node/5354447

38 Witherell, Louise R. "Camille Claudel Rediscovered", *Woman's Art Journal*, vol. 6, no. 1 (1985), p.3. JSTOR, https://www.jstor.org/stable/1358057

39 Ibid., p.7.

40 Cooper, B. "Camille Claudel: Trajectory of a Psychosis", *Medical Humanities*, vol. 34, no. 1 (2008), p.26.

41 Ibid., p.27.

42 Witherell, Louise R. "Camille Claudel Rediscovered", *Woman's Art Journal*, vol. 6, no. 1 (1985), p.6. JSTOR, https://www.jstor.org/stable/1358057

43 Cooper, B. "Camille Claudel:

Trajectory of a Psychosis", *Medical Humanities*, vol. 34, no. 1 (2008), p.28.

44 Hessel, Katy. "These Women Artists Influenced the Renaissance and Baroque", *Artsy*, 20 Dec 2016. Accessed 10 Feb 2018. https://www.artsy.net/article/artsy-editorial-these-women-artists-influenced-the-renaissance-and-baroque

45 Gaze, Delia (ed.). *Dictionary of Women Artists: Artists, J–Z*. Taylor & Francis, 1997, p.68.

46 Boccaccio, Giovanni. *Delle donne illustri.* Trans. Betussi, Giuseppe. Venice, 1545. Trans. *De claris mulieribus* (*c*.1361). Trans. of Italian text by Julia Dabbs with assistance of Pieranna Garavaso. Quoted in Dabbs, Julia. *Life Stories of Women Artists, 1550–1800*. Ashgate Publishing, 2009, p.32.

47 Ibid.

48 Ibid., p.33.

49 de Pizan, Christine. *The Book of the City of Ladies*, trans. Earl Jeffrey Richards. Persea Books, 1998. Quoted in Dabbs, Julia. *Life Stories of Women Artists, 1550–1800*. Ashgate Publishing, 2009, p.39.

50 Ibid., p.40.

51 Ibid.

52 Laden, Tanja M. "Cameron's Connections to Scientology and Powerful Men Once Drew Headlines, But Now Her Art Is Getting Its Due", *LA Weekly*, 8 Oct 2014. Accessed 25 Jan 2018. http://www.laweekly.com/arts/camerons-connections-to-scientology-and-powerful-men-once-drew-headlines-but-now-her-art-is-getting-its-due-5130928

53 Ibid.

54 Laden, Tanja M. "The Trippy Art (and Trippier Life) of Occult Artist Marjorie Cameron", *Creators*, 20 Sept 2015. Accessed 25 Jan 2018. https://creators.vice.com/en_us/article/4xqqjn/the-trippy-art-and-trippier-life-of-occult-artist-marjorie-cameron

55 Laden, Tanja M. "Cameron's Connections to Scientology and Powerful Men Once Drew Headlines, But Now Her Art Is Getting Its Due", *LA Weekly,* 8 Oct 2014. Accessed 25 Jan 2018. http://www.laweekly.com/arts/camerons-connections-to-scientology-and-powerful-men-once-drew-headlines-but-now-her-art-is-getting-its-due-5130928

56 Lunenfeld, Peter. "Season of the Witch", *Artforum*, Jan 2015, p.92.

57 Hobbs, Scott. "Cinderella of the Wastelands", *Huffington Post*, 26 Feb 2013. Accessed 25 Jan 2018. https://www.huffingtonpost.com/scott-hobbs/cinderella-of-the-wastela_b_2730500.html

58 Keuls, Eva C. *Plato and Greek Painting*. Brill, 1978, p.144.

59 Accessed 21 Apr 2018. https://st-takla.org/books/en/ecf/002/0020369.html

60 Marinella, Lucrezia. *The Nobility and Excellence of Women, and the Defects and Vices of Men*, ed. and trans. Anne Dunhill. University of Chicago Press, 1999, p.47.

61 Ibid., p.37.

62 Kilroy-Ewbank, Lauren. "Sofonisba Anguissola", *Smarthistory*, 3 (May 2016). Accessed 24 Jan 2018. https://smarthistory.org/sofonisba-anguissola/

63 Jacobs, Frederika H. "Woman's Capacity to Create: The Unusual Case of Sofonisba Anguissola", *Renaissance Quarterly*, vol. 47, no. 1 (1994): p.77.

64 Kilroy-Ewbank, Lauren. "Sofonisba Anguissola", *Smarthistory*, 3 (May 2016). Accessed 24 Jan 2018. https://smarthistory.org/sofonisba-anguissola/

65 Belinfante, Judith C E. "What Is *Life? or Theatre?*?" in *Charlotte Salomon: Life? or Theatre? A Selection of 450 Gouaches.* Taschen, 2017, p.22.

66 Bentley, Toni. "The Obsessive Art and Great Confession of Charlotte Salomon", *New Yorker*, 15 July 2017. Accessed 23 Jan 2018. https://www.newyorker.com/culture/culture-desk/the-obsessive-art-and-great-confession-of-charlotte-salomon

67 Salomon, Charlotte. *Charlotte Salomon: Life? or Theatre? A Selection of 450 Gouaches,* Taschen, 2017, p.362.

68 Belinfante, Judith C E. "What Is *Life? or Theatre?*?" in *Charlotte Salomon: Life? or Theatre? A Selection of 450 Gouaches,* Taschen, 2017, p.16.

69 Salomon, Charlotte. *Charlotte Salomon: Life? or Theatre? A Selection of 450 Gouaches,* Taschen, 2017, p.554.

70 Belinfante, Judith C E. "What Is *Life? Or Theatre?*?" in *Charlotte Salomon: Life? or Theatre? A Selection of 450 Gouaches,* Taschen, 2017, p.20.

71 Gotthardt, Alexxa. "The Erotic Artist Who Became the Queen of Bohemian New York", *Artsy*, 15 Sept 2016. Accessed 1 Feb 2018. https://www.artsy.net/article/artsy-editorial-erotic-artist-queen-bohemian-new-york

72 Quoted in Keller, Marie T. "Clara Tice, Queen of Greenwich Village" in Sawelson-Gorse, Naomi (ed.). *Women in Dada: Essays on Sex, Gender, and Identity*. MIT Press, 1999, p.430.

73 Henri, Robert. *The Art Spirit*. J B Lippincott Company, 1923.

74 Quoted in Keller, Marie T. "Clara Tice, Queen of Greenwich Village" in Sawelson-Gorse, Naomi (ed.). *Women in Dada: Essays on Sex, Gender, and Identity*. MIT Press, 1999, p.417.

75 Gotthardt, Alexxa. "The Erotic Artist Who Became the Queen of Bohemian New York", *Artsy*, 15 Sept 2016. Accessed 1 Feb 2018. https://www.artsy.net/article/artsy-editorial-erotic-artist-queen-bohemian-new-york

76 Keller, Marie T. "Clara Tice, Queen of Greenwich Village" in Sawelson-Gorse, Naomi (ed.). *Women in Dada: Essays on Sex, Gender, and Identity.* MIT Press, 1999, p.436.

77 Dalmia, Yashodhara. *Amrita Sher-Gil: A Life*. Penguin UK, 2013, p.70.

78 Ibid., p.79.

79 Ibid., p.43.

80 Ibid.

81 Ibid., p.74.

82 Ibid.

83 Ibid., p.47.

84 Hughes, Kathryn. "The Indian Frida Kahlo", *Daily Telegraph*, 3 June 2013. Accessed 23 Jan 2018. http://www.telegraph.co.uk/culture/10087130/The-Indian-Frida-Kahlo.html

85 Pound, Cath. "The Great Women Artists That History Forgot", BBC, 19 Oct 2016. Accessed 31 Jan 2018. http://www.bbc.com/culture/story/20161019-the-great-women-artists-that-history-forgot

86 Frayer, Lauren. "In a First, Spain's Prado Museum Puts the Spotlight on a Female Artist", *NPR*, 30 Nov 2016. Accessed 31 Jan 2018. https://www.npr.org/sections/parallels/2016/11/30/503129505/in-a-first-spains-prado-museum-puts-the-spotlight-on-a-woman-artist

87 Farrington, Lisa E. *Creating Their Own Image: The History of African-American Women Artist*s. Oxford University Press USA, 2005, p.65.

88 Kerr, Judith N. *God-Given Work: The Life and Times of Sculptor Meta Vaux Warrick Fuller, 1877–1968*, University of Massachusetts Amherst. 1986, p.74.

89 Farrington, Lisa E. *Creating Their Own Image: The History of African-American Women Artists*. Oxford University Press USA, 2005, p.66.

90 Kerr, Judith N. *God-Given Work: The Life and Times of Sculptor Meta Vaux Warrick Fuller, 1877–1968*. University of Massachusetts Amherst, 1986, p.4.

91 Ibid., p.viii.

92 *An Independent Woman: The Life and Art of Meta Warrick Fuller (1877–1968)*. Danforth Museum of Art, 1984, p.4. Accessed 6 Feb 2018 http://www.danforthart.org/assets/forms/meta_fuller_catalog_1984-5.pdf

93 Accessed 6 Feb 2018. http://www.emancipationtrail.org/new-page-99/

PERFORMANCE & CONCEPTUAL

1 Quoted in Gammel, Irene. *Baroness Elsa: Gender, Dada, and Everyday Modernity – A Cultural Biography*. MIT Press, 2003, p.223.

2 Steinke, Rene. "My Heart Belongs to Dada", *New York Times*, 18 Aug 2002. Accessed 2 Feb 2018. http://www.nytimes.com/2002/08/18/magazine/my-heart-belongs-to-dada.html

3 Freytag-Loringhoven, Elsa von. *Autobiography*, unpublished. Accessed 2 Feb 2018. http://www.baronesselsa.org/items/show/4#

4 Ibid.

5 Steinke, Rene. "My Heart Belongs to Dada", *New York Times*, 18 Aug 2002. Accessed 2 Feb 2018. http://www.nytimes.com/2002/08/18/magazine/my-heart-belongs-to-dada

6 Quoted in Kuenzli, Rudolf E. "Baroness Elsa von Freytag-Loringhoven and New York Dada", in Sawelson-Gorse, Naomi (ed.).*Women in Dada: Essays on Sex, Gender, and Identity*. MIT Press, 1999, p.442.

7 Ibid., p.450.

8 Ibid., p.445.

9 Ibid., p.460.

10 Ibid.

11 Freytag-Loringhoven, Elsa von. "A Dozen Cocktails – Please". Quoted in Gammel, Irene. *Baroness Elsa: Gender, Dada, and Everyday Modernity – A Cultural Biography*. MIT Press, 2003, p.377.

12 Ibid., p.454.

13 Quoted in Kuenzli, Rudolf E. "Baroness Elsa von Freytag-Loringhoven and New York Dada", in Sawelson-Gorse, Naomi (ed.). *Women in Dada: Essays on Sex, Gender, and Identity*. MIT Press, 1999, p.460.

14 Bamguartner, Frédérique.

"Reviving the Collective Body: Gina Pane's Unanesthetized Escalation", *Oxford Art Journal*, vol. 34, no. 2 (2011), p.253.
15 Accessed 10 Feb 2018. http://www.newmedia-art.org/cgi-bin/show-art.asp?LG=GBR&ID=900000000067990&na=&pna=&DOC=bio
16 Quoted in O'Dell, Kathy. *Contract with the Skin: Masochism, Performance Art, and the 1970s*. University of Minnesota Press, 1998, p.61.
17 Ibid., p.60.
18 Pane, Gina. "Lettre à un(e) inconnu(e)". Quoted in Becker, Ilka and Grosenick, Uta. *Women Artists in the 20th and 21st Century*. Taschen, 2001, p.431.
19 Hemus, Ruth. *Dada's Women*. Yale University Press, 2009, p.17.
20 http://www.tate.org.uk/art/art-terms/d/dada
21 Quoted in Rugh, Thomas F. "Emmy Hennings and the Emergence of Zurich Dada", *Woman's Art Journal*, vol. 2, no. 1 (1981), p.1. JSTOR, https://www.jstor.org/stable/1357892
22 Hemus, Ruth. *Dada's Women*. Yale University Press, 2009, p.39.
23 Ibid., p.21.
24 Ibid., p.25.
25 Ibid., p.34.
26 Ibid., p.48.
27 Parente, Letícia. "Letícia Parente. Book: Arte Novos Meios", *Letícia Parente*, exh. cat. Oi Futuro, 2011, p.98.
28 Ibid., p.100.
29 Ibid., p.90.
30 Ibid.
31 Press release, "Letícia Parente: Eu armário de mim". Galeria Jaqueline Martins, 2017. Accessed 11 Feb 2018. https://www.artforum.com/uploads/guide.004/id05802/press_release.pdf

CRAFT

1 Kinoshita, Kyoko. "The Life and Art of Tokuyama Gyokuran". Fischer, Felice, and Kinoshita, Kyoko (eds). *Ike Taiga and Tokuyama Gyokuran. Japanese Masters of the Brush*. Philadelphia Museum of Art, 2007, p.37.
2 Ibid., p.37.
3 Addis, Stephen. "The Three Women of Gion". Weidner, Marsha Smith (ed.). *Flowering in the Shadows: Women in the History of Chinese and Japanese Painting*. University of Hawaii Press, 1990, p.254.
4 Kinoshita, Kyoko. "The Life and Art of Tokuyama Gyokuran". Fischer, Felice, and Kinoshita, Kyoko (eds), *Ike Taiga and Tokuyama Gyokuran: Japanese Masters of the Brush*. Philadelphia Museum of Art, 2007, p.39.
5 Hannah Ryggen Exhibition Notes, *Modern Art Oxford*, 2017, p.2.
6 Ibid., p.1.
7 Ibid.
8 Ibid.
9 Ibid.
10 Quoted in Christianson, Karen. "Renaissance Calligraphy Books", 15 Feb 2012, *The Newberry*. Accessed 17 Feb 2018. http://www.newberry.org/renaissance-calligraphy-books
11 Frye, Susan. "Materializing Authorship in Esther Inglis's Books", *Journal of Medieval and Early Modern Studies*, vol. 32, no. 3 (2002), p.470.
12 Accessed 17 Feb 2018. https://collation.folger.edu/2012/02/spotlight-on-a-calligrapher/
13 Quoted in Dabbs, Julia K. *Life Stories of Women Artists, 1550–1800*. Ashgate, 2009, p.293.
14 Frye, Susan. "Materializing Authorship in Esther Inglis's Books". *Journal of Medieval and Early Modern Studies,* vol. 32, no. 3 (2002), p.483.
15 Ibid., p.482.
16 Adams, Renee B; Kräussl, Roman; Navone, Marco A and Verwijmeren, Patrick. "Is Gender in the Eye of the Beholder? Identifying Cultural Attitudes with Art Auction Prices", 6 Dec 2017. Accessed 17 Feb 2018. http://dx.doi.org/10.2139/ssrn.3083500
17 Miller, M H. "Georg Baselitz Says 'Women Don't Paint Very Well'", *Observer*, 29 Jan 2013. Accessed 17 Feb 2018. http://observer.com/2013/01/georg-baselitz-says-women-dont-paint-very-well/
18 Jex-Blake, K (trans.). *The Elder Pliny's Chapters on the History of Art*. 1896. Rev. edn. Argonaut, Inc., 1968. Quoted in Dabbs, Julia. *Life Stories of Women Artists, 1550–1800*. Ashgate Publishing, 2009, p.27.
19 Ibid.
20 Boccaccio, Giovanni. *Delle donne illustri*. Trans. Betussi, Giuseppe. Venice, 1545. Trans. *De claris mulieribus* (c.1361). Trans. of the Italian text by Julia Dabbs with the assistance of Pieranna Garavaso, quoted in Dabbs, Julia. *Life Stories of Women Artists, 1550–1800*. Ashgate Publishing, 2009, p.33.
21 Ibid., p.34.
22 Ibid.
23 "The character(s) of Tung Yang-tzu". *Taiwan Today*, 1 Feb 1984. Accessed 5 Apr 2018. https://taiwantoday.tw/news. php?unit=20,29,35,45&0post=25453
24 Quoted in Zong-Qi, Cai. "Poundian and Chinese Aesthetics of Dynamic Force: A Re-Discovery of Fenollosa and Pound's Theory of the Chinese Written Character", *Comparative Literature Studies*, vol. 30, no. 2 (1993), p.178. JSTOR, https://www.jstor.org/stable/40246878
25 Quoted in Shi, X. "The Aesthetic Concept of Yi in Chinese Calligraphic Creation", *Philosophy East and West*, 11 Jan 2017, p.3. Accessed 5 Apr 2018. https://muse.jhu.edu/article/646204/pdf
26 Accessed 3 Mar 2018. http://americanhistory.si.edu/collections/search/object/nmah_556462
27 Hicks, Kyra E, and Gaskins, Bill. *This I Accomplish: Harriet Powers' Bible Quilt and Other Pieces*, Black Threads Press, 2009, p.27.
28 Ibid. p.28.
29 Fry, Gladys-Marie. "New Light on Harriet Powers". Frederickson, Kristen and Webb, Sarah E (eds). *Singular Women: Writing the Artist*. University of California Press, 2003, p.93.
30 Hicks, Kyra E, and Gaskins, Bill. *This I Accomplish: Harriet Powers' Bible Quilt and Other Pieces*. Black Threads Press, 2009, p.38.
31 Daniela, Marcy. "Meet Harriet Powers Who Told Stories With Her Spectacular Quilts", *Martha Stewart*, 22 Mar 2017. Accessed 3 Mar 2018. https://www.marthastewart.com/1513455/meet-harriet-powers-who-told-stories-her-spectacular-quilts
32 Halsted, Fée. *Ardmore: We Are Because of Others*. Fernwood Press, 2012, chap. 2, par. 22.
33 Accessed 30 Jan 2018. http://ardmoreceramics.co.za/about/our-origins/
34 NZD Calendar 1997, quoted in Buckenham, Karen E. "Women's Experience, Spirituality and Theology for Liberation and Life in Contemporary South Africa as Expressed Through Visual Arts with a Focus on the Lives and Work of Two Women Artists – Dina Cormick and Bonnie Ntshalintshali". Master's Diss., University of Natal, 2001, p.75.
35 Ibid.
36 Halsted, Fée. *Ardmore: We Are Because of Others*. Fernwood Press, 2012, chap. 3, par. 8.
37 Arnold, Marion. *Women and Art in South Africa*. David Philip Publishers, 1996, p.16.
38 Accessed 30 Jan 2018. http://ardmoreceramics.co.za/artist/bonnie-ntshalinthshali/#
39 *The Art of Medieval Spain, A.D. 500–1200*. Metropolitan Museum of Art, 1993, p.156.
40 Corgnati, Martina. "Ende, God's Picture-maker", *L'Osservatore Romano*, 2 May 2016. Accessed 27 Mar 2018. http://www.osservatoreromano.va/en/news/ende-gods-picture-maker
41 Ibid., p.157.
42 Carr, Annemarie Weyl. "Women Artists in the Middle Ages", *The Feminist Art Journal*, no. 5 (Spring 1976), p.6.

PHOTOGRAPHY

1 Licter-Marck, Rose. "Vivian Maier and the Problem of Difficult Women", *New Yorker*, 9 May 2014. Accessed 22 Apr 2018. https://www.newyorker.com/culture/culture-desk/vivian-maier-and-the-problem-of-difficult-women
2 Ibid.
3 O'Donnell, Nora. "The Life and Work of Street Photographer Vivian Maier", *Chicago* magazine, 14 Dec 2010. Accessed 22 Apr 2018. http://www.chicagomag.com/Chicago-Magazine/January-2011/Vivian-Maier-Street-Photographer/
4 Ibid.
5 Rustin, Susanna. "Our Nanny, the Photographer Vivian Maier", *Guardian*, 19 July 2014. Accessed 22 Apr 2018. https://www.theguardian.com/lifeandstyle/2014/jul/19/our-nanny-vivian-maier-photographer
6 O'Donnell, Nora. "The Life and Work of Street Photographer Vivian Maier", *Chicago* magazine, 14 Dec 2010. Accessed 22 Apr 2018. http://www.chicagomag.com/Chicago-Magazine/January-2011/Vivian-Maier-Street-Photographer/
7 Rustin, Susanna. "Our Nanny, the

Photographer Vivian Maier", *Guardian*, 19 July 2014. Accessed 22 Apr 2018. https://www.theguardian.com/lifeandstyle/2014/jul/19/our-nanny-vivian-maier-photographer
8 Ferrer, Elizabeth. *Lola Alvarez Bravo*. Aperture Foundation: Center for Creative Photography, 2006, p.44.
9 Ibid., p.46.
10 Ibid., p.10.
11 Ibid., p.46.
12 Ibid., p.19.
13 Ibid., p.51.
14 Ibid., p.55.
15 Serra, Pepe. "Marianne Breslauer's photographs from the trip through our country in 1933", Museu Nacional d'Art de Catalunya blog, 10 Nov 2016. Accessed 25 Apr 2018. http://blog.museunacional.cat/en/marianne-breslauers-photographs-from-the-trip-through-our-country-in-1933/
16 Gasser, Martin and Beer, Kathrin. "Marianne Breslauer, Photographs". Cumbers, Pauline (trans.). Fotostiftung Schweiz. Accessed 25 Apr 2018. https://www.fotostiftung.ch/en/exhibitions/past/marianne-breslauer/
17 Ibid.
18 Lybeck, Marti M. *Desiring Emancipation: New Women and Homosexuality in Germany, 1890–1933*. SUNY Press, 2014, p.7.
19 Fan, Pauline. "Photo Essay: The Ravaged Angel", *Esquire*, 19 May 2017. Accessed 25 Apr 2018. https://www.esquire.my/lifestyle/entertainment-books/the-ravaged-angel#1
20 Gasser, Martin and Beer, Kathrin. "Marianne Breslauer, Photographs". Cumbers, Pauline (trans.). Fotostiftung Schweiz. Accessed 25 Apr 2018. https://www.fotostiftung.ch/en/exhibitions/past/marianne-breslauer/
21 Accessed 25 Apr 2018. http://www.museunacional.cat/en/marianne-breslauer-photographs-1927-1938
22 Morrow, Justin. "Alice Guy-Blaché, the World's First Female Filmmaker, Wrote, Directed, and Produced Over 700 Films". No Film School, 9 Mar 2017. Accessed 21 Apr 2018.
23 Kilston, Lyra. "Alice Guy Blaché", *Art in America*, 26 Apr 2010. Accessed 21 Apr 2018. https://www.artinamericamagazine.com/reviews/alice-guy-blach/
24 Morrow, Justin. "Alice Guy-Blaché, the World's First Female Filmmaker, Wrote, Directed, and Produced Over 700 Films". No Film School, 9 Mar 2017. Accessed 21 Apr 2018. https://nofilmschoo.com/2017/03/alice-guy-blache-worlds-first-woman-filmmaker
25 Ibid.
26 Meier, Allison. "Alice Guy-Blaché, the First Woman Filmmaker", *Hyperallergic*, 1 June 2017. Accessed 23 Apr 2018. https://hyperallergic.com/381372/alice-guy-blache-first-woman-filmmaker/
27 Accessed 23 Apr 2018. https:whitney.org/Exhibitions/AliceGuyBlache
28 McMahan, Alison. "Alice Guy Blaché Inducted into the DGA". Aliceguyblache.com, 6 Oct 2011. Accessed 23 Apr 2018. http://www.aliceguyblache.com/news/alice-guy-blache-inducted-dga

DESIGN

1 Merrick, Jay. "Elizabeth Wilbraham, the first lady of architecture", *The Independent*, 16 Feb 2011. Accessed 7 Apr 2018. https://www.independent.co.uk/arts-entertainment/architecture/elizabeth-wilbraham-the-first-lady-of-architecture-2215936.html
2 Quoted in Hammond, Cynthia. Architects, *Angels, Activists and the City of Bath, 1765–1965: Engaging with Women's Spatial Interventions in Buildings and Landscape*. Routledge, 2017, p 57.
3 Ibid.
4 Ibid.
5 "Rare letters of Weston Park aristocrat donated to public records", The Free Library. 2008 Birmingham Post & Mail Ltd. Accessed 7 Apr 2018. https://www.thefreelibrary.com/Rare+letters+of+Weston+Park+aristocrat+donated+to+public+records.-a018973073
6 Rowan Moore, *Why We Build, Pan Macmillan*, 2012, p 18.
7 Domus, "Lina Bo Bardi: The Last Lesson", 8 Mar 2016. Accessed 8 Apr 2018. http://loves.domusweb.it/lina-bo-bardi-the-last-lesson/
8 Ibid.
9 Werbler, Annie. "Prolific Midcentury Brazilian Architect Lina Bo Bardi is Having a Moment", *Curbed*, 24 Mar 2015. Accessed 8 Apr 2018. https://www.curbed.com/2015/3/24/9977684/lina-bo-bardi
10 Farago, Jason. "Lina Bo Bardi: Brazil's Best-Kept Secret", BBC, 11 June 2014. Accessed 8 Apr 2018. http://www.bbc.com/culture/story/20140611-brazils-best-kept-secret
11 Ferraz, Marcelo. "The Making of SESC Pompéia." Accessed 8 Apr 2018. http://linabobarditogether.com/2012/08/03/the-making-of-sesc-pompeia-by-marcelo-ferraz/
12 Lima, Zeuler R M de A. "Lina Bo Bardi and the Architecture of Everyday Culture", *Places Journal*, Nov 2013. Accessed 8 Apr 2018. https://placesjournal.org/article/lina-bo-bardi-and-the-architecture-of-everyday-culture/
13 Bremmer, Rolf H, Jr. "Hermes-Mercury and Woden-Odin as Inventors of Alphabets: A Neglected Parallel", in Bammesberger, Alfred. *Old English Runes and Their Continental Background*. Carl Winter, 1991, p 409.
14 Spurkland, Terje. *Norwegian Runes and Runic Inscriptions*. Boydell Press, 2005, p 15.
15 Caban, Geoffrey. *A Fine Line*. Hale & Iremonger, 1983, p 72.
16 Ibid., p 72.
17 Ibid., p 71.
18 Ibid., p 73.
19 Bremer, Veronica. "Dahl Collings (1909–1988) and her Itinerary: Australia, England, and Back" in Groot, Marjan; Seražin, Helena; Franchini, Caterina; Garda, Emilia; and Di Battista, Alenka (eds). *MOMOWO: Women Designers, Craftswomen, Architects and Engineers between 1918 and 1945*, ZRC Publishing House, 2017, p 60.
20 Talmor, Ruti. "Introductory Essay." Accessed 6 Apr 2018. https://web.archive.org/web/20110723212742/http://www.haverford.edu:80/HHC/rtalmor/essay.html
21 Ibid.
22 Ibid.
23 Quist-Arcton, Ofeibea. "Ghana: Building from the Ground Up – With Local Earth", *AllAfrica*, 17 Sept 2002. Accessed 6 Apr 2018. http://allafrica.com/stories/200209170002.html
24 Ibid.
25 Talmor, Ruti. "Kokrobitey Institute." Accessed 6 Apr 2018. https://web.archive.org/web/20110723212757/http://www.haverford.edu:80/HHC/rtalmor/kokrobitey.html
26 Walker, Alissa. "Corita Kent: How a Screenprinting Nun Changed the Course of Modern Art", *Gizmodo*, 2 Oct 2013. Accessed 7 Apr 2018. https://gizmodo.com/how-a-screenprinting-nun-changed-the-course-of-modern-a-1412576274
27 Ibid.
28 Shaw, Jonathan. "Corita Shaw", *Harvard Magazine*, Sept–Oct 2015. Accessed 7 Apr 2018. https://harvardmagazine.com/2015/08/corita-kent-nun-with-a-pop-art-habit
29 "Biography." Corita Art Center. Accessed 7 Apr 2018. http://corita.org/about-corita
30 Barnett, David C. "A Nun Inspired By Warhol: The Forgotten Pop Art of Sister Corita Kent", *NPR*, 8 Jan 2015. Accessed 7 Apr 2018. https://www.npr.org/2015/01/08/375856633/a-nun-inspired-by-warhol-the-forgotten-pop-art-of-sister-corita-kent.
31 Gotthardt, Alexa. "How to Free Your Creative Spirit, According to Sister Corita Kent", *Artsy*, 7 July 2017. Accessed 7 Apr 2018. https://www.artsy.net/article/artsy-editorial-free-creative-spirit-1960s-radical-nun
32 Pacatte, Rose. "The Tumultuous Times of Corita Kent", *National Catholic Reporter*, 3 Aug 2016. Accessed 7 Apr 2018. https://www.ncronline.org/books/2017/08/tumultuous-times-corita-kent
33 Barnett, David C. "A Nun Inspired By Warhol: The Forgotten Pop Art of Sister Corita Kent", *NPR*, 8 Jan 2015. Accessed 7 Apr 2018. https://www.npr.org/2015/01/08/375856633/a-nun-inspired-by-warhol-the-forgotten-pop-art-of-sister-corita-kent
34 Ibid.
35 Quoted in Gotthardt, Alexa. "How to Free Your Creative Spirit, According to Sister Corita Kent", *Artsy*, 7 July 2017. Accessed 7 Apr 2018. https://www.artsy.net/article/artsy-editorial-free-creative-spirit-1960s-radical-nun

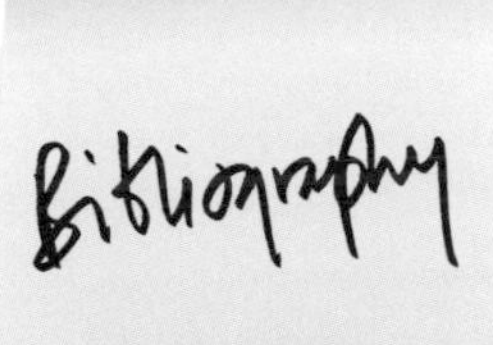

ABSTRACT

Janet Sobel

Hawlin, Thea. "Five Forgotten Female Artists of Abstract Expressionism", *Another*, 23 Sept 2016. Accessed 20 Jan 2018. http://www.anothermag.com/art-photography/9101/the-forgotten-female-artists-of-abstract-expressionism

Hutter, Hillary. "Which Artist Began Experimenting with Drip Painting First: Janet Sobel or Jackson Pollock?" Crystal Bridges Museum of American Art. Accessed 20 Jan 2018. https://crystalbridges.org/blog/significant-careers-determined-artists-janet-sobel/

Levin, Gail. "Janet Sobel: Primitivist, Surrealist, and Abstract Expressionist", *Woman's Art Journal*, vol. 26, no. 1 (2005). JSTOR, http://www.jstor.org/stable/3566528.

Seaberg, Libby. *Will the Real Janet Sobel Please Stand Up*? Accessed 20 Jan 2018. http://www.janetsobel.com/SiteJuly24/1.html

"Services Held for Mrs. Sobel", *Courier News*, 12 Nov 1968.

Smith, Roberta. "Janet Sobel", *New York Times*, 15 Feb 2002. Accessed 20 Jan 2018. http://www.nytimes.com/2002/02/15/arts/art-in-review janet-sobel.html

Sweeney, Kim. "The Forgotten Female Artist: Janet Sobel's Struggle within the Abstract Expressionist Movement", *The Artifice*, 13 Apr 2014. Accessed 20 Jan 2018. https://the-artifice.com/janet-sobel-abstract-expressionist-movement/

Emily Kame Kngwarreye

Batty, Philip. "Selling Emily: Confessions of a white advisor", *Artlink*, vol. 27, no. 2 (2007).

Benjamin, Roger. "Emily Kame Kngwarreye". Vizard Foundation Art Collection. Accessed 14 Jan 2018. http://www.vizardfoundationartcollection.com.au/the-nineties/explore/emily-kame-kngwarreye/

"Emily Kame Kngwarreye". DACOU Australia. Accessed 14 Jan 2018. http://dacou.com.au/aboriginal-artists/emily-kame-kngwarreye/cat_36359.html

Green, Jenny. "Holding the Country: Art from Utopia and the Sandover" in Perkins, Hetti (ed.). *One Sun One Moon: Aboriginal Art in Australia*. Art Gallery of New South Wales, 2007.

Green, Jenny. "World of Dreamings: Traditional and Modern Art of Australia". National Gallery of Australia. Accessed 14 Jan 2018. https://nga.gov.au/Dreaming/Index.cfm?Refrnc=Ch6

Hodges, C. "Alhalkere" in Neale, M (ed.). *Emily Kame Kngwarreye, Alhalkere: Paintings from Utopia*. Queensland Art Gallery, Brisbane, 1998.

Hossack, Rachel. "Obituary: Emily Kngwarreye", *Independent*, 5 Sept 1996. Accessed 14 Jan 2018. http://www.independent.co.uk/news/people/obituary-emily-kngwarreye-1362024.html

McCulloch, Susan. "A New Way of Seeing: Emily Kame Kngwarreye's Significance in Australian Art". DACOU Australia. Accessed 14 Jan 2018. http://dacou.com.au/aboriginal-art-articles/emily-kame-kngwarreye-s-significance-in-australian-art/cat_36361.html

McKenzie, Janet. "Utopia: The Genius of Emily Kame Kngwarreye", *Studio International*, 10 Nov 2008. Accessed 14 Jan 2018. http://www.studiointernational.com/index.php/utopia-the-genius-of-emily-kame-kngwarreye

Myers, Fred R. *Painting Culture: The Making of an Aboriginal High Art*. Duke University Press Books, 2002.

Neale, Margo. "Emily Kame Kngwarreye: The Impossible Modernist", *Artlink*, vol. 37, no. 2 (June 2017).

Schwartzkoff, Louise. "Stroke of Genius as Unseen Emilys Go on Display", *Sydney Morning Herald*, 20 Dec 2007. Accessed 14 Jan 2018. http://www.smh.com.au/news/arts/stroke-of-genius-as-unseen-emilys-go-on-display/2007/12/19/1197740378161.html

Skelton, Russell. "Japan Takes Emily to Heart", *Sydney Morning Herald*, 31 May 2008. Accessed 13 Jan 2018. http://www.smh.com.au/news/arts/japan-takes-emily-tohea rt/2008/05/30/1211654305476.html

Smith, Sue. "Emily Kame Kngwarreye", *Graffico Topico*, 1998. Accessed 14 Jan 2018. http://www.grafico-qld.com/content/emily-kame-kngwarreye

Stevenson, M. "Utopia Women's Batik Group, Northern Territory, 1970s–1980s". Museums Victoria Collections, 2015. Accessed 14 Jan 2018. https://collections.museumvictoria.com.au/articles/14272

Sylvester, Rachel. "Conmen Make a Killing on Aboriginal Art Market", *Sunday Telegraph*, 17 Sept 1995. Accessed 18 Feb 2018. https://www.rebeccahossack.com/usr/documents/press/download_url/539/the-sunday-telegraph-17-sept-1995-.pdf

"Utopia: the Genius of Emily Kame Kngwarreye". National Museum of Australia. Accessed 14 Jan 2018. http://www.nma.gov.au/exhibitions/utopia_the_genius_of_emily_kame_kngwarreye/emily_kame_kngwarreye

Hilma af Klint

Birnbaum, Daniel; Obrist, Hans-Ulrich; Higgie, Jennifer; Peyton-Jones, Julia; and Voss, Julia. *Hilma af Klint: Painting the Unseen*. Verlag der Buchhandlung Walther Konig, 2016.

Higgie, Jennifer. "Highlights 2013", *Frieze*, 7 Jan 2014. Accessed 14 Jan 2018. https://frieze.com/article/highlights-2013-jennifer-higgie?language=en

Higgie, Jennifer. "Hilma af Klint", *Frieze*, 18 May 2013. Accessed 14 Jan 2018. https://frieze.com/article/hilma-af-klint-0

Higgie, Jennifer. "Longing for Light: The Art of Hilma af Klint" in *Hilma af Klint: Painting the Unseen*. Serpentine Sackler Galleries, 2015.

Judah, Hettie. "Rediscovering Hilma Af Klint: The Original Abstract Painter", *Independent*, 21 Feb 2016. Accessed 14 Jan 2018. http://www.independent.co.uk/arts-entertainment/art/features/rediscovering-hilma-af-klin-the-original-abstract-painter-a6885826.html

Voss, Julia. "The First Abstract Artist? (And It's Not Kandinsky)", *Tate Etc*, issue 27 (spring 2013). Accessed 14 Jan 2018. http://www.tate.org.uk/context-comment/articles/first-abstract-artist-and-its-not-kandinsky

Nasreen Mohamedi

Clayton, Eleanor. "Seeking 'A Blazing Reality': Nasreen Mohamedi's Photographs". Accessed 13 Jan 2018. http://www.tate.org.uk/whats-on/tate-liverpool/exhibition/nasreen-mohamedi/blazing-reality

Cotter, Holland. "Art in Review, Nasreen Mohamedi", *New York Times*, 10 Oct 2003. Accessed 13 Jan 2018. http://www.nytimes.com/2003/10/10/arts/art-in-review-nasreen-mohamedi.html

Kapur, Geeta. "Elegy for an Unclaimed Beloved: Nasreen Mohamedi 1937–1990". Accessed 13 Jan 2018. http://www.tate.org.uk/whats-on/tate-liverpool/exhibition/nasreen-mohamedi/elegy-for-unclaimed-beloved

Pundir, Pallavi. "A Life on the Lines: Celebrating Three Decades of Nasreen Mohamedi's Work", *Indian Express*, 22 Nov 2015. Accessed 13 Jan 2018. http://indianexpress.com/article/lifestyle/art-and-culture/a-life-on-the-lines-celebrating-three-decades-of-nasreen-mohamedis-work/

Singh, Kishore. "Celebrating Minimalism with Nasreen Mohamedi", *Forbes India*, 5 July 2016. Accessed 13 Jan 2018. http://www.forbesindia.com/article/think/celebrating-minimalism-with-nasreen-mohamedi/43697/1

Spence, Rachel. "Nasreen Mohamedi, Tate Liverpool, UK – Review", *Financial Times*, 30 June 2014. Accessed 13 Jan 2018. https://www.ft.com/content/6715ad90-f2ea-11e3-a3f8-00144feabdc0

Yau, John. "India's Nasreen Mohamedi Belongs to Everyone", *Hyperallergic*, 17 Nov 2013. Accessed 13 Jan 2018. https://hyperallergic.com/93951/indias-nasreen-mohamedi-belongs-to-everyone/

Accessed on 13 Jan 2018 via http://www.tate.org.uk/whats-on/tate liverpool/exhibition/nasreen-mohamedi

Alma Thomas

Budick, Ariella. "Alma Thomas Defied Gravity and Reached for the Stars", *Financial Times*, 19 Aug 2016. Accessed 20 Jan 2018. https://www.ft.com/content/15ac0118-645d-11e6-8310-ecf0bddad227

Embuscado, Rain. "Celebrate Alma Thomas's 125th Birthday With Five Remarkable Facts", *Artnet*, 22 Sept 2016. Accessed 20 Jan 2018. https://news.artnet.com/exhibitions/alma-thomas-birthday-facts-660602

Johnson, Ken. "Alma Thomas, an Incandescent Pioneer", *New York Times*, 4 Aug 2016. Accessed 20 Jan 2018. https://www.nytimes.com/2016/08/05/arts/design/alma-thomas-an-incandescent-pioneer.html

Kalina, Richard. "Through Color", *Art in America*, 20 July 2016. Accessed 20 Jan 2018. http://www.artinamericamagazine.com/news-features/magazines/through-color/

Perry, Regenia A. *Free within Ourselves: African-American Artists in the Collection of the National Museum of American Art*. National Museum of American Art/Pomegranate Art Books, 1992. Accessed 20 Jan 2018. https://americanart.si.edu/artist/alma-thomas-4778

Quinn, Kelly. "Alma Thomas's March on Washington …with 250,000 Others", *Archives of American Art*, 9 Aug 2013. Accessed 20 Jan 2018. https://www.aaa.si.edu/blog/2013/08/alma-thomas%E2%80%99s-march-on-washington-%E2%80%A6with-250000-others

Schjeldahl, Peter. "Alma Thomas's Late Blooms", *New Yorker*, 25 July 2016. Accessed 20 Jan 2018. https://www.newyorker.com/magazine/2016/07/25/alma-thomas-and-sports-photography

Sheets, Hilarie. "Museums Bring Pioneering Painter Alma Thomas out of Storage for Her First Major Retrospective in Over 30 Years", *Artsy*, 21 Jan 2016. Accessed 20 Jan 2018. https://www.artsy.net/article/artsy-editorial-pioneering-painter-alma-thomas-is-making-a-comeback-over-30-years-since-her-last-major-retrospective

Carol Rama

Budick, Ariella. "Carol Rama – Her Dark Materials", *Financial Times*, 30 June 2017. Accessed 14 Jan 2018. https://www.ft.com/content/7abfe792-461c-11e7-8d27-59b4dd6296b8

Farago, Jason. "The Psychosexual World of Carol Rama Still Shocks", *New York Times*, 11 May 2017. Accessed 14 Jan 2018. https://www.nytimes.com/2017/05/11/arts/design/the-psychosexual-world-of-carol-rama-still-shocks.html?mtrref=undefined

Fossati, Filippo, and Levi, Corrado. "An Interview with Carol Rama". Accessed 14 Jan 2018. https://zoltanjokay.de/zoltanblog/2013/09/carol-rama-half-3/

Gotthardt, Alexxa. "For Carol Rama, Art was a Way to Process Life's Pleasure and Pain", *Artsy*, 5 May 2017. Accessed 14 Jan 2018. https://www.artsy.net/article/artsy-editorial-carol-rama-art-way-process-lifes-pleasure-pain

Grandas, Teresa. "The Rest Can Go to Hell. Other Possible Tales of Carol Rama and Turin" in Dressen, Anne; Grandas, Teresa; and Preciado, Beatriz. *The Passion According to Carol Rama*. Museu d'Art Contemporani de Barcelona (MACBA), 2015.

Lloyd, Ann Wilson. "ART/ARTCHITECTURE; Brushwork With a Certain Fine Madness", *New York Times*, 1 Nov 1998. Accessed 14 Jan 2018. http://www.nytimes.com/1998/11/01/arts/art-artchitecture-brushwork-with-a-certain-fine-madness.html

Lubow, Arthur. "The Renaissance of Marisa Merz, Carol Rama, and Carla Accardi: Three Italian Women Artists Having a Moment", *W Magazine*, 10 Feb 2017. Accessed 14 Jan 2018. https://www.wmagazine.com/story/the-renaissance-of-marisa-merz-carol-rama-and-carla-accardi-italian-women-artists

Spence, Rachel. "A Tormented, Original Talent: Carol Rama in Venice", *Financial Times*, 5 July 2017. Accessed 14 Jan 2018. https://www.ft.com/content/0f63fc4e-5c1b-11e7-b553-e2df1b0c3220

Charlotte Posenenske

Charlotte Posenenske. "Statement", *Art International*, no. 5 (May 1968). Accessed 13 Jan 2018. http://artistsspace.org/exhibitions/charlotte-posenenske

"Charlotte Posenenske an einen Bauunternehmer", *EgoIst*, vol. 1, no. 17 (1970). Quoted in Mehring, Christine. "Public Options", *Art Forum*, Sept 2010. Accessed 13 Jan 2018.

Garcia-Fenech, Giovanni. "Goodbye to All That: Why Do Artists Reject the Art World?" *Hyperallergic*, 7 Mar 2017. Accessed 13 Jan 2018. https://hyperallergic.com/363448/goodbye-to-all-that-why-do-artists-reject-the-art-world/

Judah, Hettie. "Don't Look Now: The Artists Who Turn their Backs on the World", *Guardian*, 20 Apr 2017. Accessed 13 Jan 2018. https://www.theguardian.com/artanddesign/2017/apr/20/tell-them-i-said-no-artists-who-turn-backs-on-world-martin-herbert

Kleinman, Adam. "Charlotte Posenenske at Artists Space, New York", *Art Agenda*, 23 June–15 Aug 2010. Accessed 13 Jan 2018. http://www.art-agenda.com/reviews/charlotte-posenenske-at-artists-spacenew-york/

Pesch, Martin. "Charlotte Posenenske", *Frieze*, 3 Mar 2000. Accessed 13 Jan 2018. https://frieze.com/article/charlotte-posenenske

Smith, Roberta. "Hands-On Reassembly in Stripped-Down Gallery", *New York Times*, 9 Aug 2010. Accessed 13 Jan 2018. http://www.nytimes.com/2010/08/10/arts/design/10charlotte.html?module=ArrowsNav&contentCollection=Art%20%26%20Design&action=keypress®ion=FixedLeft&pgtype=article Accessed 13 Jan 2018. http://www.tate.org.uk/art/artworks/posenenske-prototype-for-revolving-vane-t12773

Fahrelnissa Zeid

Ellis-Petersen, Hannah. "Fahrelnissa Zeid: Tate Modern Resurrects Artist Forgotten by History", *Guardian*, 12 June 2017. Accessed 21 Jan 2018. https://www.theguardian.com/artanddesign/2017/jun/12/fahrelnissa-zeid-tate-modern-resurrects-artist-forgotten-by-history

"Fahrelnissa Zeid: City by City". Accessed 21 Jan 2018. http://www.tate.org.uk/art/artists/fahrelnissa-zeid-22764/quick-read/city-by-city

"Fahrelnissa Zeid in Four Key Works". Accessed 21 Jan 2018. http://www.tate.org.uk/art/artists/fahrelnissa-zeid-22764/lists/four-key-works

Gauntlett, Suzy. "The Painter Princess", *Tate Etc*, 7 June 2017. Accessed 21 Jan 2018. http://www.tate.org.uk/art/artists/fahrelnissa-zeid-22764/tate-etc/fahrelnissa-zeid-the-painter-princess

G-H, G. "The Fusion Paintings of Fahrelnissa Zeid", *Economist*, 14 June 2017. Accessed 21 Jan 2018. https://www.economist.com/blogs/prospero/2017/06/canvasses-nowhere

Luke, Ben. "Fahrelnissa Zeid, Exhibition Review: A Wonderful Abstract Artist Who Later Lost Her Way", *Evening Standard*, 13 June 2017. Accessed 21 Jan 2018. https://www.standard.co.uk/go/london/arts/fahrelnissa-zeid-exhibition-review-a-wonderful-abstract-artist-who-later-lost-her-way-a3681346.html

Spence, Rachel. "Fahrelnissa Zeid, Tate Modern, London – Journey into Abstraction", *Financial Times*, 28 June 2017. Accessed 21 Jan 2018. https://www.ft.com/content/ca4d57b8-5be8-11e7-b553-e2df1b0c3220

Marlow Moss

Chodha, Dal. "Marlow Moss: Constructivism, Mondrian & Gender Politics", *AnOther*, 29 Sept 2014. Accessed 19 Jan 2018. http://www.anothermag.com/art-photography/3952/marlow-moss-constructivism-mondrian-gender-politics

Howarth, Lucy. *Marlow Moss (1889–1958)*. Diss., University of Plymouth, 2008.

Marlow Moss, exhibition catalogue Amsterdam, Stedelijk Museum, 1962. Cited in Howarth, Lucy. "Marlow Moss: Dress Address Name" in Kane, Nina, and Woods, Jude (eds). *Reflections on Female and Trans* Masculinities and Other Queer Crossings*.

FIGURATIVE

Prehistoric cave painters

Barriaux, Marianne. "To Unlock the Secrets of Prehistoric Hand Paintings, Experts Catalog Them in 3D". Agence France-Presse (AFP), 5 Jan 2017. Accessed 21 Jan 2018. https://www.seeker.com/culture/archaeology/to-unlock-the-secrets-of-prehistoric-hand-paintings-experts-catalog-them-in-3d

Corbett, Rachel. "A Journey Deep Inside Spain's Temple of Cave Art". BBC, 19 Nov 2014. Accessed 21 Jan 2018. http://www.bbc.com/travel/story/20141027-a-journey-deep-inside-spains-temple-of-cave-art

Frank, Priscilla. "Let's Stop Assuming The Early Cave Painters Were Dudes", *Huffington Post*, 14 Oct 2015. Accessed 21 Jan 2018. http://www.huffingtonpost.co.uk/entry/lets-stop-assuming-the-early-cave-painters-were-dudes_us_561e6ebce4b050c6c4a39bf3

Hughes, Virginia. "Were the First Artists Mostly Women?", *National Geographic*, 9 Oct 2013. Accessed 21 Jan 2018. https://news.nationalgeographic.com/news/2013/10/131008-women-handprints-oldest-neolithic-cave-art/

Messer, A'ndrea Elyse. "Women Leave Their Handprints on the Cave Wall", *Penn State News*, 15 Oct 2013. Accessed 21 Jan 2018. http://news.psu.edu/story/291423/2013/10/15/research/women-leave-their-handprints-cave-wall

Penn State, "Women Leave Their Handprints on the Cave Wall", *ScienceDaily*, 15 Oct 2013. Accessed 21 Jan 2018. https://www.sciencedaily.com/releases/2013/10/131015113909.htm

Snow, Dean R. "Sexual Dimorphism in European Upper Paleolithic Cave Art", *American Antiquity*, vol. 78, no. 4 (Oct 2013). Accessed 21 Jan 2018. http://cuevas.culturadecantabria.com/el-castillo-2/

Chen Shu

Lee, Lily Xiao Hong Lee; Lau, Clara; and Stefanowsky, A D. *Biographical Dictionary of Chinese Women: Vol. 1: The Qing Period, 1644–1911*. Routledge, 1998.

Smith, Bonnie G. *The Oxford Encyclopedia of Women in World History, Volume 1*. Oxford University Press, 2008.

Sung, Doris Ha Lin. "Redefining Female Talent: Chinese Women Artists in the National and Global Art Worlds, 1900s–1970s". Dissertation, York University, 2012.

Weidner, Martha. "The Conventional Success of Ch'en Shu", *Flowering in the Shadows: Women in the History of Chinese and Japanese Painting*. University of Hawaii Press, 1990.

Weidner, Martha. *Views from Jade Terrace: Chinese Women Artists, 1300–1912*. Indianapolis Museum of Art, 1988.

Tina Blau

Belvedere Museum, "Masterpieces in Focus: Tina Blau". Accessed 31 Jan

2018. https://www.belvedere.at/jart/prj3/belvedere/data/documents/presse-dokumente/projekte_2016/PM_Tina_Blau_en.pdf
Ben-Eli, Birgit. "Tina Blau: 1845–1916", *Jewish Women's Archive*. Accessed 31 Jan 2018. https://jwa.org/encyclopedia/article/blau-tina
Harriman, Helga H. "Olga Wisinger-Florian and Tina Blau: Painters in 'Fin de Siècle' Vienna", *Woman's Art Journal*, vol. 10, no. 2 (1989). JSTOR, http://www.jstor.org/stable/1358208
Johnson, Julie M. "Writing, Erasing, Silencing: Tina Blau and the (Woman) Artist's Biography", *Nineteenth Century Art Worldwide*, vol. 4, no. 3 (autumn 2005). Accessed 31 Jan 2018. http://www.19thc-artworldwide.org/index.php/autumn05/208-writing-erasing-silencing-tina-blau-and-the-woman-artists-biography

Jo Hopper
Levin, Gail. *Edward Hopper: An Intimate Biography*. University of California Press, 1998.
https://www.theguardian.com/artanddesign/2004/apr/25/art1
http://publishing.cdlib.org/ucpressebooks/view?docId=kt5b69q3pk&doc.view=content&chunk.id=ch10&toc.depth=100&brand=ucpress
http://www.telegraph.co.uk/culture/art/10157460/Edward-Hoppers-art-through-his-wifes-eyes.html

Elisabetta Sirani
Heller, Nancy G. "Artist Spotlight: Elisabetta Sirani". National Museum of Women in the Arts, 23 Dec 2009. Accessed 2 Feb 2018. https://nmwa.org/explore/artist-profiles/elisabetta-sirani
Modesti, Adelina. *Elisabetta Sirani "Virtuosa": Women's Cultural Production in Early Modern Bologna*. Brepolis, 2014.

Sylvia Sleigh
Grimes, William. "Sylvia Sleigh, Provocative Portraitist and Feminist Artist, Dies at 94", *New York Times*, 25 Oct 2010. Accessed 23 Jan 2018. http://www.nytimes.com/2010/10/26/arts/design/26sleigh.html
Hughes, Maggie. "Sylvia Sleigh and Lawrence Alloway, Mutual Muses", *The Iris*, 21 June 2012. Accessed 23 Jan 2018. http://blogs.getty.edu/iris/treasures-from-the-vault-sylvia-sleigh-and-lawrence-alloway-mutual-muses/
Latimer, Quinn. "A Step Out of Time", *Frieze*, 7 Mar 2013. Accessed 23 Jan 2018. https://frieze.com/article/step-out-time
Simavi, Zeynep. "Remembering Sylvia Sleigh". National Museum of Women in the Arts, 9 Nov 2010. Accessed 23 Jan 2018. https://nmwa.org/blog/2010/11/09/remembering-sylvia-sleigh/
"Sylvia Sleigh, Lawrence Alloway, and The Turkish Bath". Smart Blog, 24 Mar 2015. Accessed 23 Jan 2018. https://arts.uchicago.edu/blogs/smart/sylvia-sleigh-lawrence-alloway-and-turkish-bath
Accessed 23 Jan 2018. https://www.brooklynmuseum.org/eascfa/feminist_art_base/sylvia-sleigh

Camille Claudel
Akbar, Arifa. "How Rodin's Tragic Lover Shaped the History of Sculpture", *Independent*, 10 Aug 2012. Accessed 4 Feb 2018. http://www.independent.co.uk/arts-entertainment/art/features/how-rodins-tragic-lover-shaped-the-history-of-sculpture-8026836.html
Cooper, B. "Camille Claudel: Trajectory of a Psychosis", *Medical Humanities*, vol. 34, no. 1 (2008).
Economist. "The Triumph of Tragedy", 5 Jan 2006. Accessed 4 Feb 2018. http://www.economist.com/node/5354447
Delistraty, Cody. "Rediscovering the Overlooked Talent of French Sculptor Camille Claudel", *Frieze*, 26 Jan 2018. Accessed 4 Feb 2018. https://frieze.com/article/rediscovering-overlooked-talent-french-sculptor-camille-claudel
Katz, Brigit. "Museum Devoted to Camille Claudel, Long Overshadowed by Rodin, Opens in France", *Smithsonian*, 30 Mar 2017. Accessed 4 Feb 2018. https://www.smithsonianmag.com/smart-news/museum-devoted-camille-claudel-overshadowed-rodin-opens-france-180962718/
Kennedy, Maeve. "Museum Rescues Sculptor Camille Claudel from Decades of Obscurity", *Guardian*, 25 Mar 2017. Accessed 4 Feb 2018. https://www.theguardian.com/artanddesign/2017/mar/25/museum-rescues-sculptor-camille-claudel-from-decades-of-obscurity
Lampert, Catherine. "The genius of Camille Claudel", *Apollo*, 13 May 2017. Accessed 4 Feb 2018. https://www.apollo-magazine.com/the-genius-of-camille-claudel/
Webster, Paul. "Fame at last for Rodin's lost muse", *Guardian*, 23 Mar 2003. Accessed 4 Feb 2018. https://www.theguardian.com/world/2003/mar/23/arts.artsnews
Witherell, Louise R. "Camille Claudel Rediscovered", *Woman's Art Journal*, vol. 6, no. 1 (1985). JSTOR, http://www.jstor.org/stable/1358057.

Catharina van Hemessen
Buchholz, Elke Linda. *Women Artists*. Prestel, 2003.
Gaze, Delia (ed.). *Dictionary of Women Artists: Artists, J–Z*. Taylor & Francis, 1997.
Hessel, Katy. "These Women Artists Influenced the Renaissance and Baroque", *Artsy*, 20 Dec 2016. Accessed 10 Feb 2018. https://www.artsy.net/article/artsy-editorial-these-women-artists-influenced-the-renaissance-and-baroque
Weidemann, Christiane; Larass, Petra; and Klier, Melanie. *50 Women Artists You Should Know*. Prestel, 2008.

Timarete
Cheney, Liana De Girolami; Faxon, Alicia Craig; and Russo, Kathleen Lucey. *Self-Portraits by Women Painters*. Ashgate, 2000.
Dabbs, Julia. *Life Stories of Women Artists, 1550–1800*. Ashgate Publishing, 2009.
Gurewitsch, Matthew. "True Colours", *Smithsonian Magazine*, July 2008. Accessed 29 Jan 2018. https://www.smithsonianmag.com/arts-culture/true-colors-17888/
Havice, Christine. "Women and the Production of Art in the Middle Ages: The Significance of Context" in Bluestone, Natalie Harris (ed.). *Double Vision*. Associated University Presses, 1995.

Marjorie Cameron
Blanks, Tim. "Witches Crew", *W Magazine*, Mar 2013.
Duncan, Michael. "Cameron", Cameron Parsons Foundation. Accessed 25 Jan 2018. http://observer.com/2015/10/deitch-projects-presents-the-uncensored-story-of-la-artistoccultist-marjorie-cameron/
Garrova, Robert. "Dark Arts: Artist, Occultist Marjorie Cameron Featured in New Book, MOCA show", *Off-Ramp*, 24 July 2014. Accessed 25 Jan 2018. http://www.scpr.org/programs/offramp/2014/07/24/38528/dark-arts-artist-occultist-marjorie-cameron-featur/
Hobbs, Scott. "Cinderella of the Wastelands", *Huffington Post*, 26 Feb 2013. Accessed 25 Jan 2018. https://www.huffingtonpost.com/scott-hobbs/cinderella-of-the-wastela_b_2730500.html
Laden, Tanja M. "Cameron's Connections to Scientology and Powerful Men Once Drew Headlines, But Now Her Art Is Getting Its Due", *LA Weekly*, 8 Oct 2014. Accessed 25 Jan 2018. http://www.laweekly.com/arts/camerons-connections-to-scientology-and-powerful-men-once-drew-headlines-but-now-her-art-is-getting-its-due-5130928
Laden, Tanja M. "The Trippy Art (and Trippier Life) of Occult Artist Marjorie Cameron", *Creators*, 20 Sept 2015. Accessed 25 Jan 2018. https://creators.vice.com/en_us/article/4xqqjn/the-trippy-art-and-trippier-life-of-occult-artist-marjorie-cameron
Lunenfeld, Peter. "Season of the Witch", *Artforum*, Jan 2015.
Martinez, Alanna. "Deitch Projects Presents the Uncensored Story of LA Artist/Occultist Marjorie Cameron", *Observer*, 10 Feb 2015. Accessed 25 Jan 2018. http://observer.com/2015/10/deitch-projects-presents-the-uncensored-story-of-la-artistoccultist-marjorie-cameron/

Anaxandra
"Anaxandra – Fl. 220S BCE – Greece". Rebel Women Embroidery, 29 Sept 2015. Accessed 21 April 2018. https://rebelwomenembroidery.wordpress.com/2015/09/29/anaxandra-fl-220s-bce-greece/
Kampen, Natalie. "Hellenistic Artists: Female", *Archeologia Classica*, vol. 27, no. 1, 1975. JSTOR, http://www.jstor.org/stable/44366491
Keuls, Eva C. *Plato and Greek Painting*. Brill, 1978.
Marinella, Lucrezia. *The Nobility and Excellence of Women, and the Defects and Vices of Men*. Dunhill, Anne (ed. and trans.). University of Chicago Press, 1999.

Sofonisba Anguissola
Fortune, Jane. "Deeper Study, Greater Grace?" *The Florentine*, issue 182 (25 Apr 2013). Accessed 24 Jan 2018. http://www.theflorentine.net/art-culture/2013/04/deeper-study-greater-grace/
Fortune, Jane. "Michelangelo Buonarroti and his Women", *The Florentine*, issue 239 (2 Nov 2017). Accessed 24 Jan 2018. http://www.theflorentine.net/art-culture/2017/11/michelangelo-buonarroti-women/
Jacobs, Frederika H. "Woman's Capacity to Create: The Unusual Case of Sofonisba Anguissola", *Renaissance Quarterly*, vol. 47, no. 1 (1994).
Kilroy-Ewbank, Lauren. "Sofonisba Anguissola", *Smarthistory*, 3 May 2016. Accessed 24 Jan 2018. https://smarthistory.org/sofonisba-anguissola/
Slobogin, Christie. "Painting with Confidence: Early Female Self-Portraiture". National Museum of

Women in the Arts, 15 July 2015. Accessed 24 Jan 2018. https://nmwa.org/blog/2015/07/15/painting-with-confidence-early-female-self-portraiture/
Accessed 24 Jan 2018. http://clara.nmwa.org/index.php?g=entity_detail&entity_id=116
Accessed 24 Jan 2018. http://web-archives.mansfield.edu/~art/Papyrus2AnnabellaLajuzensofoisba_anguissola_the.htm
Accessed 24 Jan 2018. https://www.oneonta.edu/faculty/farberas/arth/arth200/artist/sofonisba.htm

Charlotte Salomon
Bentley, Toni. "The Obsessive Art and Great Confession of Charlotte Salomon", *New Yorker*, 15 July 2017. Accessed 23 Jan 2018. https://www.newyorker.com/culture/culture-desk/the-obsessive-art-and-great-confession-of-charlotte-salomon
Levitt, Aimee. "Charlotte Salomon's Life? or Theater?: Painting for her Life, Literally", *Chicago Reader*, 27 June 2014. Accessed 22 Jan 2018. https://www.chicagoreader.com/Bleader/archives/2014/06/27/charlotte-salomons-life-or-theater-painting-for-her-life-literally
Pollock, Griselda. "Recalling Charlotte Salomon", *TLS*, 14 Nov 2017. Accessed 22 Jan 2018. https://www.the-tls.co.uk/articles/public/charlotte-salomon-life-theatre/
Pound, Cath. "Tragedy and the Will to Live: The Obsessive Art of Charlotte Salomon", *New York Times*, 23 Oct 2017. Accessed 22 Jan 2018. https://www.nytimes.com/2017/10/23/arts/design/charlotte-salomon-life-or-theater.html
Salomon, Charlotte. *Charlotte Salomon: Life? or Theatre? A Selection of 450 Gouaches*. Taschen, 2017.

Clara Tice
Frank, Priscilla. "Meet Clara Tice, The Erotic Illustrator Who Scandalized 20th-Century New York", *Huffington Post*, 24 Apr 2017. Accessed 1 Feb 2018. http://www.huffingtonpost.co.uk/entry/clara-tice-honest-erotica_us_58fa216ae4b06b9cb916396f
Gotthardt, Alexxa. "The Erotic Artist Who Became the Queen of Bohemian New York", *Artsy*, 15 Sept 2016. Accessed 1 Feb 2018. https://www.artsy.net/article/artsy-editorial-erotic-artist-queen-bohemian-new-york
Guenter, Patricia. "Clara Tice Rediscovered". ClaraTice.com, 12 Jan 2012. Accessed 1 Feb 2018. http://www.claratice.com/Biography.html
Henri, Robert. *The Art Spirit*. J B Lippincott Company, 1923.
Keller, Marie T. "Clara Tice, Queen of Greenwich Village" in Sawelson-Gorse, Naomi (ed.). *Women in Dada: Essays on Sex, Gender, and Identity*. MIT Press, 1999.

Amrita Sher-Gil
Alok, Nupur Preeti. "Life of Amrita Sher-Gil: An Artist Way Ahead of her Time", *Feminism in India*, 30 Jan 2017. Accessed 23 Jan 2018. https://feminisminindia.com/2017/01/30/amrita-sher-gil-artist-life/
Dalmia, Yashodhara. *Amrita Sher-Gil: A Life*. Penguin UK, 2013.
Garcia, Meryl. "Google's Doodle Honours Amrita Sher-Gil. Here Are 5 Things You Should Know about Her", *The Better India*, 30 Jan 2016. Accessed 23 Jan 2018. https://www.thebetterindia.com/44577/googles-doodle-indian-painter-amrita-shergil/
Hughes, Kathryn. "The Indian Frida Kahlo", *Telegraph*, 3 June 2013. Accessed 23 Jan 2018. http://www.telegraph.co.uk/culture/10087130/The-Indian-Frida-Kahlo.html
Pillai, Manu S. "Why Amrita Sher-Gil's Wry Nationalism is Relevant", *LiveMint*, 9 Dec 2016. Accessed 23 Jan 2018. http://www.livemint.com/Leisure/C4Jg2hzHX46whzvx1bJXCL/Why-Amrita-SherGils-wry-nationalism-is-relevant.html
Punjab Monitor. "Amrita Shergill: The Pioneer Artist". Accessed 23 Jan 2018. http://www.punjabmonitor.com/2013/04/amrita-shergill-pioneer-artist.html
Accessed 23 Jan 2018. http://www.tate.org.uk/whats-on/tate-modern/exhibition/amrita-sher-gil/amrita-sher-gil-room-1-early-years-paris
http://www.tate.org.uk/whats-on/tate-modern/exhibition/amrita-sher-gil/amrita-sher-gil-room-2-return-india

Clara Peeters
Brusati, Celeste. "Stilled Lives: Self-Portraiture and Self-Reflection in Seventeenth-Century Netherlandish Still-Life Painting", *Simiolus: Netherlands Quarterly for the History of Art*, vol. 20, no. 2/3 (1990). JSTOR, http://www.jstor.org/stable/3780741
Frayer, Lauren. "In A First, Spain's Prado Museum Puts the Spotlight on a Female Artist", *NPR*, 30 Nov 2016. Accessed 31 Jan 2018. https://www.npr.org/sections/parallels/2016/11/30/503129505/in-a-first-spains-prado-museum-puts-the-spotlight-on-a-woman-artist
Hofrichter, Frima Fox. "Clara Peeters, 1594–ca. 1640", *Woman's Art Journal*, vol. 16, no. 2 (1995). JSTOR, http://www.jstor.org/stable/1358580
Murphy, Kathryn. "More to Cheese than Meets the Eye?" *Apollo*, 11 Mar 2017. Accessed 1 Feb 2018. https://www.apollo-magazine.com/cheese-meets-eye-dutch-still-life/
Pound, Cath. "The Great Women Artists That History Forgot". BBC, 19 Oct 2016. Accessed 31 Jan 2018. http://www.bbc.com/culture/story/20161019-the-great-women-artists-that-history-forgot
Accessed 1 Feb 2018. https://www.museodelprado.es/en/whats-on/exhibition/the-art-of-clara-peeters/e4628dea-9ffd-4632-85c9-49367e86959?searchid=2b30ffbc-455e-736b-e5d8-bc363c4ac1cd

Meta Warrick Fuller
Ater, Renee. "Meta Warrick Fuller's Ethiopia and the America's Making Exposition of 1921" in Kirschke, Amy Helene (ed.), *Women Artists of the Harlem Renaissance*. University Press of Mississippi, 2014.
Farrington, Lisa E. *Creating Their Own Image: The History of African-American Women Artists*. Oxford University Press, 2005.
Finkelman, Paul, and Wintz, Cary D. *Encyclopedia of the Harlem Renaissance: A–J*. Taylor & Francis, 2004.
Green, Carol Hurd, and Sicherman, Barbara. *Notable American Women: The Modern Period: A Biographical Dictionary*. Harvard University Press, 1980.
An Independent Woman: The Life and Art of Meta Warrick Fuller (1877–1968). Danforth Museum of Art, 1984. Accessed 6 Feb 2018. http://www.danforthart.org/assets/forms/meta_fuller_catalog_1984-5.pdf
Kerr, Judith N. *God-Given Work: The Life and Times of Sculptor Meta Vaux Warrick Fuller, 1877–1968*. University of Massachusetts Amherst, 1986.
Accessed 6 Feb 2018. http://www.edwardianpromenade.com/women/fascinating-women-meta-warrick-fuller
Accessed 6 Feb 2018. http://www.emancipationtrail.org/new-page-99/

PERFORMANCE & CONCEPTUAL
Baroness Elsa Von Freytag-Loringhoven
Cotter, Holland. "The Mama of Dada", *New York Times*, 19 May 2002. Accessed 2 Feb 2018. http://www.nytimes.com/2002/05/19/books/the-mama-of-dada.html
Freytag-Loringhoven, Elsa von. *Autobiography*, unpublished. Accessed 2 Feb 2018. http://www.baronesselsa.org/items/show/4#
Freytag-Loringhoven, Elsa von. *Body Sweats: The Uncensored Writings of Elsa von Freytag-Loringhoven*. MIT Press, 2011.
Freytag-Loringhoven, Elsa von. "A Dozen Cocktails – Please". Quoted in Gammel, Irene. *Baroness Elsa: Gender, Dada, and Everyday Modernity – A Cultural Biography*. MIT Press, 2003.
Gammel, Irene. *Baroness Elsa: Gender, Dada, and Everyday Modernity – A Cultural Biography*. MIT Press, 2003.
Kuenzli, Rudolf E. "Baroness Elsa von Freytag-Loringhoven and New York Dada." Sawelson-Gorse, Naomi (ed). *Women in Dada: Essays on Sex, Gender, and Identity*. MIT Press, 1999.
Mann, Jon. "How Duchamp's Urinal Changed Art Forever", *Artsy*, 9 May 2017. Accessed 2 Feb 2018. https://www.artsy.net/article/artsy-editorial-duchamps-urinal-changed-art-forever
Mifflin, Margot. "Bride Stripped Bare", *Bookforum*, Fall 2002. Accessed 2 Feb 2018. http://www.bookforum.com/archive/fall_02/mifflin.html
Steinke, Rene. "My Heart Belongs to Dada", *New York Times*, 18 Aug 2002. Accessed 2 Feb 2018. http://www.nytimes.com/2002/08/18/magazine/my-heart-belongs-to-dada.html

Gina Pane
Bamguartner, Frédérique. "Reviving the Collective Body: Gina Pane's Unanesthetized Escalation", *Oxford Art Journal*, vol. 34, no. 2 (2011).
Blessing, Jennifer. "Gina Pane's Witnesses: The Audience and Photography", *Performance Research*, vol. 7, no. 4 (2002).
"Gina Pane at Kamel Mennour", *Contemporary Art Daily*, 15 Apr 2016. Accessed 10 Feb 2018. http://www.contemporaryartdaily.com/2016/04/gina-pane-at-kamel-mennour/
Graves, Jen. "Currently Hanging: Gina Pane's Steel Stairs and Locked-In Hurt", *The Stranger*, 2 Apr 2014. Accessed 10 Feb 2018. https://www.thestranger.com/slog/archives/2014/04/02/currently-hanging-gina-panes-steel-stairs-and-locked-in-hurt
Johnson Sam. "Five Radical Female Artists Who Used Their Body as a Canvas", *AnOther*, 21 Oct 2015. Accessed 10 Feb 2018. http://www.anothermag.com/art-photography/7942/five-radical-female-artists-who-used-their-body-as-a-canvas
Koebel, Caroline. "Parallel Practices: Joan Jonas & Gina Pane", *Glasstire*, 8 June 2013. Accessed 10 Feb 2018. http://glasstire.com/2013/06/08/parallel-practices-joan-jonas-gina-pane/

Leszkowicz, Paweł. “Female St Sebastian: Parallel Lines in the Radical Lesbian Art of Gina Pane and Catherine Opie”, *Interalia, A Journal of Queer Studies*, 2010, http://interalia.org.pl/en/artykuly/2010_5/07_female_st_sebastian_parallel_lines_in_the_radical_lesbian_art_of_gina_pane.htm.

Lombardi, Monica. “Gina Pane: The Vulnerability of Human Body”, *The Blogazine*, 25 June 2016. Accessed 10 Feb 2018. http://www.theblogazine.com/2012/06/gina-pane-the-vulnerability-of-human-body/

O'Dell, Kathy. *Contract with the Skin: Masochism, Performance Art, and the 1970s*. University of Minnesota Press, 1998.

Pane, Gina. “Lettre à un(e) inconnu(e)”. Quoted in Becker, Ilka, and Grosenick, Uta. *Women Artists in the 20th and 21st Century*. Taschen, 2001.

Perel, Marissa. “A Brief History of Sacrifice”, *Art 21*, 14 June 2013. Accessed 10 Feb 2018. http://magazine.art21.org/2013/06/14/a-brief-history-of-sacrifice/#.WnzBy5OFiRs

Platt, Susan Noyes. “Feminism and Performance: Joan Jonas and Gina Pane”, *Art and Politics Now*, 10 Apr 2014. Accessed 10 Feb 2018. http://www.artandpoliticsnow.com/2014/04/feminism-and-performance-joan-jonas-and-gina-pane/

Voss, Kelly. *Valie Export, Gina Pane, and Orlan: Pain, Body Art, and the Question of the Feminine*. University of Cincinnati, 2014.

Emmy Hennings

Ghanem, Nadia. “Cabaret Voltaire”, trans. from the French text, published in the catalogue Dada (Editions du Centre Pompidou, Paris, 2005). The translation was part of the Press Pack, published by MNAM Centre Pompidou 2005. Accessed 10 Feb 2018. http://www.dada-companion.com/cabaret/

Heiser, Jorg. “Mad World”, *Frieze*, 8 Dec 2015. Accessed 10 Feb 2018. https://frieze.com/article/mad-world-0

Hemus, Ruth. *Dada's Women*. Yale University Press, 2009.

Hubert, Renee Riese. “Zurich Dada and its Artist Couples” in Sawelson-Gorse, Naomi (ed). *Women in Dada: Essays on Sex, Gender, and Identity*. MIT Press, 1999.

O'Reilly, Sally. “Dada's Women”, *Frieze*, 5 May 2009. Accessed 10 Feb 2018. https://frieze.com/article/dada%E2%80%99s-women?language=de

Rugh, Thomas F. “Emmy Hennings and the Emergence of Zurich Dada”, *Woman's Art Journal*, vol. 2, no. 1, 1981, JSTOR, http://www.jstor.org/stable/1357892

Letícia Parente

Gurba, Myriam. “Images of Torture in Videos by Letícia Parente in Radical Women”. Hammer Museum, 21 Nov 2017. Accessed 11 Feb 2018. https://hammer.ucla.edu/blog/2017/11/images-of-torture-in-videos-by-leticia-parente-in-radical-women/

Marti, Silas. “Letícia Parente”, *ArtReview*, Summer 2017. Accessed 11 Feb 2018. https://artreview.com/reviews/ar_summer_2017_review_letcia_parente/

Meigh-Andrews, Chris. *A History of Video Art*. A&C Black, 2013.

Press release, “Letícia Parente: Eu armário de mim”. Galeria Jaqueline Martins, 2017. Accessed 11 Feb 2018. https://www.artforum.com/uploads/guide.004/id05802/press_release.pdf

Shtromberg, Elena. “Bodies in Peril: Enacting Censorship in Early Brazilian Video Art (1974–1978)”. The Aesthetics of Risk: SoCCAS Symposium. Vol. 3.

CRAFT

Tokuyama Gyokuran

Addis, Stephen. “The Three Women of Gion” in Weidner, Marsha Smith (ed.). *Flowering in the Shadows: Women in the History of Chinese and Japanese Painting*. University of Hawaii Press, 1990.

Kinoshita, Kyoko. “The Life and Art of Tokuyama Gyokuran” in Fischer, Felice, and Kinoshita, Kyoko (eds). *Ike Taiga and Tokuyama Gyokuran: Japanese Masters of the Brush*. Philadelphia Museum of Art, 2007.

Smith, Roberta. “In Japan, When Word Was Wed to Image”, *New York Times*, 18 May 2007. Accessed 2 Apr 2018. https://www.nytimes.com/2007/05/18/arts/design/18nang.html

Accessed 2 Apr 2018. https://collections.artsmia.org/art/116887/akashi-bay-ike gyokuran

Hannah Ryggen

Attlee, James. “Hannah Ryggen”, *Frieze*, 23 Jan 2018. Accessed 4 Mar 2018. https://frieze.com/article/hannah-ryggen

Chivers, Clara. “The Revolutionary Craft of Hannah Ryggen”, *Apollo Magazine*, 5 Feb 2018. Accessed 4 Mar 2018. https://www.apollo-magazine.com/the-revolutionary-craft-of-hannah-ryggen/

“Hannah Ryggen”, *Art in America*, 2 Oct 2015. Accessed 4 March 2018. https://www.artinamericamagazine.com/reviews/hannah-ryggen/

Hannah Ryggen Exhibition Notes, *Modern Art Oxford*, 2017. Jackson Lesley. “Ryggen's Riposte”, *Crafts*, issue 269 (Nov/Dec 2017). Accessed 4 Mar 2018. http://www.craftscouncil.org.uk/articles/ryggens-riposte/

Judah, Hettie. “Hannah Ryggen Wove Politics into her Gorgeous Tapestries”, *New York Times*, 1 Dec 2017. Accessed 4 Mar 2018. https://www.nytimes.com/2017/12/01/arts/hannah-ryggen-wove-politics-into-her-gorgeous-tapestries.html

Sherwin, Skye. “The Woman Who Kept Hitler and Churchill in Stitches: Hannah Ryggen *Woven Histories* Review”, *Guardian*, 14 Nov 2017. Accessed 4 Mar 2018. https://www.theguardian.com/artanddesign/2017/nov/14/hannah-ryggen-woven-histories-review-modern-art-oxford

Esther Inglis

Christianson, Karen. “Renaissance Calligraphy Books”, 15 Feb 2012, *The Newberry*. Accessed 17 Feb 2018. http://www.newberry.org/renaissance-calligraphy-books

Clement, Taylor. “Selfie Fashioning and the Self-Portraits of Calligrapher Esther Inglis”, *Early Modern Women: Lives, Texts, Objects*, 15 June 2017. Accessed 17 Feb 2018. https://martinevanelk.wordpress.com/2017/06/15/selfie-fashioning-and-the-self-portraits-of-calligrapher-esther-inglis/

Dabbs, Julia K. *Life Stories of Women Artists, 1550–1800*. Ashgate, 2009.

Emzell, Margaret J M. “Invisibility Optics”, in Phillippy, Patricia (ed.). *A History of Early Modern Women's Literature*. Cambridge University Press, 2018.

Frye, Susan. “Materializing Authorship in Esther Inglis's Books”, *Journal of Medieval and Early Modern Studies*, vol. 32, no. 3 (2002).

Yeo, Elspeth. “Inglis, Esther (1570/71–1624)” in Goldman, Lawrence (ed.). *Oxford Dictionary of National Biography*. Oxford University Press, 2004. Accessed 17 Feb 2018 http://collections.vam.ac.uk/item/O696575/esther-kello-nee-english-inglis-print-aikman-george-w/

Ziegler, Georgianna. “Spotlight on a Calligrapher”, *The Collation*, 27 Feb 2012. Accessed 17 Feb 2018. https://martinevanelk.wordpress.com/2017/06/15/selfie-fashioning-and-the-self-portraits-of-calligrapher-esther-inglis/

Iaia

Adams, Renee B; Kräussl, Roman; Navone, Marco A; and Verwijmeren, Patrick. “Is Gender in the Eye of the Beholder? Identifying Cultural Attitudes with Art Auction Prices”, 6 Dec 2017. Accessed 17 Feb 2018. http://dx.doi.org/10.2139/ssrn.3083500

Dabbs, Julia. *Life Stories of Women Artists, 1550–1800*. Ashgate Publishing, 2009.

Kleiner, Fred S. *Gardner's Art through the Ages: The Western Perspective, Volume 1*. Cengage Learning, 2013.

Miller, M H. “Georg Baselitz Says 'Women Don't Paint Very Well'”, *Observer*, 29 Jan 2013. Accessed 17 Feb 2018. http://observer.com/2013/01/georg-baselitz-says-women-dont-paint-very-well/

Sutton, Benjamin. “Art by Women Sells for 47.6% Less than Works by Men, Study Finds”, *Hyperallergic*, 14 Dec 2017. Accessed 18 Feb 2018. https://hyperallergic.com/417356/art-by-women-gender-study-sexism/

Wei Shuo

“Ancient Calligrapher Madame Wei”, *Women of China*, 29 Mar 2007. Accessed 5 Apr 2018. http://www.womenofchina.cn/womenofchina/html1/people/history/7/4420-1.htm

Chang, Serena. “Madame Wei, Ancient Calligrapher”, *World of Chinese*, 17 June 2015. Accessed 5 Apr 2018. http://www.theworldofchinese.com/2015/06/madame-wei-ancient-calligrapher/

“The Character(s) of Tung Yang-tzu”, *Taiwan Today*, 1 Feb 1984. Accessed 5 Apr 2018. https://taiwantoday.tw/news.hp?unit=20,29,35,45&post=25453

Delbanco, Dawn. “Chinese Calligraphy” in *Heilbrunn Timeline of Art History*. Metropolitan Museum of Art, 2000. Accessed 5 Apr 2018. http://www.metmuseum.org/toah/hd/chcl/hd_chcl.htm

Lachman, Charles. “Chinese Calligraphy”. Asia Society. Accessed 5 Apr 2018. https://asiasociety.org/education/chinese-calligraphy

Lee, Lily Xiao Hong, and Stefanowska, A D. *Biographical Dictionary of Chinese Women: Antiquity Through Sui, 1600 BCE–618 CE*. Routledge, 2015.

Shi, X. “The Aesthetic Concept of Yi in Chinese Calligraphic Creation”, *Philosophy East and West*, 11 Jan 2017. Accessed 5 Apr 2018. https://muse.jhu.edu/article/646204/pdf

Weidner, Marsha Smith (ed.). *Flowering in the Shadows: Women in the History of Chinese and Japanese Painting*. University of Hawaii Press, 1990.

Zong-Qi, Cai. “Poundian and Chinese Aesthetics of Dynamic Force: A Re-

Discovery of Fenollosa and Pound's Theory of the Chinese Written Character", *Comparative Literature Studies*, vol. 30, no. 2, 1993. JSTOR, http://www.jstor.org/stable/40246878

Harriet Powers

Breneman, Judy Anne. "Harriet Powers: A Freed Slave Tells Stories Through Quilting", *History of Quilts*, 2009. Accessed 3 Mar 2018. http://www.historyofquilts.com/hpowers.html

Callahan, Ashley. "Harriet Powers (1837–1910)", *New Georgia Encyclopedia*, 1 Aug 2017. Accessed 22 February 2018. http://www.georgiaencyclopedia.org/articles/arts-culture/harriet-powers-1837-1910

Chevalier, Tracy. "The Craft that is Now Art", *RA Magazine*, Spring 2014. Accessed 3 Mar 2018. https://www.royalacademy.org.uk/article/the-craft-that-is-now-art

Daniela, Marcy. "Meet Harriet Powers Who Told Stories With Her Spectacular Quilts", *Martha Stewart*, 22 Mar 2017. Accessed 3 Mar 2018. https://www.marthastewart.com/1513455/meet-harriet-powers-who-told-stories-her-spectacular-quilts

Fry, Gladys-Marie. "New Light on Harriet Powers". Frederickson, Kristen, and Webb, Sarah E (eds). *Singular Women: Writing the Artist*. University of California Press, 2003.

Hicks, Kyra E, and Gaskins, Bill. *This I Accomplish: Harriet Powers' Bible Quilt and Other Pieces*. Black Threads Press, 2009.

Bonnie Ntshalintshali

Arnold, Marion. *Women and Art in South Africa*. David Philip Publishers, 1996.

Buckenham, Karen E. "Women's Experience, Spirituality and Theology for Liberation and Life in Contemporary South Africa as Expressed Through Visual Arts with a Focus on the Lives and Work of Two Women Artists – Dina Cormick and Bonnie Ntshalintshali". Master's Diss., University of Natal, 2001.

Cruise, Wilma. "Breaking the Mould: Women Ceramists in KwaZulu-Natal" in Arnold, Marion, and Schmahmann, Brenda (eds). *Between Union and Liberation: Women Artists in South Africa 1910–1994*. Ashgate, 2005.

Cruise, Wilma. *Contemporary Ceramics in South Africa*. Struik Winchester, 1991.

Doherty, Helen. "Upcycling Stereotypes – Telling Stories of Africa", *Interpreting Ceramics*, issue 16 (2015). Accessed 30 Jan 2018. http://interpretingceramics.com/issue016/articles/02.htm#b12

Dougan, Leila. "Bonnie Ntshalintshali: Rising Above The Chaos", *The Journalist*. Accessed 30 Jan 2018. http://www.thejournalist.org.za/art/bonnie-ntshalintshali

Halsted, Fée. *Ardmore: We Are Because of Others*. Fernwood Press, 2012.

Holm, Lyn. "Ardmore's Bonnie Ntshalintshali", *South African Art Times*, Oct 2014. Accessed 30 Jan 2018. https://issuu.com/arttimes/docs/the_south_african_art_times_october/10

Luxford, Charlotte. "Empowering Zulu Women Through Design: The Story Behind Cole & Son's Ardmore Collection", *The Culture Trip*, 11 May 2017. Accessed 30 Jan 2018. https://theculturetrip.com/africa/south-africa/articles/empowering-zulu-women-through-design-the-amazing-story-behind-cole-sons-ardmore-collection/

Martin, Marilyn. "Death in Venice", *ArtThrob*, issue 73 (Sept 2003). Accessed 30 Jan 2018. https://artthrob.co.za/03sept/news/deathinvenice.html

Ende

The Apocalypse, Then and Now. University of Santa Cruz. Accessed 27 Mar 2018. http://exhibits.library.ucsc.edu/exhibits/show/havc-winter2015/religious-books/the-apocalypse--then-and-now

The Art of Medieval Spain, A.D. 500–1200. Metropolitan Museum of Art, 1993.

Carr, Annemarie Weyl. "Women as Artists in the Middle Ages", *The Feminist Art Journal*, spring 1976.

Corgnati, Martina. "Ende, God's Picture-maker", *L'Osservatore Romano*, 2 May 2016. Accessed 27 Mar 2018. http://www.osservatoreromano.va/en/news/ende-gods-picture-maker

Gaze, Delia. *Concise Dictionary of Women Artists*. Taylor & Francis, 2001.

Gaze, Delia. *Dictionary of Women Artists: Artists, J–Z*. Taylor & Francis, 1997.

PHOTOGRAPHY

Vivian Maier

Bannos, Pamela. "The Life and Afterlife of Vivian Maier", *The Paris Review*, 20 Nov 2017. Accessed 22 Apr 2018. https://www.theparisreview.org/blog/2017/11/20/the-life-and-afterlife-of-vivian-maier/

Licter-Marck, Rose. "Vivian Maier and the Problem of Difficult Women", *New Yorker*, 9 May 2014. Accessed 22 Apr 2018. https://www.newyorker.com/culture/culture-desk/vivian-maier-and-the-problem-of-difficult-women

O'Donnell, Nora. "The Life and Work of Street Photographer Vivian Maier", *Chicago* magazine, 14 Dec 2010. Accessed 22 Apr 2018. http://www.chicagomag.com/Chicago-Magazine/January-2011/Vivian-Maier-Street-Photographer/

Rustin, Susanna. "Our Nanny, the Photographer Vivian Maier", *Guardian*, 19 July 2014. Accessed 22 Apr 2018. https://www.theguardian.com/lifeandstyle/2014/jul/19/our-nanny-vivian-maier-photographer

Accessed 22 Apr 2018. http://www.vivianmaier.com/about-vivian-maier/

Lola Álvarez Bravo

Ferrer, Elizabeth. *Lola Alvarez Bravo*. Aperture Foundation: Center for Creative Photography, 2006.

Gonzalez, David. "A Mexican Photographer, Overshadowed but Not Outdone", *New York Times*, 20 Feb 2013. Accessed 24 Mar 2018. https://lens.blogs.nytimes.com/2013/02/25/a-mexican-photographer-overshadowed-but-not-outdone/

"Lola Alvarez Bravo". Center for Creative Photography. Accessed 24 Mar 2018. https://ccp.arizona.edu/artists/lola-alvarez-bravo

Marianne Breslauer

Beckers, Marion. "Marianne Breslauer 1909–2001". Jewish Women's Archive. Accessed 25 Apr 2018. https://jwa.org/encyclopedia/article/breslauer-marianne

Debraine, Luc. "Rediscovering Marianne Breslauer", *The Eye of Photography*, 20 Jan 2017. Accessed 25 Apr 2018. https://loeildelaphotographie.com/en/a-la-redecouverte-de-marianne-breslauer/

Fan, Pauline. "Photo Essay: The Ravaged Angel", *Esquire*, 19 May 2017. Accessed 25 Apr 2018. https://www.esquire.my/lifestyle/entertainment-books/the-ravaged-angel#1

Frost, Amber. "Marianne Breslauer's Gorgeous Photos of Queer, Androgynous and Butch Women of the 1930s", *Dangerous Minds*, 30 June 2016. Accessed 25 Apr 2018. https://dangerousminds.net/comments/marianne_breslauers_gorgeous_photos_of_queer_androgynous_and_butch_women_of

Gasser, Martin, and Beer, Kathrin. "Marianne Breslauer, Photographs". Cumbers, Pauline (trans.). Fotostiftung Schweiz. Accessed 25 Apr 2018. https://www.fotostiftung.ch/en/exhibitions/past/marianne-breslauer/

Lybeck, Marti M. *Desiring Emancipation: New Women and Homosexuality in Germany, 1890–1933*. SUNY Press, 2014.

Rycroft, Sophie. "Self-expression and Profession: Female photographers' Self-portraits in Berlin 1929–1933". Diss. University of Birmingham, 2014.

Serra, Pepa. "Marianne Breslauer's Photographs from the Trip through our Country in 1933". Museu Nacional d'Art de Catalunya blog, 10 Nov 2016. Accessed 25 Apr 2018. http://blog.museunacional.cat/en/marianne-breslauers-photographs-from-the-trip-through-our-country-in-1933/

"November 20: Marianne Breslauer (1909–2001)", *Gay Girls*, 21 Nov 2017. Accessed 25 Apr 2018. https://gaygirls.blogabode.com/category/marianne-breslauer/

Accessed 25 Apr 2018. https://www.berlinischegalerie.de/en/exhibitions/archives/2010/marianne-breslauer/

Alice Guy-Blaché

Arnold, Amanda. "The Forgotten Revolutionary Filmmaker Whose Name Was Replaced by her Husband's", *Broadly*, 27 Jan 2016. Accessed 23 April 2018. https://broadly.vice.com/en_us/article/785y5y/the-forgotten-revolutionary-filmmaker-whose-name-was-replaced-by-her-husbands

Kilston, Lyra. "Alice Guy Blaché", *Art in America*, 26 Apr 2010. Accessed 21 Apr 2018. https://www.artinamericamagazine.com/reviews/alice-guy-blach/

Kizirian, Shari. "The Solax Films of Alice Guy Blaché". Presented at Silent Winter 2009. Accessed 23 Apr 2018. http://www.silentfilm.org/the-solax-films-of-alice-guy-blache

McMahan, Alison. "Alice Guy Blaché" in Gaines, Jane; Vatsal, Radha; and Dall'Asta, Monica (eds). *Women Film Pioneers Project*. Center for Digital Research and Scholarship. Columbia University Libraries, 2013. Accessed 23 Apr 2018. https://wfpp.cdrs.columbia.edu/pioneer/ccp-alice-guy-blache/

McMahan, Alison. "Alice Guy Blaché Inducted into the DGA". Aliceguyblache.com, 6 Oct 2011. Accessed 23 Apr 2018. http://www.aliceguyblache.com/news/alice-guy-blache-inducted-dga

Meier, Allison. "Alice Guy-Blaché, the First Woman Filmmaker", *Hyperallergic*, 1 June 2017. Accessed 23 Apr 2018. https://hyperallergic.com/381372/alice-guy-blache-first-woman-filmmaker/

Milam, Whitney. "Meet Alice Guy-Blaché: The First Female Director", *Amy Poehler's Smart Girls*, 27 Jan 2016. Accessed 23 Apr 2018. https://amysmartgirls.com/meet-alice-guy-blach%C3%A9-the-first-female-director-

4cc0e5753817
Morrow, Justin. "Alice Guy-Blaché, the World's First Female Filmmaker, Wrote, Directed, and Produced Over 700 Films". No Film School, 9 Mar 2017. Accessed 21 Apr 2018. https://nofilmschool.com/2017/03/alice-guy-blache-worlds-first-woman-filmmaker
Slide, Anthony. *The Silent Feminists: America's First Women Directors*. Scarecrow Press, 1996.

DESIGN
Lady Elizabeth Wilbraham
Álvarez, Eva, and Gomez, Carlos."The Invisible Women: How Female Architects Were Erased from History", *Architectural Review*, 8 Mar 2017. Accessed 7 Apr 2018. https://www.architectural-review.com/rethink/the-invisible-women-how-female-architects-were-erased-from-history/10017481.article
Hammond, Cynthia. *Architects, Angels, Activists and the City of Bath, 1765–1965: Engaging with Women's Spatial Interventions in Buildings and Landscape*. Routledge, 2017.
Kahn, Eve M. "Maybe a Lady Taught Christopher Wren", *New York Times*, 8 Mar 2012. Accessed 7 Apr 2018. https://www.nytimes.com/2012/03/09/arts/design/the-case-for-a-17th-century-female-british-architect.html
Laurence, Anne. "Women Using Building in Seventeenth-Century England: A Question of Sources?" *Transactions of the Royal Historical Society*, vol. 13 (2003). http://JSTOR, www.jstor.org/stable/3679259
Merrick, Jay. "Elizabeth Wilbraham, the First Lady of Architecture", *Independent*, 16 Feb 2011. Accessed 7 Apr 2018. https://www.independent.co.uk/arts-entertainment/architecture/elizabeth-wilbraham-the-first-lady-of-architecture-2215936.html
Millar, John. "The First Woman Architect", *The Architects' Journal*, 11 Nov 2010. Accessed 7 Apr 2018. https://www.architectsjournal.co.uk/the-first-woman-architect/8608009.article
"Rare Letters of Weston Park Aristocrat Donated to Public Records", *Birmingham Post & Mail Ltd*, 2008. Accessed 7 Apr 2018. http://www.thefreelibrary.com/Rare+letters+of+Weston+Park+aristocrat+donated+to+public+records.-a018973073

Lina Bo Bardi
Domus, "Lina Bo Bardi: The Last Lesson", 8 Mar 2016. Accessed 8 Apr 2018. http://loves.domusweb.it/lina-bo-bardi-the-last-lesson/
Farago, Jason. "Lina Bo Bardi: Brazil's Best-Kept Secret". BBC, 11 June 2014. Accessed 8 Apr 2018. http://www.bbc.com/culture/story/20140611-brazils-best-kept-secret
Ferraz, Marcelo. "The Making of SESC Pompéia". Accessed 8 Apr 2018. http://linabobarditogether.com/2012/08/03/the-making-of-sesc-pompeia-by-marcelo-ferraz/
Heet, Erica. "Why Brazilian Modernist Lina Bo Bardi Is 'Among the Most Important Architects of the 20th Century'", *Dwell*, 12 Dec 2015. Accessed 8 Apr 2018. https://www.dwell.com/article/why-brazilian-modernist-lina-bo-bardi-is-among-the-most-important-architects-of-the-20th-century-7573e127
Lima, Zeuler R M de A. "Lina Bo Bardi and the Architecture of Everyday Culture", *Places Journal*, Nov 2013. Accessed 8 Apr 2018. https://placesjournal.org/article/lina-bo-bardi-and-the-architecture-of-everyday-culture/
Moore, Rowan. "Lina Bo Bardi (1914–1992)", *Architectural Review*, 24 July 2012. Accessed 8 Apr 2018. https://www.architectural-review.com/rethink/reputations-pen-portraits-/lina-bo-bardi-1914-1992/8633391.article
Moore, Rowan. "Lina Bo Bardi: Buildings Shaped by Love", *Guardian*, 9 Sept 2012. Accessed 8 Apr 2018. https://www.theguardian.com/artanddesign/2012/sep/09/lina-bo-bardi-together-review
Werbler, Annie. "Prolific Midcentury Brazilian Architect Lina Bo Bardi is Having a Moment", *Curbed*, 24 Mar 2015. Accessed 8 Apr 2018. https://www.curbed.com/2015/3/24/9977684/lina-bo-bardi

Gunnborga the Good
Bremmer, Rolf H, Jr. "Hermes-Mercury and Woden-Odin as Inventors of Alphabets: A Neglected Parallel", in Bammesberger, Alfred. *Old English Runes and Their Continental Background*. Carl Winter, 1991.
Elliott, Ralph W V. "Runes, Yews, and Magic", *Speculum*, vol. 32, no. 2, 1957. JSTOR, http://www.jstor.org/stable/2849116.
Ferguson, Robert. *The Hammer and the Cross: A New History of the Vikings*. Penguin UK, 2009.
Koefoed, H A. "The Heroic Age in Scandinavia in Light of the Danish Inscriptions in the Younger Runes", *Scandinavian Studies*, vol. 35, no. 2 (1963). http://JSTOR, http://www.jstor.org/stable/40916452
Pruitt, Sarah. "What Was Life Like for Women in the Viking Age?" *History*, 18 Nov 2016. Accessed 18 Apr 2018. https://www.history.com/news/what-was-life-like-for-women-in-the-viking-age
Spurkland, Terje. *Norwegian Runes and Runic Inscriptions*. Boydell Press, 2005, p.15.
Accessed 18 Apr 2018. https://en.natmus.dk/historical-knowledge/denmark/prehistoric-period-until-1050-ad/the-viking-age/power-and-aristocracy/rune-stones/

Dahl Collings
Bremer, Veronica. "Dahl Collings (1909–1988) and her Itinerary: Australia, England, and Back" in Groot, Marjan; Seražin, Helena; Franchini, Caterina; Garda, Emilia; and Di Battista, Alenka (eds). *MOMOWO: Women Designers, Craftswomen, Architects and Engineers between 1918 and 1945*. ZRC Publishing House, 2017.
Caban, Geoffrey. *A Fine Line*. Hale & Iremonger, 1983.
Robinson, Max. "Hall of Fame: Geoffrey (1905–2000) and Dahl (1909–1988) Collings". AGDA, 2002. Accessed 20 Apr 2018. https://www.agda.com.au/inspiration/hall-of-fame/geoffrey-(1905-2000)-and-dahl-(1909-1988)-collings/
Stephen, Ann; Goad, Philip; and McNamara, Andrew. *Modern Times: The Untold Story of Modernism in Australia*. The Miegunyah Press, 2008.
Van de Ven, Anne-Marie. "Dahl Collings (1909–1988)". Re:collection, 2012. Accessed 20 Apr 2018. https://recollection.com.au/biographies/dahl-collings
Accessed 20 Apr 2018. https://www.daao.org.au/bio/dahl-collings/biography/

Alero Olympio
Quaye, Audrey. "Alero 'Woman 7' Olympio Passes Away", *GhanaWeb*, 29 Aug 2005. Accessed 6 Apr 2018. https://www.ghanaweb.com/GhanaHomePage/diaspora/artikel.php?ID=89021
Talmor, Ruti. "Building Africa: The Work of Alero Olympio". Accessed 6 Apr 2018. https://web.archive.org/web/20110723212747/http://www.haverford.edu:80/HHC/rtalmor/index.html
Talmor, Ruti. "Introductory Essay". Accessed 6 Apr 2018. https://web.archive.org/web/20110723212742/http://www.haverford.edu:80/HHC/rtalmor/essay.html
Talmor, Ruti. "Kokrobitey Institute". Accessed 6 Apr 2018. https://web.archive.org/web/20110723212757/http://www.haverford.edu:80/HHC/rtalmor/kokrobitey.html

Corita Kent
Barnett, David C. "A Nun Inspired by Warhol: The Forgotten Pop Art of Sister Corita Kent", *NPR*, 8 Jan 2015. Accessed 7 Apr 2018.
"Biography." Corita Art Center. Accessed 7 Apr 2018. http://corita.org/about-corita
Bourton, Lucy. "'The grandmother of socially active art': the generous work of Sister Corita Kent", *It's Nice That*, 8 Mar 2018. Accessed 7 Apr 2018. https://www.itsnicethat.com/features/corita-kent-ray-smith-art-international-womens-day-080318
"Corita Kent, Warhol's Kindred Spirit in the Convent", *New York Times*, 10 Apr 2015. Accessed 7 Apr 2018. https://www.nytimes.com/2015/04/10/magazine/corita-kent-warhols-kindred-spirit-in-the-convent.html
Gotthardt, Alexa. "How to Free Your Creative Spirit, According to Sister Corita Kent", *Artsy*, 7 July 2017. Accessed 7 Apr 2018. https://www.artsy.net/article/artsy-editorial-free-creative-spirit-1960s-radical-nun
Pacatte, Rose. "The Tumultuous Times of Corita Kent", *National Catholic Reporter*, 3 Aug 2016. Accessed 7 Apr 2018. https://www.ncronline.org/books/2017/08/tumultuous-times-corita-kent
Shaw, Jonathan. "Corita Shaw", *Harvard Magazine*, Sept–Oct 2015. Accessed 7 Apr 2018. https://harvardmagazine.com/2015/08/corita-kent-nun-with-a-pop-art-habit
Trinder, Kington. "The Radical Art of Sister Mary Corita Kent", *AnOther*, 20 Jan 2016. Accessed 7 Apr 2018. http://www.anothermag.com/art-photography/8228/the-radical-art-of-sister-mary-corita-kent
Walker, Alissa. "Corita Kent: How a Screenprinting Nun Changed the Course of Modern Art", *Gizmodo*, 2 Oct 2013. Accessed 7 Apr 2018. https://gizmodo.com/how-a-screenprinting-nun-changed-the-course-of-modern-a-1412576274

Allegra Lockstadt

Allegra Lockstadt was born in Canada, raised in the southeastern United States, and currently resides in Minneapolis, Minnesota, US. She currently works as freelance illustrator and designer. To see more of Allegra's work visit **www.allegralockstadt.com**

Sara Netherway

Sara Netherway is an illustrator from the Isle of Wight. Originally trained in fine art, she enjoys creating images with rich textures and detail. To see more of Sara's work visit **www.saranetherway.co.uk**

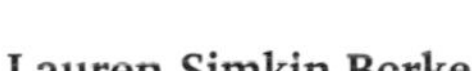

Lauren Simkin Berke

Lauren Simkin Berke is an American artist and illustrator based in Brooklyn, NY. Working in ink on paper, Lauren draws for clients such as *The New York Times*, *Smithsonian* magazine, Simon & Schuster publishers and Rémy Martin.
www.simkinberke.com

María Hergueta

María Hergueta is a freelance illustrator from a small village in north Spain. She has been working as an illustrator for five years now and her work has been published in different publishing houses and magazines such as Oxford University Press, Penguin Books and *The New York Times*.

She currently lives between Barcelona and the Swedish countryside.

Miriam Castillo

Miriam Castillo is an illustrator based in Brooklyn and Mexico. Her whimsical hand-drawn illustrations explore the intersection in between yoga, spirituality and nature. For more of her world, visit
www.miriamcastillo.com

Marcela Quiroz

Marcela works as an illustrator for publishing projects and print media. Her day is divided between books and pencils, searching for new words, memorizing them and writing them over and over again until they become drawings and part of some of her alphabets of illustrated words.

www.do-re-mi.co

Shreyas R Krishnan

Shreyas is an illustrator-designer from Chennai, India. She is curious about the ways in which art, design and gender intersect. Through drawing and writing, she tries to understand how, why and what we remember.

www.shreyasrkrishnan.com

Grace Helmer

Grace Helmer is a Brighton-born, London-based illustrator. She has put her paintbrushes to work for a range of clients, including Apple, Google, HarvardX and *Marie Claire*.

www.gracehelmer.co.uk

Tanya Heidrich

Tanya is a Swiss, American and German graphic designer and illustrator who designs in colour and illustrates in black and white drawing inspiration from patterns and details in everyday life.

www.tanyaheidri.ch

W T Frick

Winnie T Frick is a comic artist and illustrator currently based in Brooklyn. Her interests include, cross-hatching, architecture and doppelgängers. Her illustrations and webcomics can be found on **www.ipsumlorum.com**

Hélène Baum

Hélène Baum is a Berlin-based illustrator. "There are no lines in nature, only areas of colour, one against another" (Manet). This principle guides her work and life. With her diverse cultural background and much travelling, she creates a cosmic space through which humour, idealism and elements from diferent cultures co-exist in vibrant images.

Contributors

The New Historia

In creating this series, the author and publisher have worked with Gina Luria Walker, Professor of Women's Studies at The New School, New York City, and Director of The New Historia, carefully building, curating and editing the list of 48 women within this book to ensure that we uncovered as many lost female histories as possible. The New Historia's ongoing work is dedicated to the discovery, recovery and authoritative reclamation of women of the past through time and around the globe, and honour earlier women by telling their stories and sharing their strategies that inspire us to be sturdy and brave. In them we find our foremothers, transforming and remaking our ideas about history and ourselves.

"It is imperative that we galvanize what we know so that women's legacy is acknowledged as essential to the continuum of human enlightenment. Activating what we know will also keep us from making contemporary women invisible – waiting to be brought to life 50 or 100 years from now."
Gina Luria Walker,
The New Historia

www.thenewhistoria.com

Index

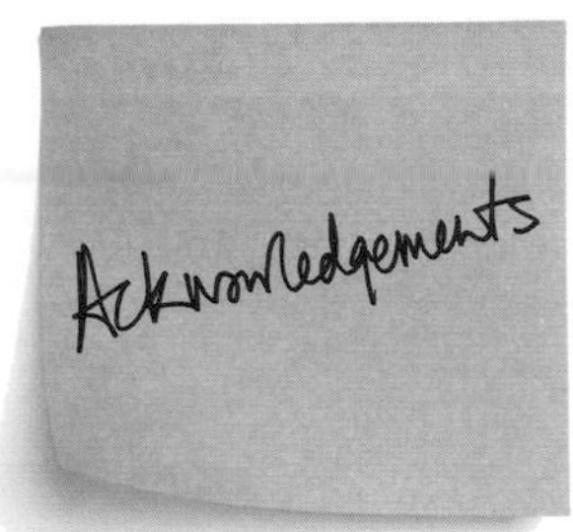

First off, I want to thank my mother. You never stopped encouraging me to express myself, whether it was through art or writing, and I will always be grateful for that.

Thank you to everyone at Octopus including, but most especially, Romilly Morgan and Pauline Bache. To my agent at Rogers, Coleridge & White, Emma Paterson, and my constant source of support, Daniel Johnson – I couldn't have done this without either of you. To Dr Gina Luria Walker at the New Historia, for her insight, wit and assistance. To all the Women Who Draw illustrators, who have done such incredible work to bring the series to life.

Finally, I would like to thank my former editors at *Wonderland* and *Dazed* who taught me so much about art, fashion and creativity when I was starting out in journalism. To Adam Welch, Charlie Robin Jones and Tim Noakes – thank you.

Zing Tsjeng

The Publisher would like to thank the entire team involved in curating the list of women featured in *Forgotten Women: The Artists*, and in particular would like to praise The New Historia centre's ongoing work in rediscovering women's contributions throughout history.